BRIAN WOOD
WRITER

RICCARDO BURCHIELLI
BRIAN WOOD
ARTISTS

JEROMY COX
COLORIST

JARED K. FLETCHER
LETTERER

BRIAN WOOD
ORIGINAL SERIES COVERS

DMZ CREATED BY
BRIAN WOOD AND
RICCARDO BURCHIELLI

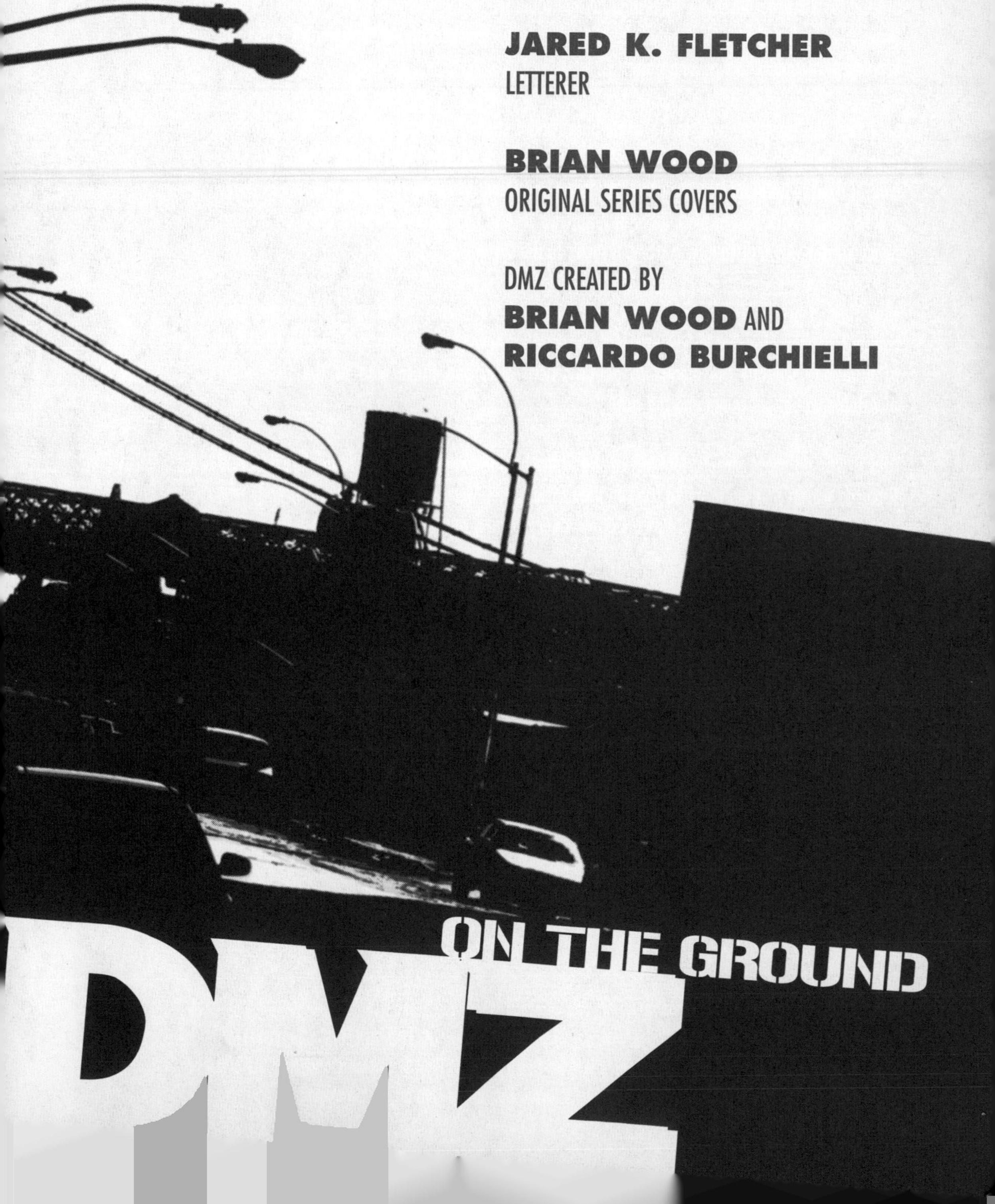

DMZ
ON THE GROUND

"I'll see you later," he said, and I could taste the disgust. "I'm gonna catch a ride back to Brooklyn with these guys." I tried to grin, though I'm sure the bruises made my mouth look like it was doing something vile. "I didn't get to say enough," I coughed while sizing up the "these guys," not sure whose side they were on, and watched Brian Wood fade away into the New York night with them.

Another missed opportunity, I thought to myself, making my way back into the bar I used to like, a bar like so many in a great city that had caved. At a table filthy with Italians I looked around for Riccardo Burchielli, thinking maybe I could tell him what I was feeling about his and Brian's book, but that opportunity was missed as well. Riccardo had a sentimental thing for breakfast, meaning he was long gone.

So I fled the bar that used to be something, and I started walking east. My handler was nervous, but then given my mood, she had every right to believe I was going to war. Ah, yes, war... I tried to imagine New York the way Brian and Riccardo were presenting it to me in DMZ. A New York smack dab in the middle of America's Second Civil War. A New York where around every corner was a discovery, a story, a shock to the system.

New York, a great, big, unruly beauty, brimming with iconoclasts, artists and visionaries who couldn't dream of living anywhere else, no matter how shitty things get in the city. Full of humanity without the means to go anywhere else, and those who at the first whiff of trouble would get mean and get out.

And it was on those streets, looking at the lights behind windows, that I realized Brian and Riccardo weren't trying to make me see their vision; they were pointing out what already was there. New York defines itself. Put a Gap on every corner, and a Starbuck's across the street, it'll still be New York.

Put it at ground zero, it won't change what it is.

Brian Wood & Riccardo Burchielli's DMZ caught me off guard. On Lafayette and Houston, I came across a couple of New York's Finest, but at that moment, I needed them to be the two men who created this book in your hands. I wasn't about to miss another opportunity.

"You guys— the two of you— do good work. Thank you."

They looked at me like they couldn't care less about my opinion.

Azz 03.24.06

Brian Azzarello is the Eisner and Harvey award-winning author of 100 BULLETS and LOVELESS, both series he created for DC/Vertigo. He's left his mark on SUPERMAN, BATMAN and HELLBLAZER. He lives in Chicago with his wife, two cats, a car, a corner bar, and a chip on his big shoulder.

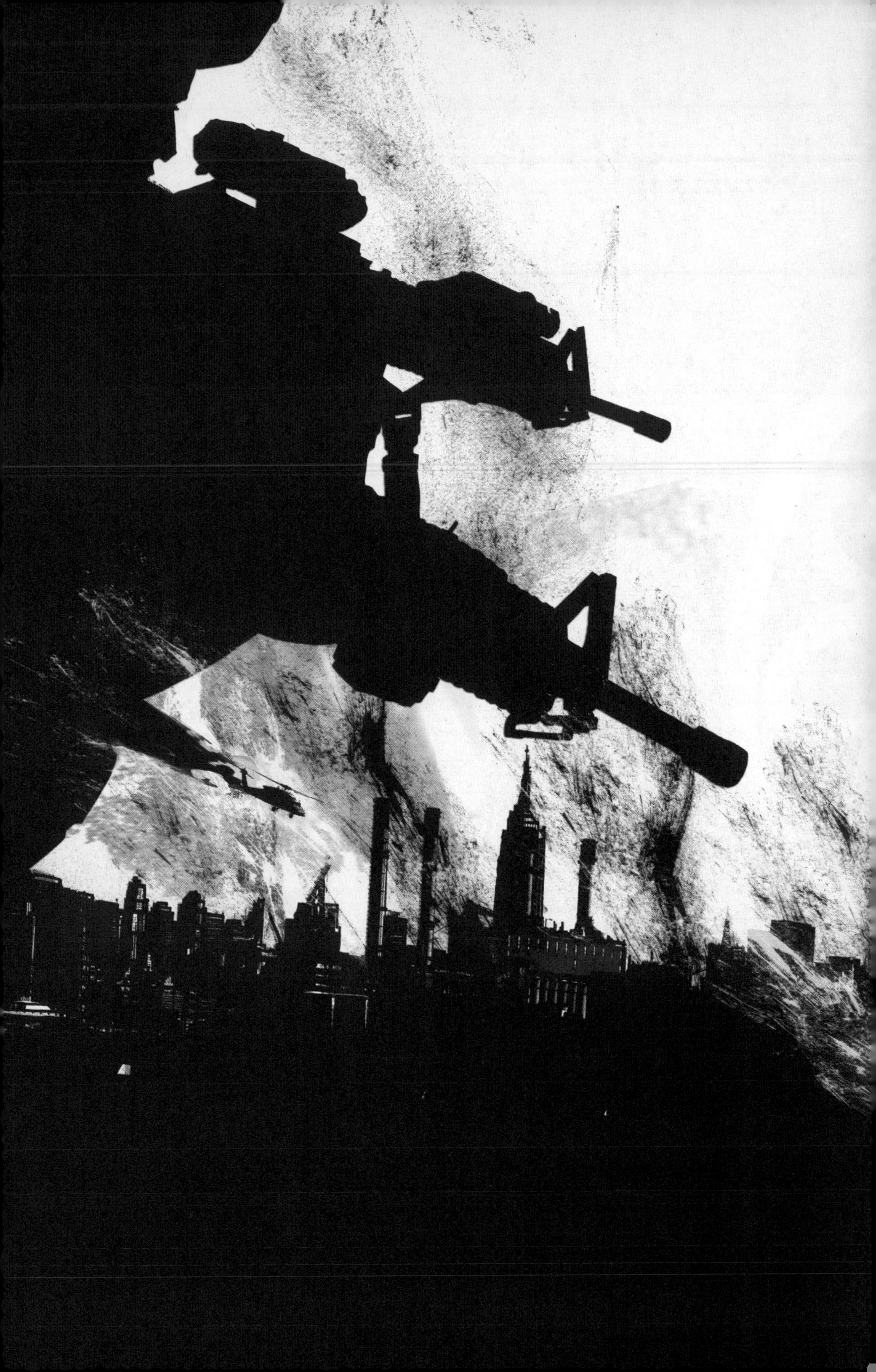

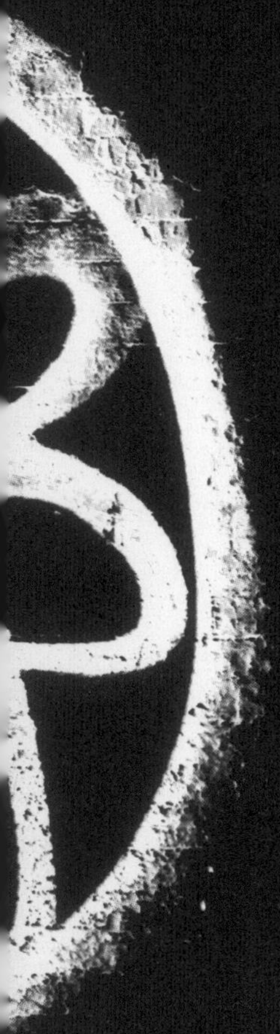

DMZ
ON THE GROUND

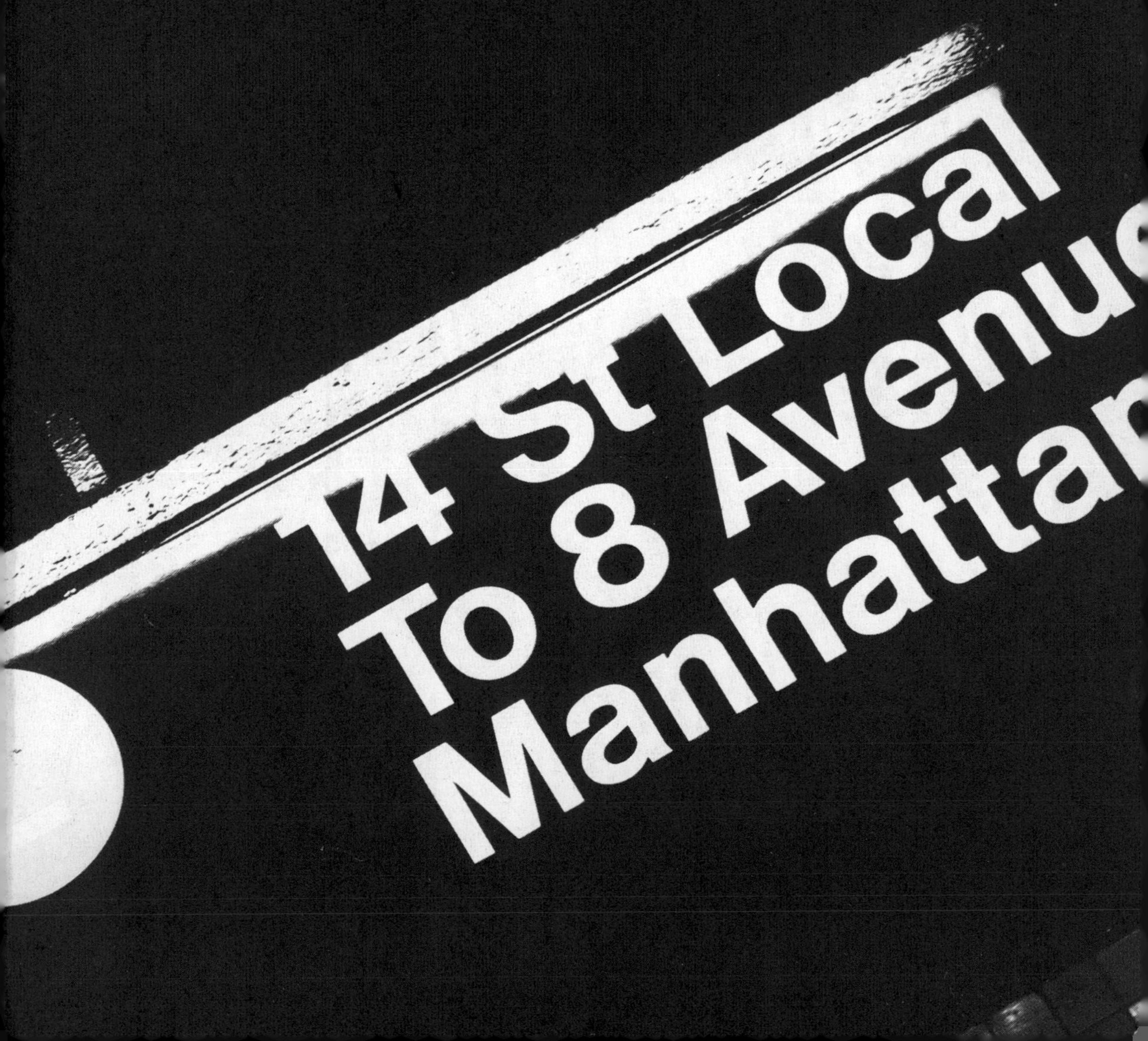

14 St Local
To 8 Avenu
Manhatta

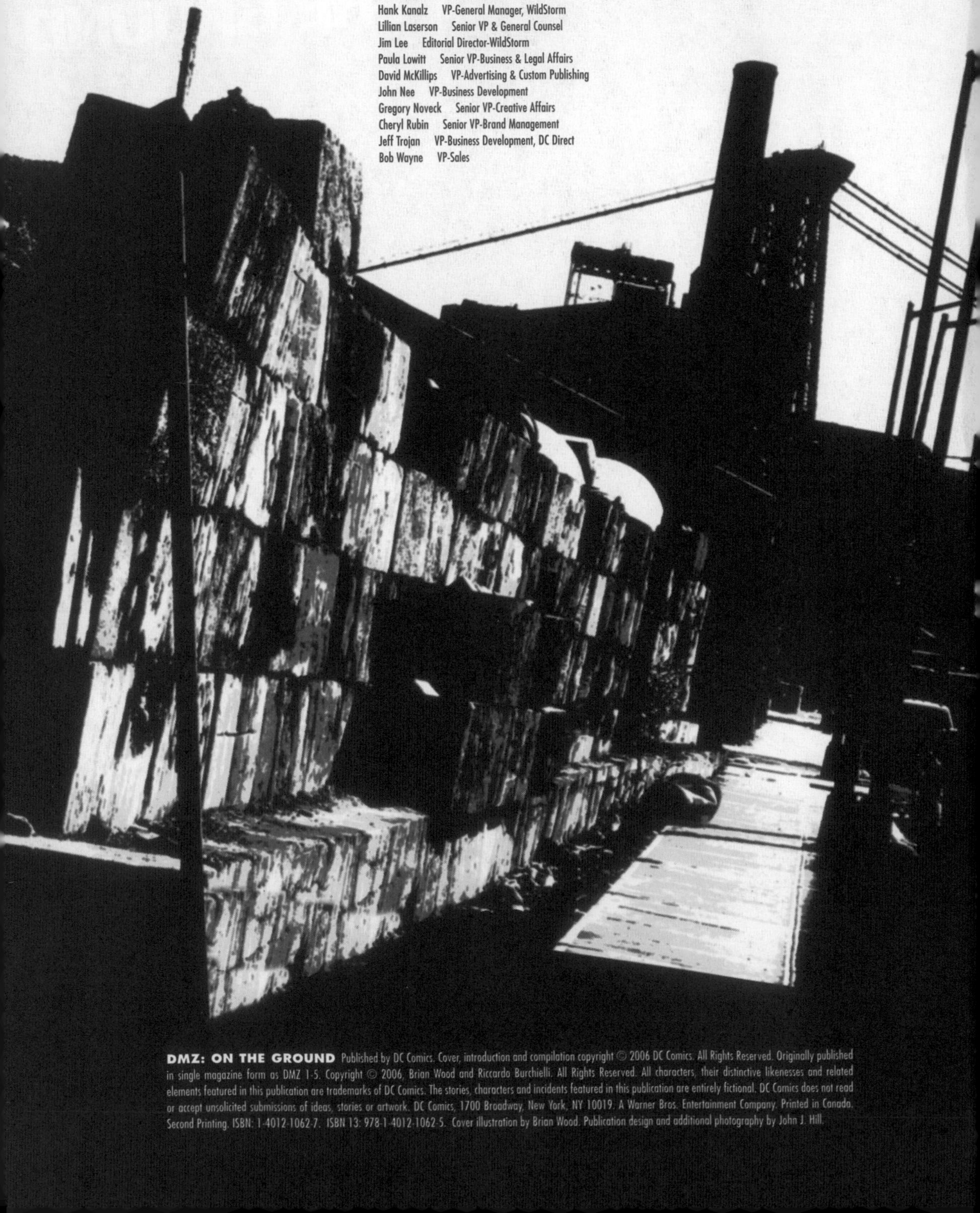

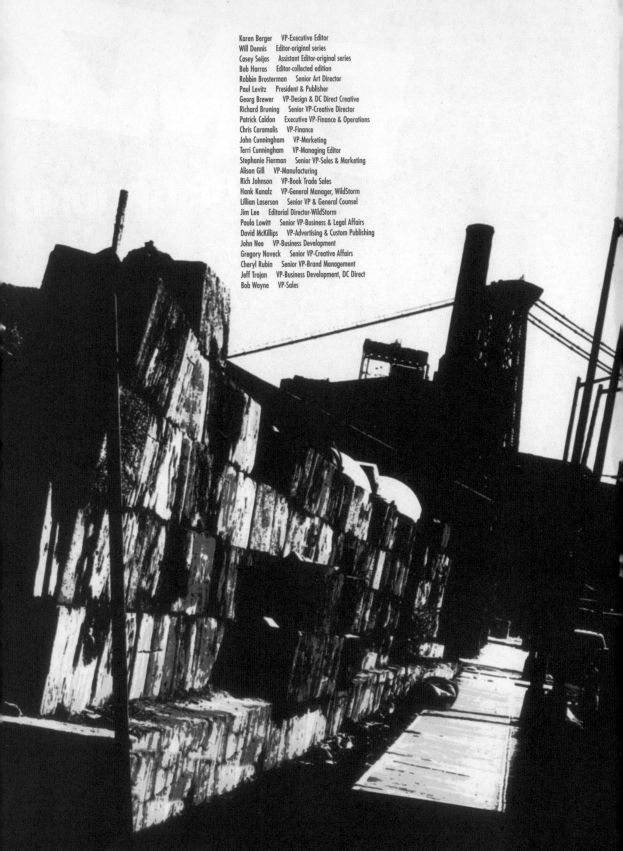

DMZ: ON THE GROUND Published by DC Comics. Cover, introduction and compilation copyright © 2006 DC Comics. All Rights Reserved. Originally published in single magazine form as DMZ 1-5. Copyright © 2006, Brian Wood and Riccardo Burchielli. All Rights Reserved. All characters, their distinctive likenesses and related elements featured in this publication are trademarks of DC Comics. The stories, characters and incidents featured in this publication are entirely fictional. DC Comics does not read or accept unsolicited submissions of ideas, stories or artwork. DC Comics, 1700 Broadway, New York, NY 10019. A Warner Bros. Entertainment Company. Printed in Canada. Second Printing. ISBN: 1-4012-1062-7. ISBN 13: 978-1-4012-1062-5. Cover illustration by Brian Wood. Publication design and additional photography by John J. Hill.

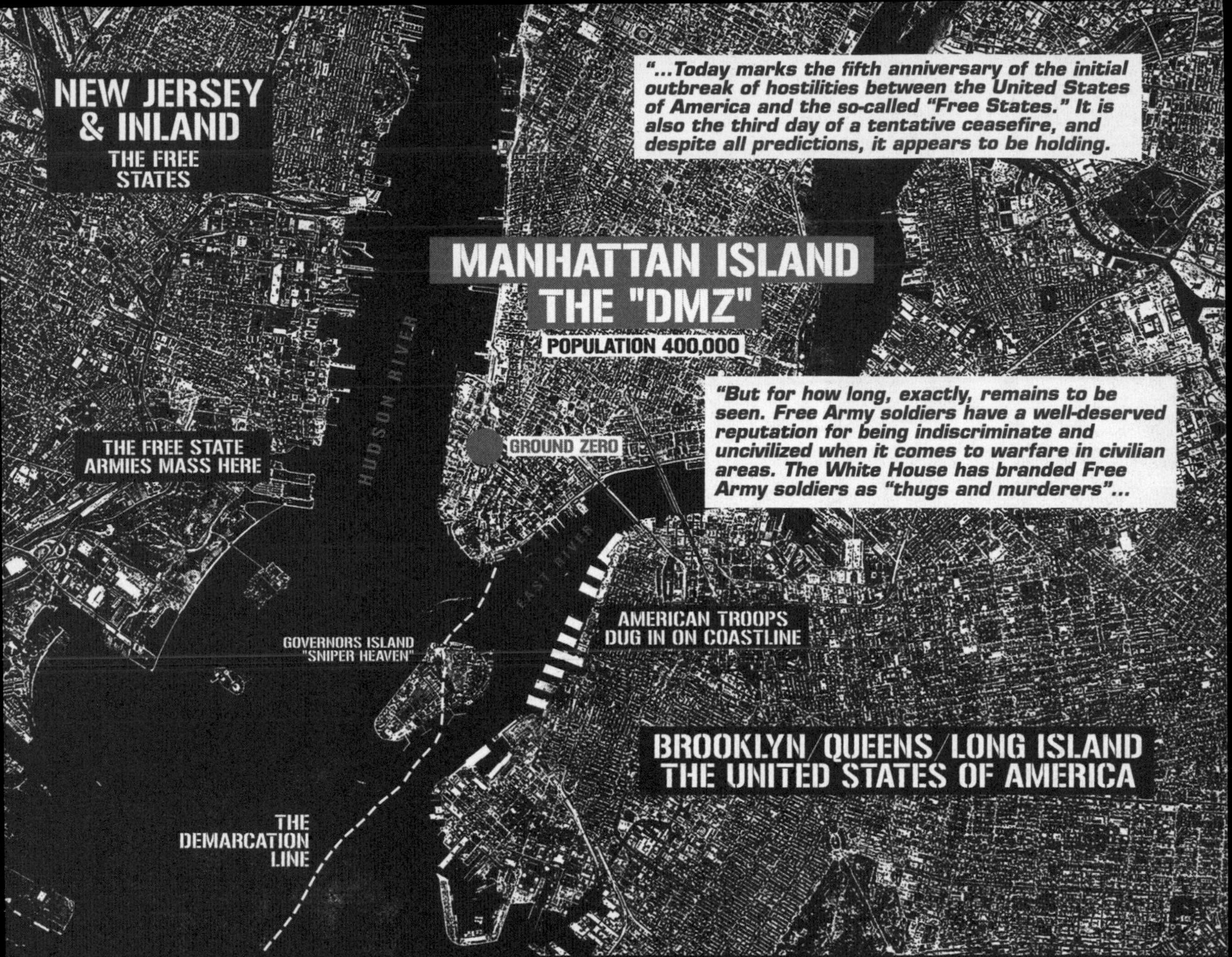
NEW JERSEY & INLAND
THE FREE STATES
"...Today marks the fifth anniversary of the initial outbreak of hostilities between the United States of America and the so-called "Free States." It is also the third day of a tentative ceasefire, and despite all predictions, it appears to be holding.
MANHATTAN ISLAND THE "DMZ"
POPULATION 400,000
HUDSON RIVER
"But for how long, exactly, remains to be seen. Free Army soldiers have a well-deserved reputation for being indiscriminate and uncivilized when it comes to warfare in civilian areas. The White House has branded Free Army soldiers as "thugs and murderers"...
THE FREE STATE ARMIES MASS HERE
GROUND ZERO
EAST RIVER
AMERICAN TROOPS DUG IN ON COASTLINE
GOVERNORS ISLAND "SNIPER HEAVEN"
BROOKLYN/QUEENS/LONG ISLAND THE UNITED STATES OF AMERICA
THE DEMARCATION LINE

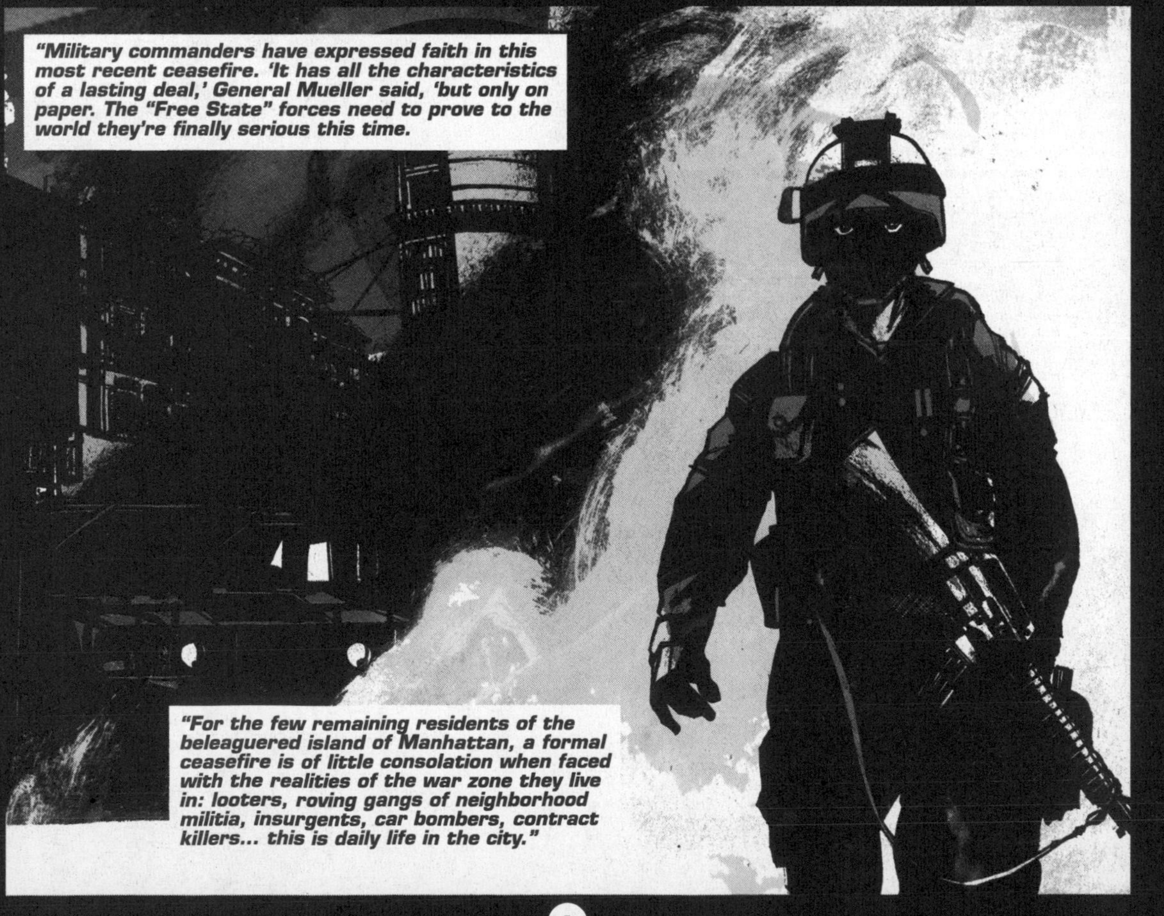
"Military commanders have expressed faith in this most recent ceasefire. 'It has all the characteristics of a lasting deal,' General Mueller said, 'but only on paper. The "Free State" forces need to prove to the world they're finally serious this time.
"For the few remaining residents of the beleaguered island of Manhattan, a formal ceasefire is of little consolation when faced with the realities of the war zone they live in: looters, roving gangs of neighborhood militia, insurgents, car bombers, contract killers... this is daily life in the city."

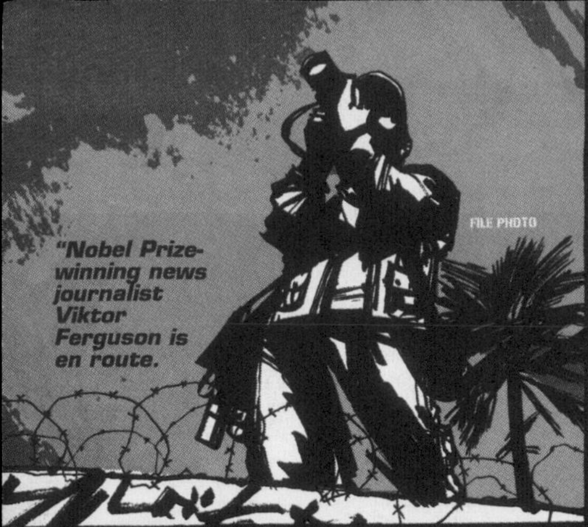
"Nobel Prize-winning news journalist Viktor Ferguson is en route.
FILE PHOTO

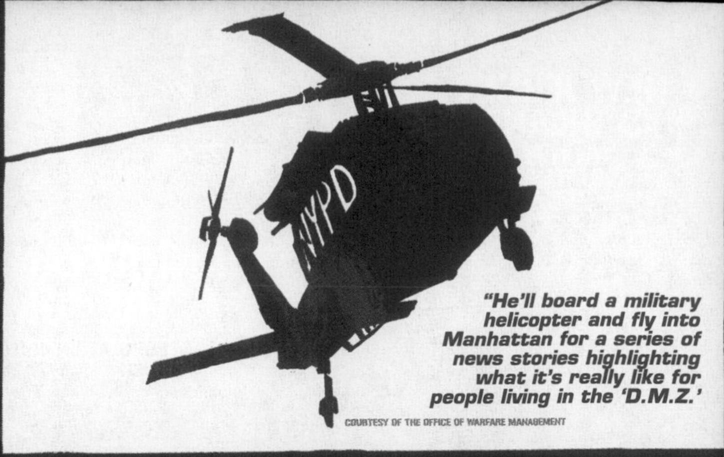
NYPD
"He'll board a military helicopter and fly into Manhattan for a series of news stories highlighting what it's really like for people living in the 'D.M.Z.'
COURTESY OF THE OFFICE OF WARFARE MANAGEMENT

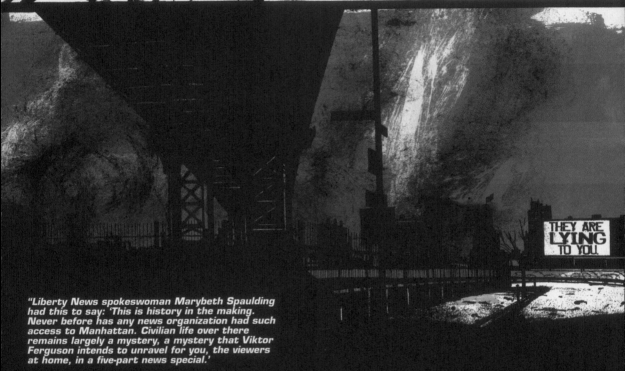

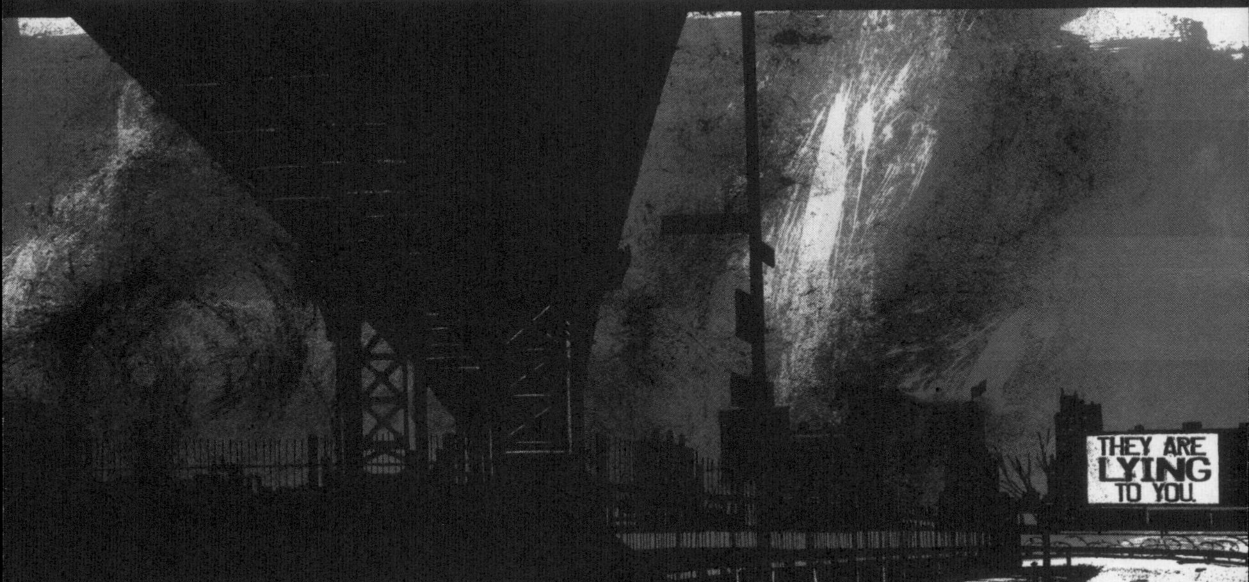
THEY ARE LYING TO YOU.

"Liberty News spokeswoman Marybeth Spaulding had this to say: 'This is history in the making. Never before has any news organization had such access to Manhattan. Civilian life over there remains largely a mystery, a mystery that Viktor Ferguson intends to unravel for you, the viewers at home, in a five-part news special.'

"In regard to safety concerns, that remains to be seen. If the ceasefire holds, as all parties pledge it will, they should be perfectly safe with the military bodyguards attached. Mr. Ferguson will broadcast, live, twice daily on this station, starting tomorrow evening.

"Tune in then for what will be, we're sure, unforgettable television.

"This is the LIberty News service, broadcasting from the United States of America, Long Island, New York."

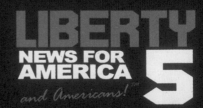

LIBERTY
NEWS FOR AMERICA 5
and Americans!™

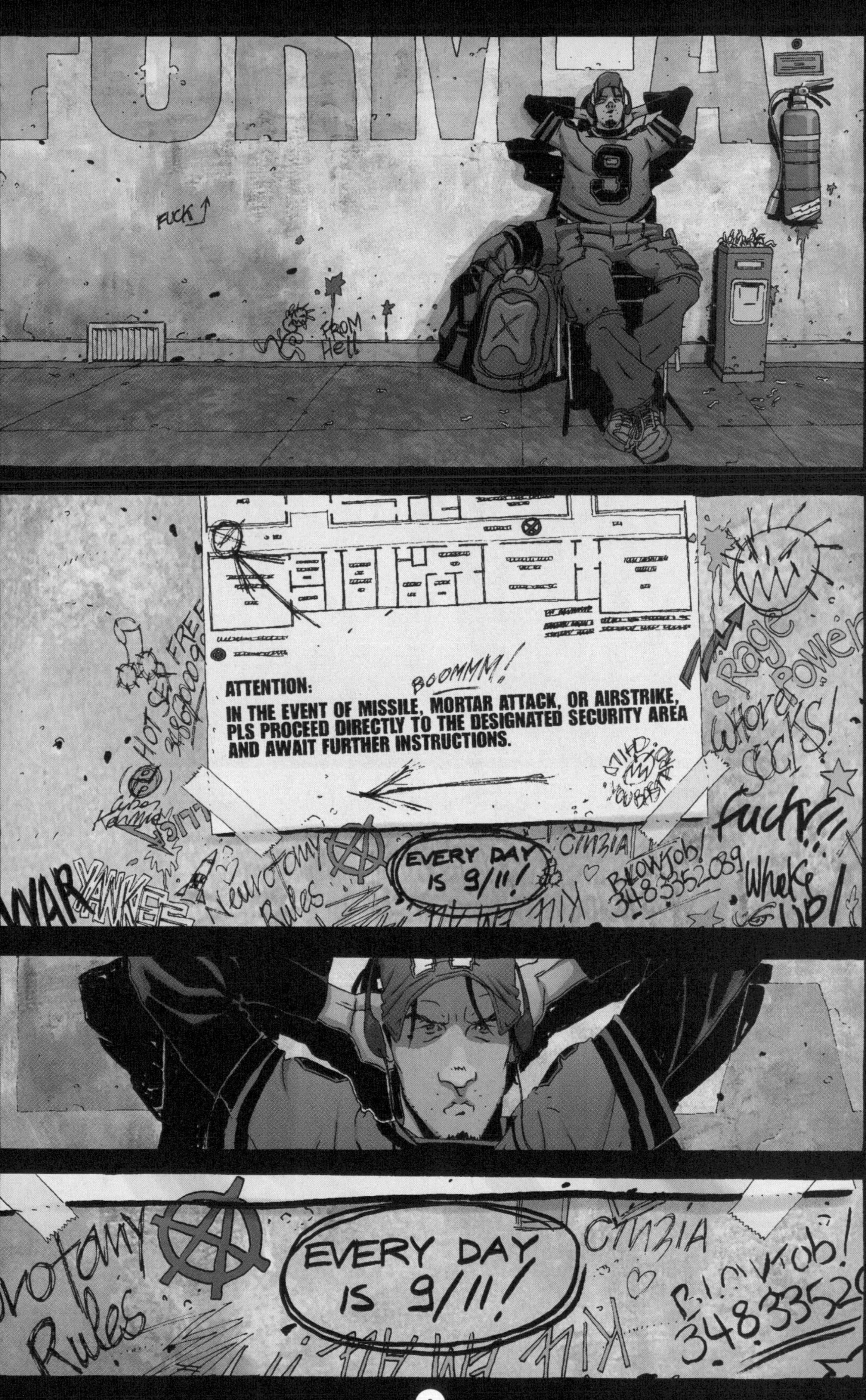
FUCK
FROM Hell
BOOMMM!
ATTENTION:
IN THE EVENT OF MISSILE, MORTAR ATTACK, OR AIRSTRIKE, PLS PROCEED DIRECTLY TO THE DESIGNATED SECURITY AREA AND AWAIT FURTHER INSTRUCTIONS.
HOT SEX FREE
Rage
Power
Whore
SUCKS!
fuck
EVERY DAY IS 9/11!
WAR
YANKEE
Neurotomy Rules
CINZIA
BLOWJOB! 3483352089
Wake Up!
EVERY DAY IS 9/11!
Neurotomy Rules
CINZIA

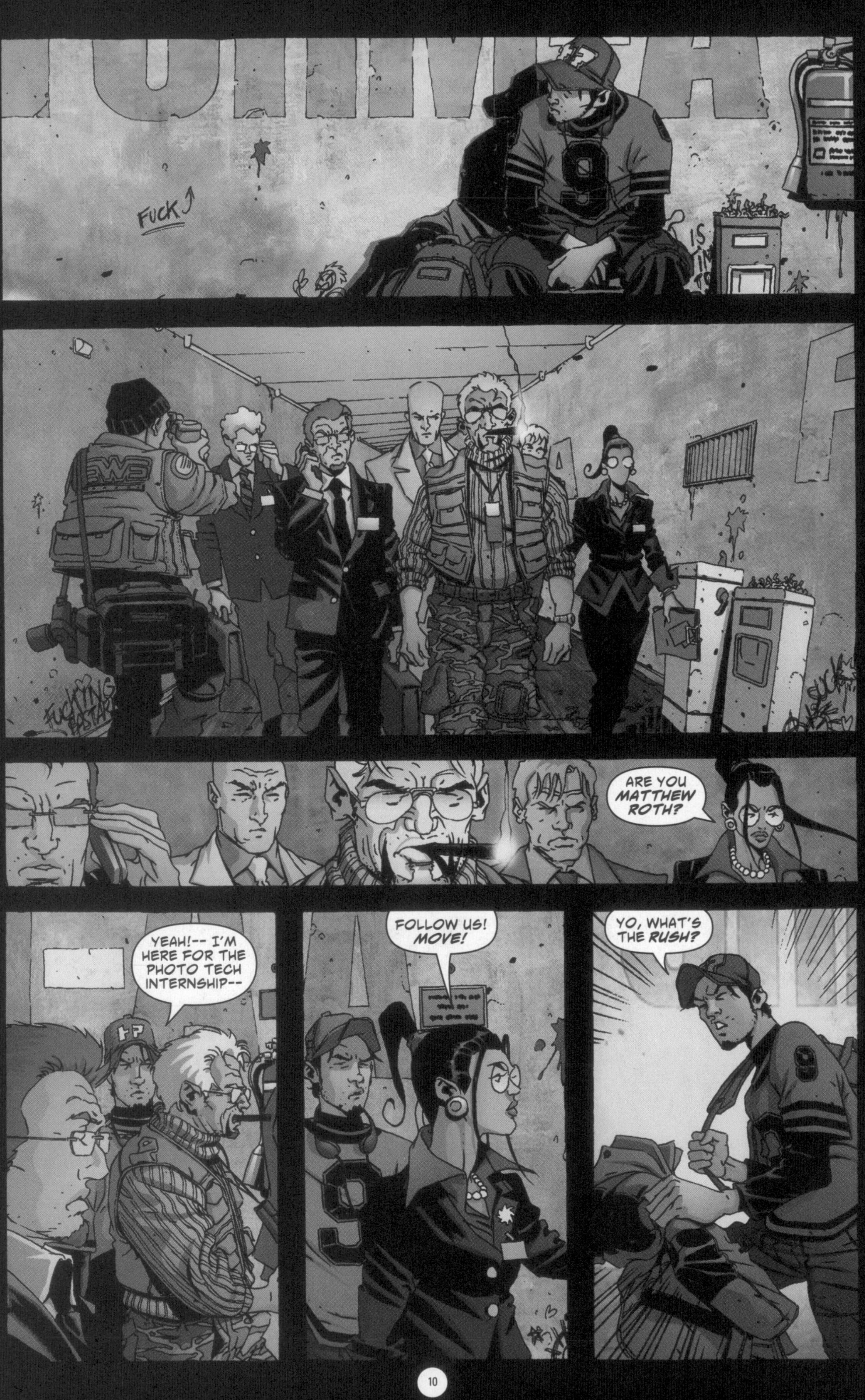
FUCK
FUCKING BASTARD
SUCK
ARE YOU MATTHEW ROTH?
YEAH!-- I'M HERE FOR THE PHOTO TECH INTERNSHIP--
FOLLOW US! MOVE!
YO, WHAT'S THE RUSH?

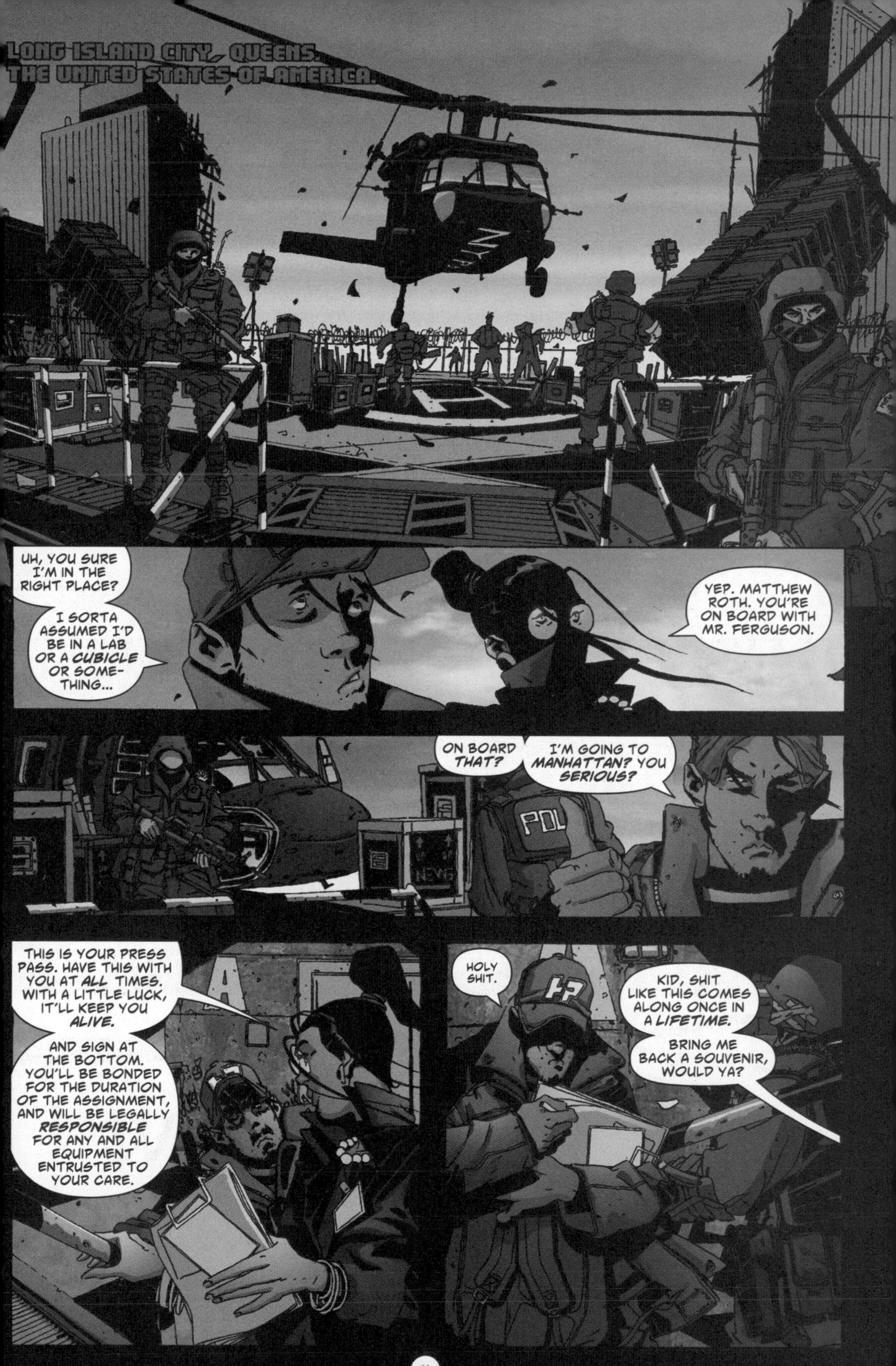
LONG ISLAND CITY, QUEENS.
THE UNITED STATES OF AMERICA.
UH, YOU SURE I'M IN THE RIGHT PLACE?
I SORTA ASSUMED I'D BE IN A LAB OR A CUBICLE OR SOME-THING...
YEP. MATTHEW ROTH. YOU'RE ON BOARD WITH MR. FERGUSON.
ON BOARD THAT?
I'M GOING TO MANHATTAN? YOU SERIOUS?
POL
THIS IS YOUR PRESS PASS. HAVE THIS WITH YOU AT ALL TIMES. WITH A LITTLE LUCK, IT'LL KEEP YOU ALIVE.
AND SIGN AT THE BOTTOM. YOU'LL BE BONDED FOR THE DURATION OF THE ASSIGNMENT, AND WILL BE LEGALLY RESPONSIBLE FOR ANY AND ALL EQUIPMENT ENTRUSTED TO YOUR CARE.
HOLY SHIT.
KID, SHIT LIKE THIS COMES ALONG ONCE IN A LIFETIME.
BRING ME BACK A SOUVENIR, WOULD YA?

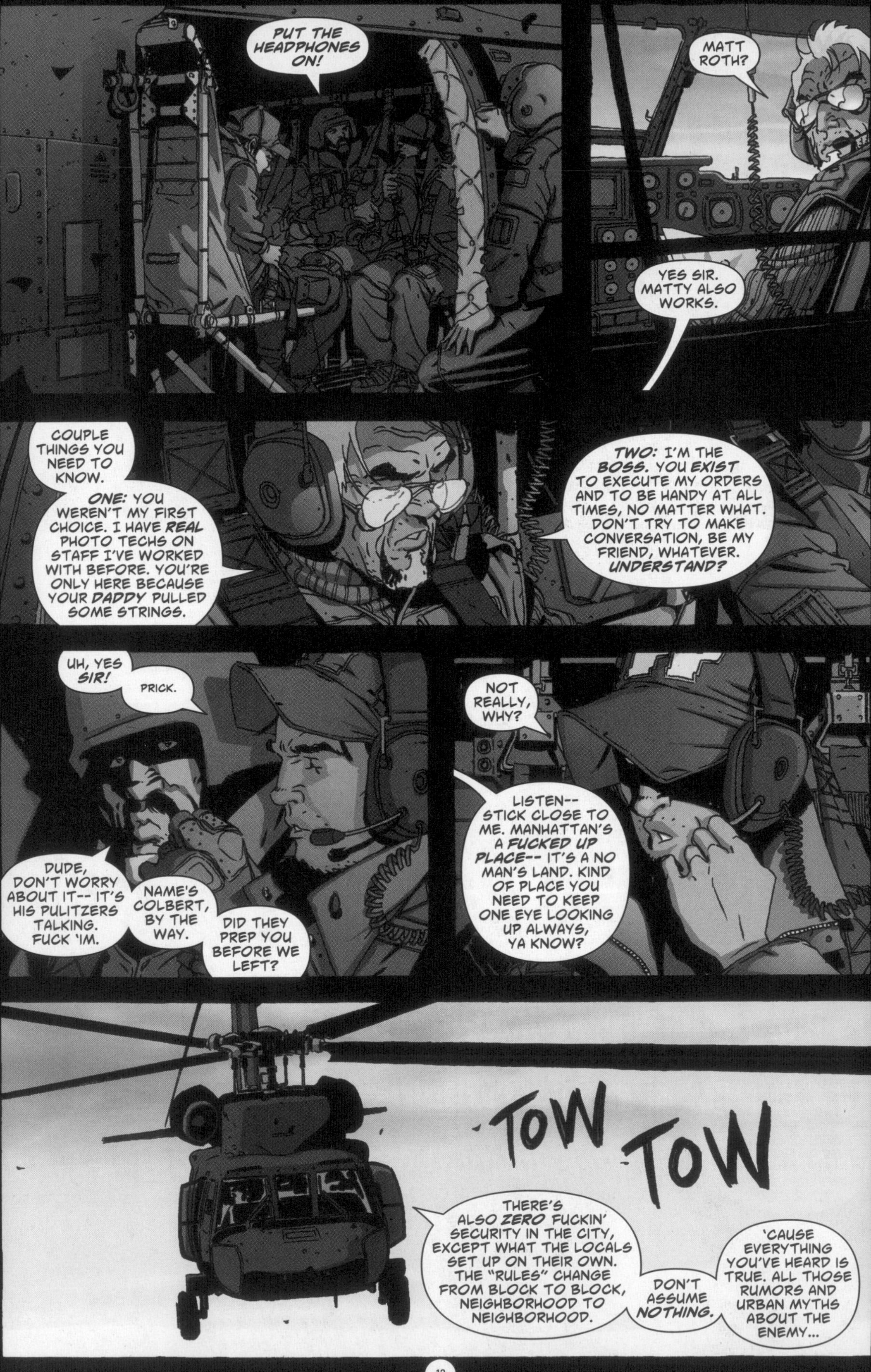
PUT THE HEADPHONES ON!
MATT ROTH?
YES SIR. MATTY ALSO WORKS.
COUPLE THINGS YOU NEED TO KNOW.
ONE: YOU WEREN'T MY FIRST CHOICE. I HAVE REAL PHOTO TECHS ON STAFF I'VE WORKED WITH BEFORE. YOU'RE ONLY HERE BECAUSE YOUR DADDY PULLED SOME STRINGS.
TWO: I'M THE BOSS. YOU EXIST TO EXECUTE MY ORDERS AND TO BE HANDY AT ALL TIMES, NO MATTER WHAT. DON'T TRY TO MAKE CONVERSATION, BE MY FRIEND, WHATEVER. UNDERSTAND?
UH, YES SIR!
PRICK.
DUDE, DON'T WORRY ABOUT IT-- IT'S HIS PULITZERS TALKING. FUCK 'IM.
NAME'S COLBERT, BY THE WAY.
DID THEY PREP YOU BEFORE WE LEFT?
NOT REALLY, WHY?
LISTEN-- STICK CLOSE TO ME. MANHATTAN'S A FUCKED UP PLACE-- IT'S A NO MAN'S LAND. KIND OF PLACE YOU NEED TO KEEP ONE EYE LOOKING UP ALWAYS, YA KNOW?
TOW
TOW
THERE'S ALSO ZERO FUCKIN' SECURITY IN THE CITY, EXCEPT WHAT THE LOCALS SET UP ON THEIR OWN. THE "RULES" CHANGE FROM BLOCK TO BLOCK, NEIGHBORHOOD TO NEIGHBORHOOD.
DON'T ASSUME NOTHING.
'CAUSE EVERYTHING YOU'VE HEARD IS TRUE. ALL THOSE RUMORS AND URBAN MYTHS ABOUT THE ENEMY...

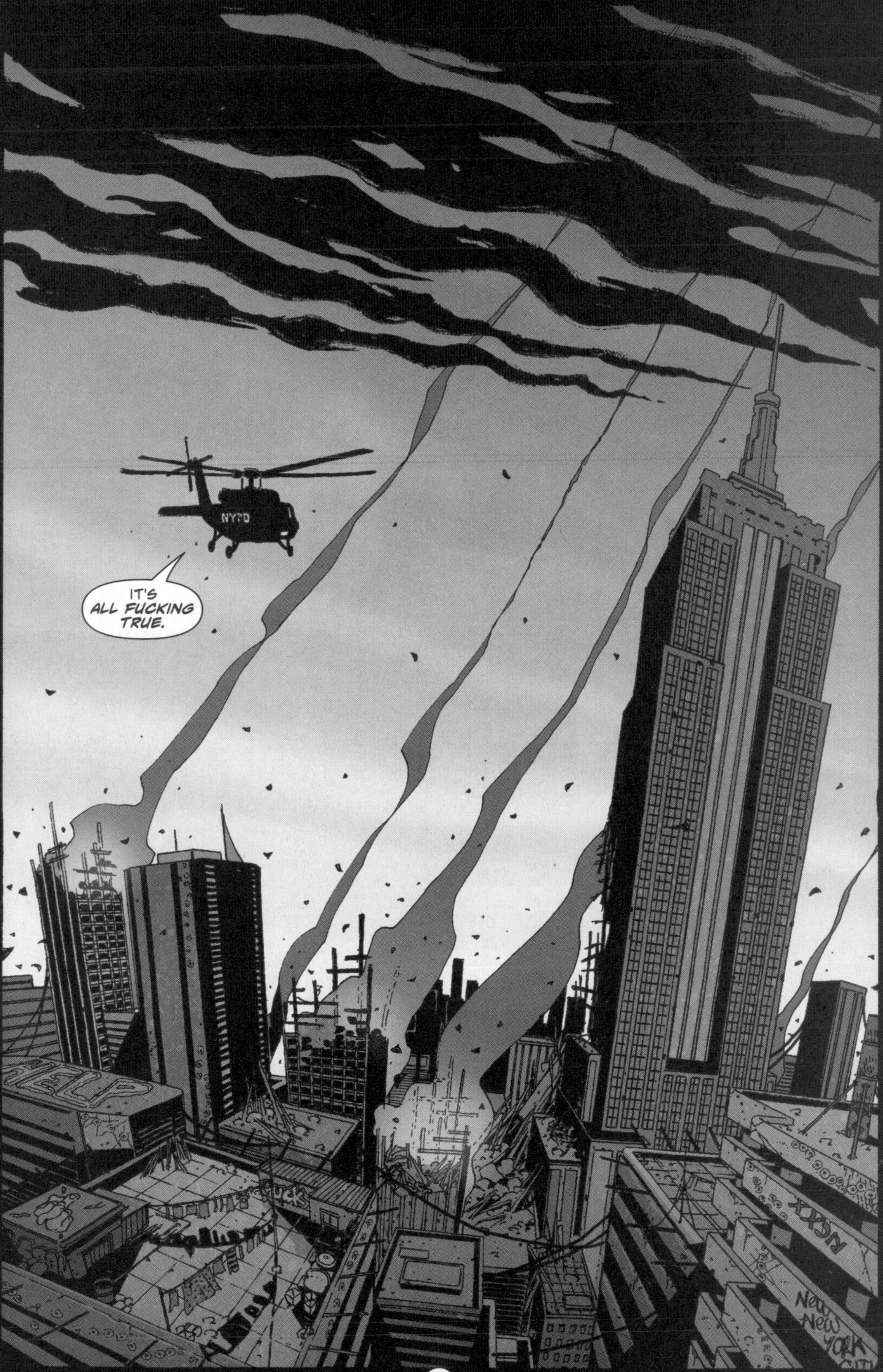
NYPD
IT'S ALL FUCKING TRUE.

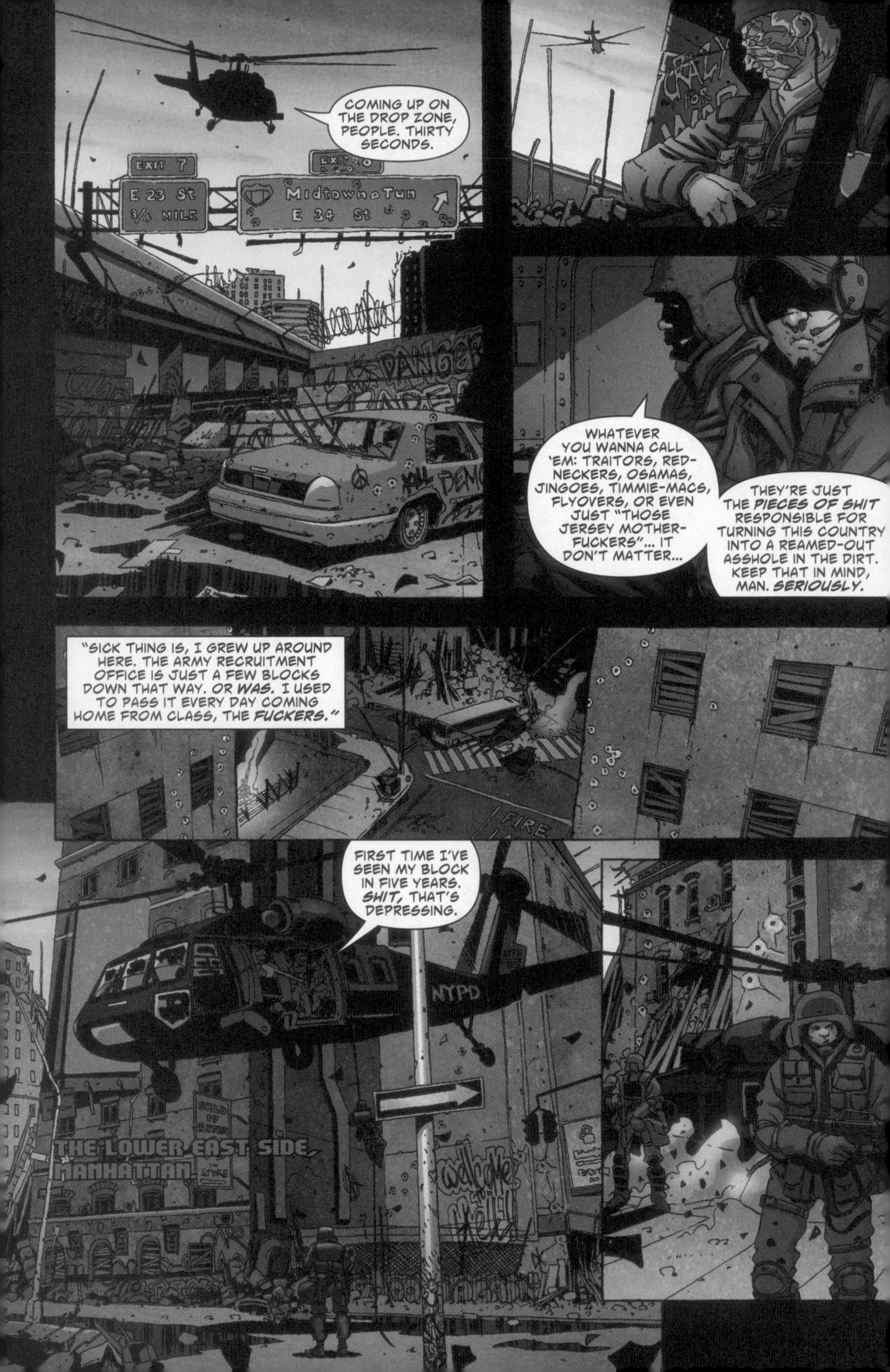
COMING UP ON THE DROP ZONE, PEOPLE. THIRTY SECONDS.
EXIT 7
E 23 St 3/4 MILE
Midtown Tun E 34 St
DANGER
WHATEVER YOU WANNA CALL 'EM: TRAITORS, RED-NECKERS, OSAMAS, JINGOES, TIMMIE-MACS, FLYOVERS, OR EVEN JUST "THOSE JERSEY MOTHER-FUCKERS"... IT DON'T MATTER...
THEY'RE JUST THE PIECES OF SHIT RESPONSIBLE FOR TURNING THIS COUNTRY INTO A REAMED-OUT ASSHOLE IN THE DIRT. KEEP THAT IN MIND, MAN. SERIOUSLY.
"SICK THING IS, I GREW UP AROUND HERE. THE ARMY RECRUITMENT OFFICE IS JUST A FEW BLOCKS DOWN THAT WAY. OR WAS. I USED TO PASS IT EVERY DAY COMING HOME FROM CLASS, THE FUCKERS."
FIRST TIME I'VE SEEN MY BLOCK IN FIVE YEARS. SHIT, THAT'S DEPRESSING.
NYPD
THE LOWER EAST SIDE, MANHATTAN

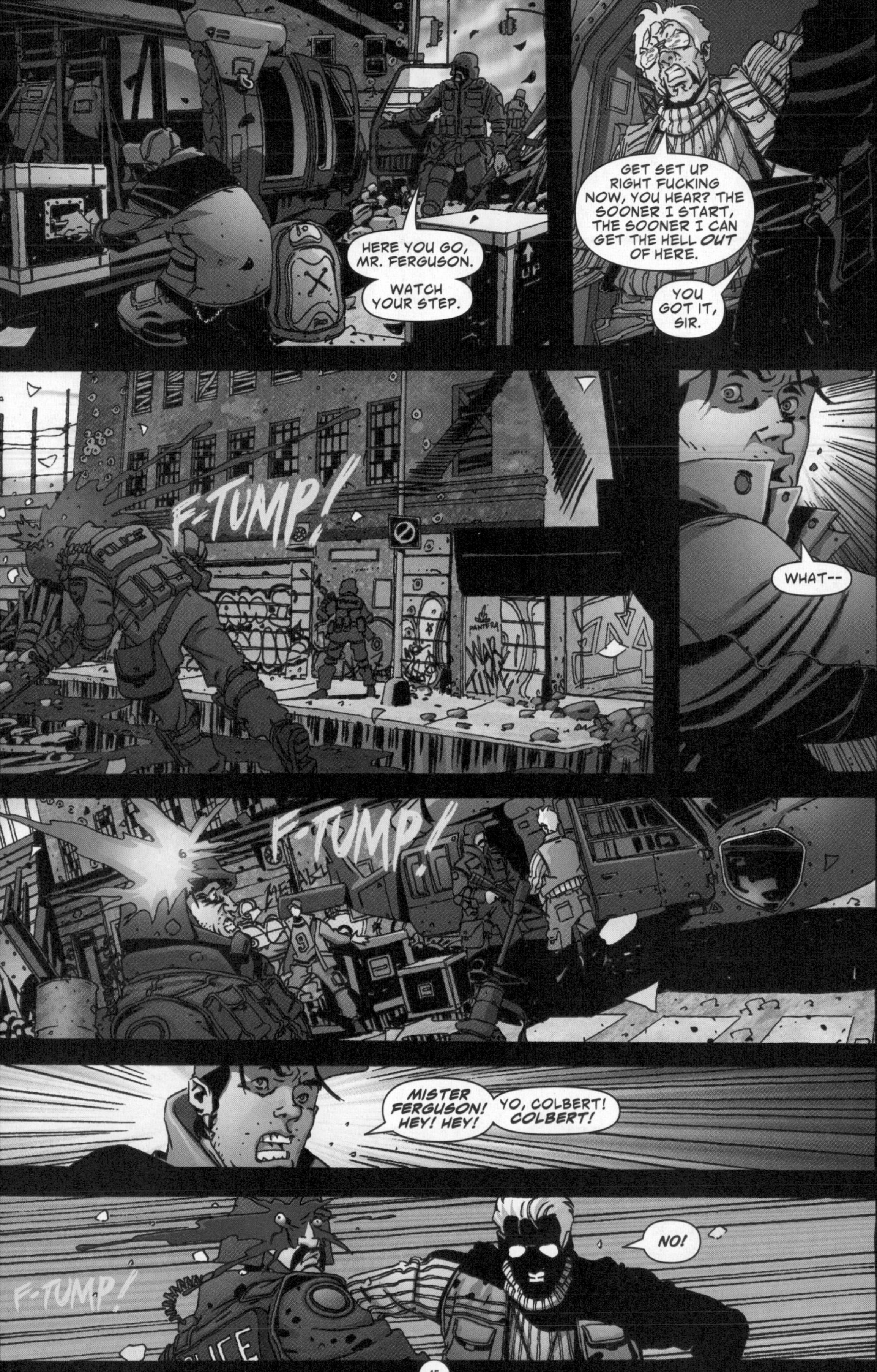
HERE YOU GO, MR. FERGUSON.
WATCH YOUR STEP.
UP
GET SET UP RIGHT FUCKING NOW, YOU HEAR? THE SOONER I START, THE SOONER I CAN GET THE HELL *OUT* OF HERE.
YOU GOT IT, SIR.
POLICE
F-TUMP!
PANTERA
WHAT--
F-TUMP!
MISTER FERGUSON! HEY! HEY!
YO, COLBERT! COLBERT!
NO!
F-TUMP!

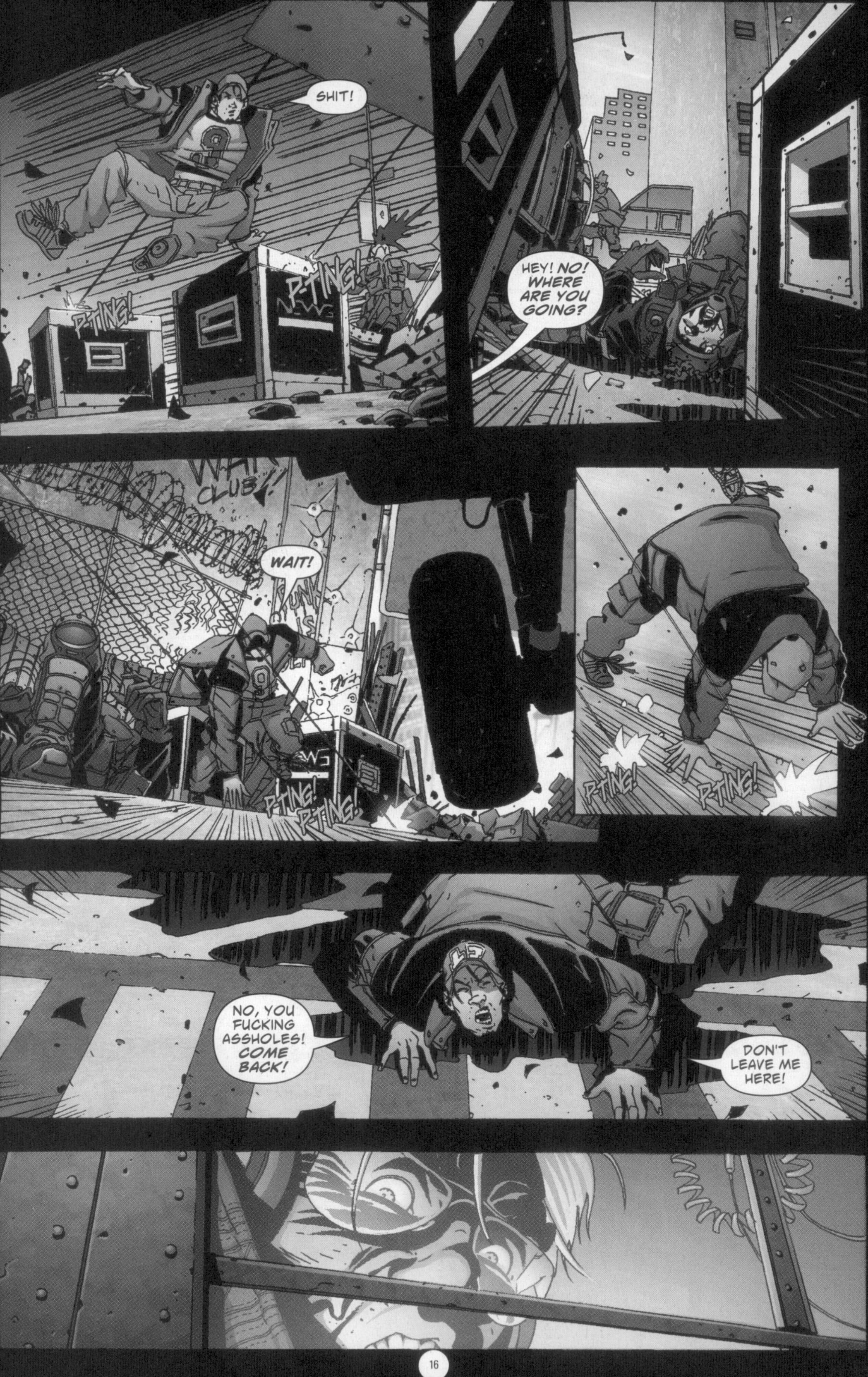
SHIT!
P-TING!
P-TING!
HEY! NO! WHERE ARE YOU GOING?
WAIT!
P-TING!
P-TING!
P-TING!
P-TING!
NO, YOU FUCKING ASSHOLES! COME BACK!
DON'T LEAVE ME HERE!

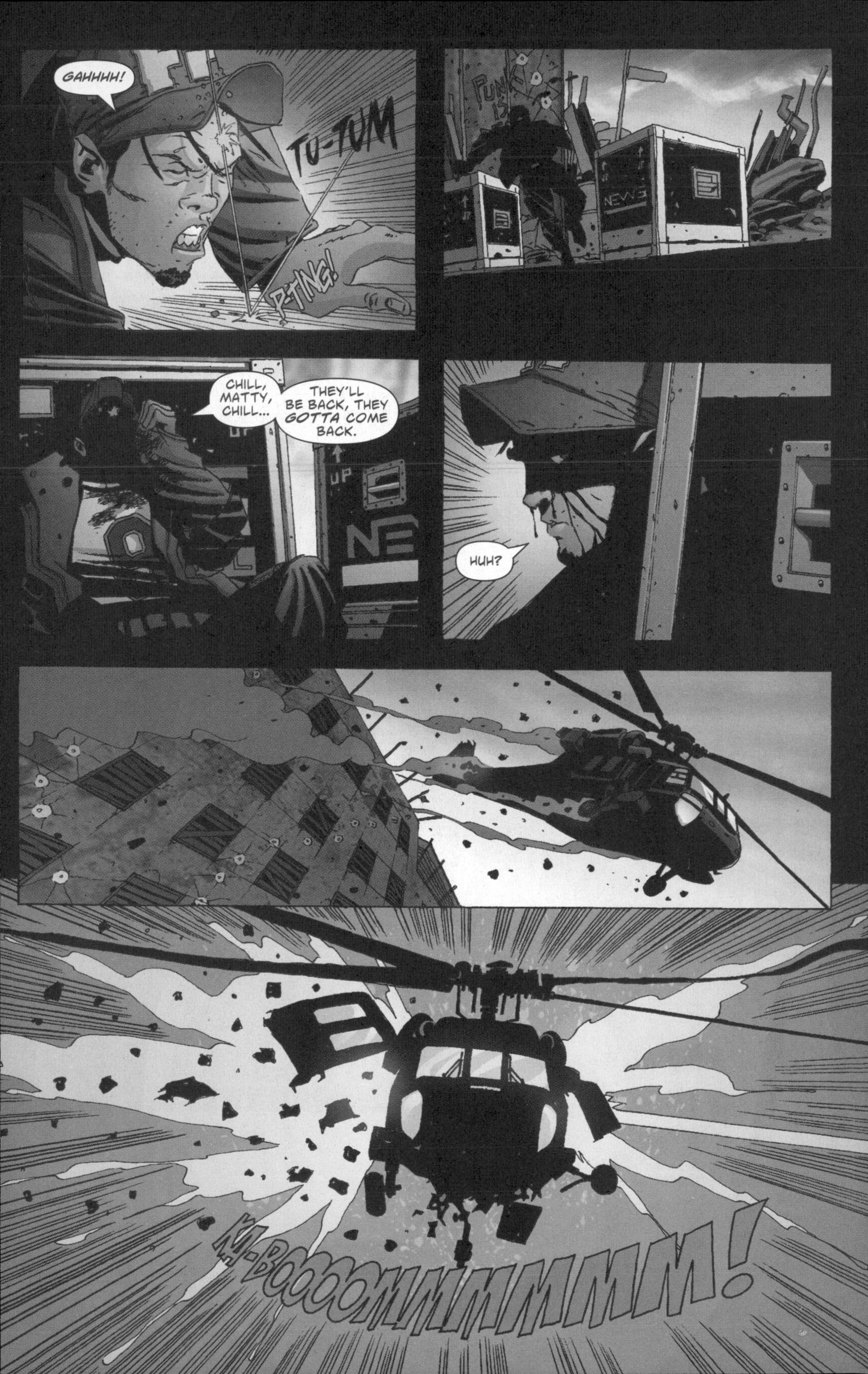
GAHHHH!
TU-TUM
P'TING!
PUNK IS
CHILL, MATTY, CHILL...
THEY'LL BE BACK, THEY GOTTA COME BACK.
HUH?
K-BOOOOMMMMMMMMMM!

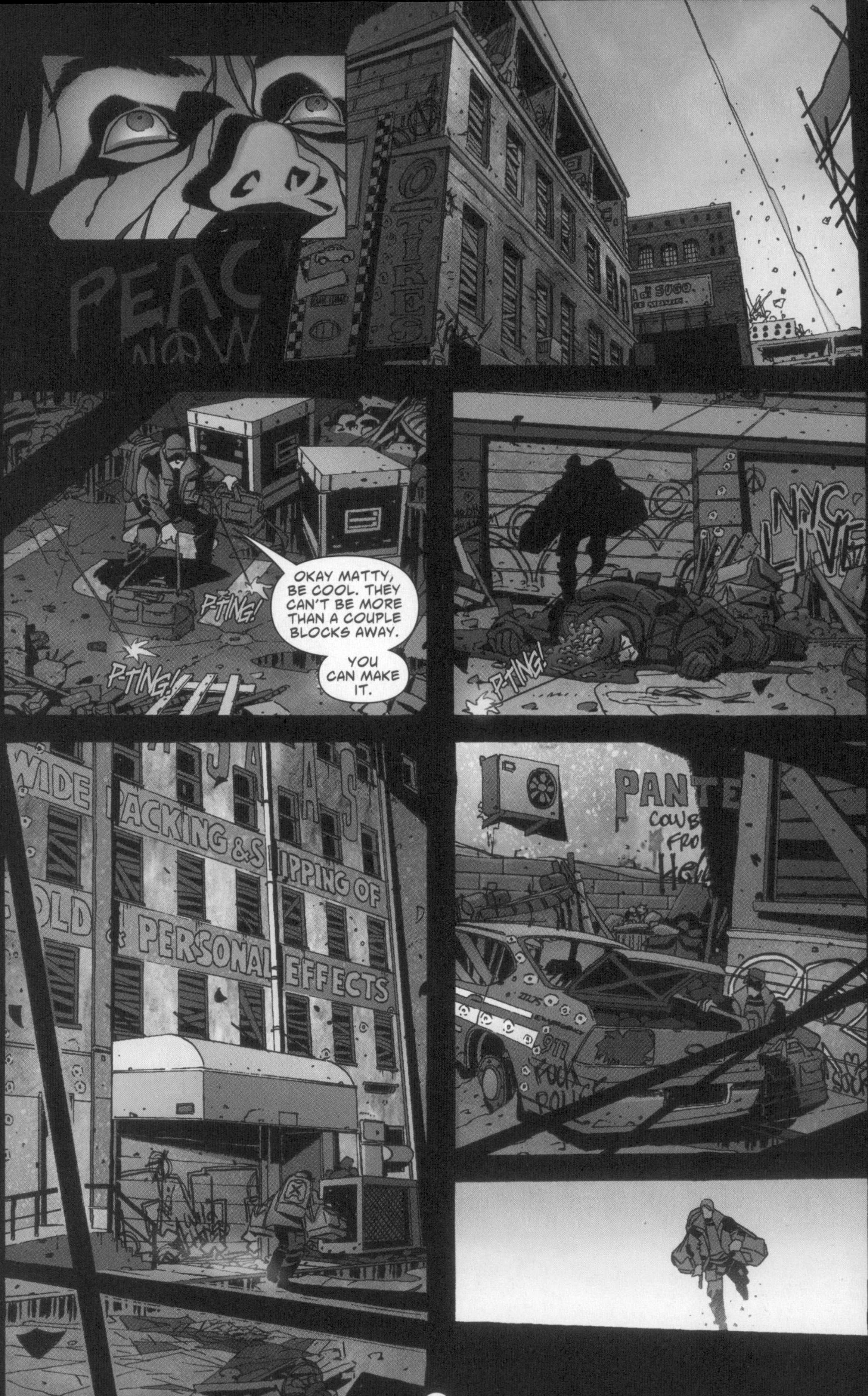
PEAC
NOW
TIRES
OKAY MATTY, BE COOL. THEY CAN'T BE MORE THAN A COUPLE BLOCKS AWAY.
YOU CAN MAKE IT.
P-TING!
P-TING!
P-TING!
NYC
WIDE PACKING & SHIPPING OF
OLD
& PERSONAL EFFECTS
PANTE
911
POLICE

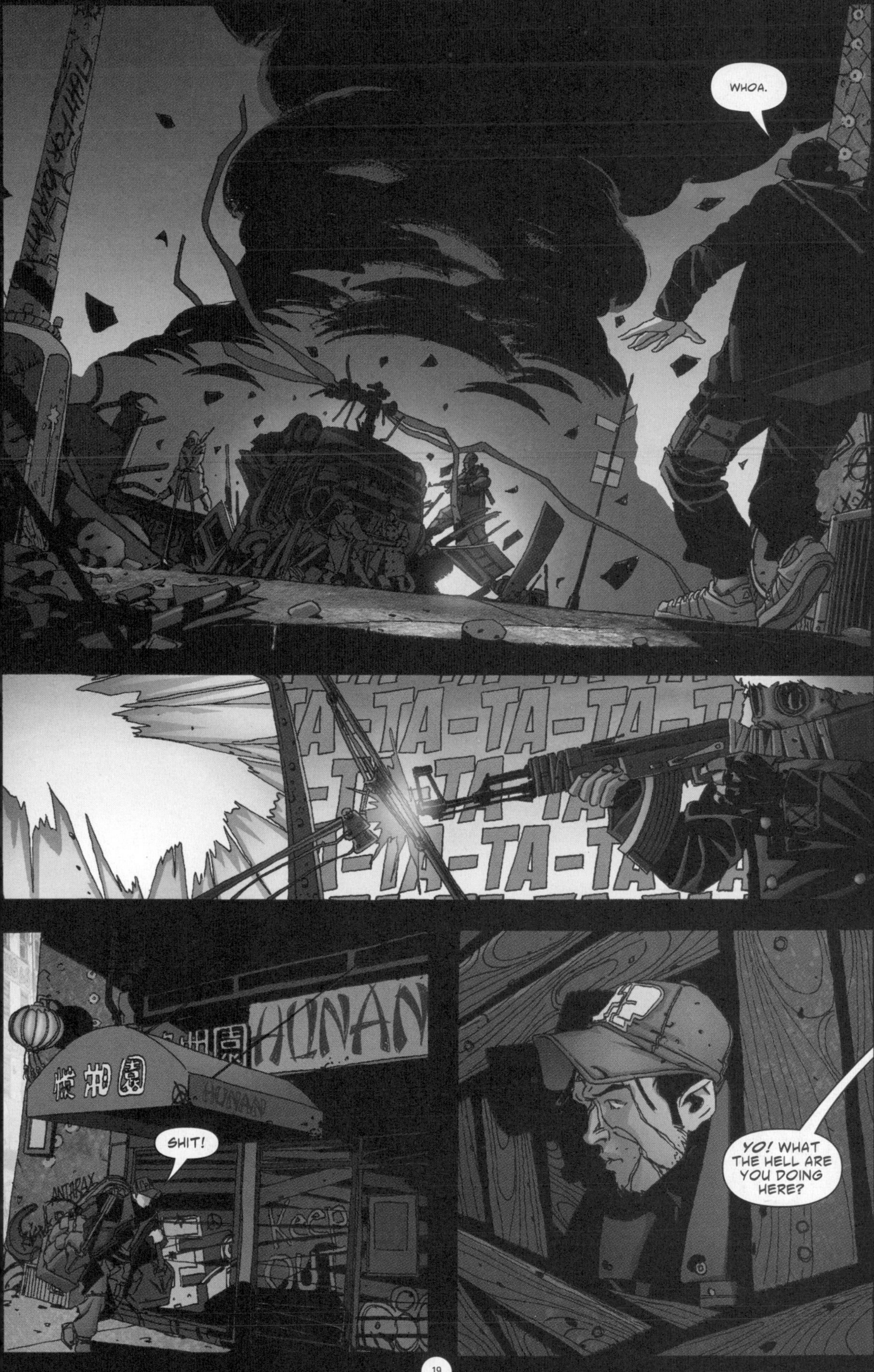
WHOA.
TA-TA-TA-TA-
HUNAN
SHIT!
YO! WHAT THE HELL ARE YOU DOING HERE?

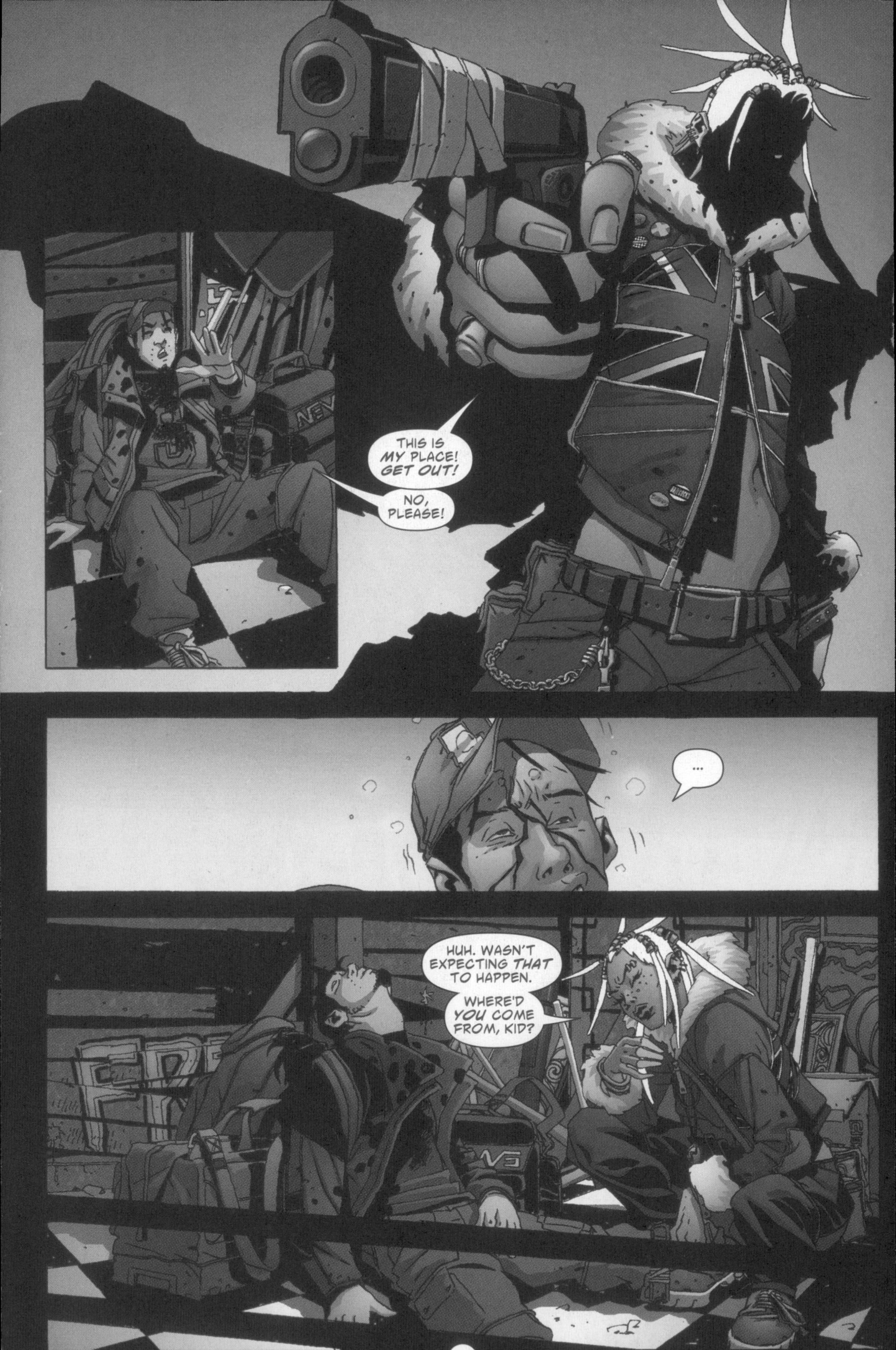
THIS IS MY PLACE! GET OUT!
NO, PLEASE!
...
HUH. WASN'T EXPECTING THAT TO HAPPEN.
WHERE'D YOU COME FROM, KID?

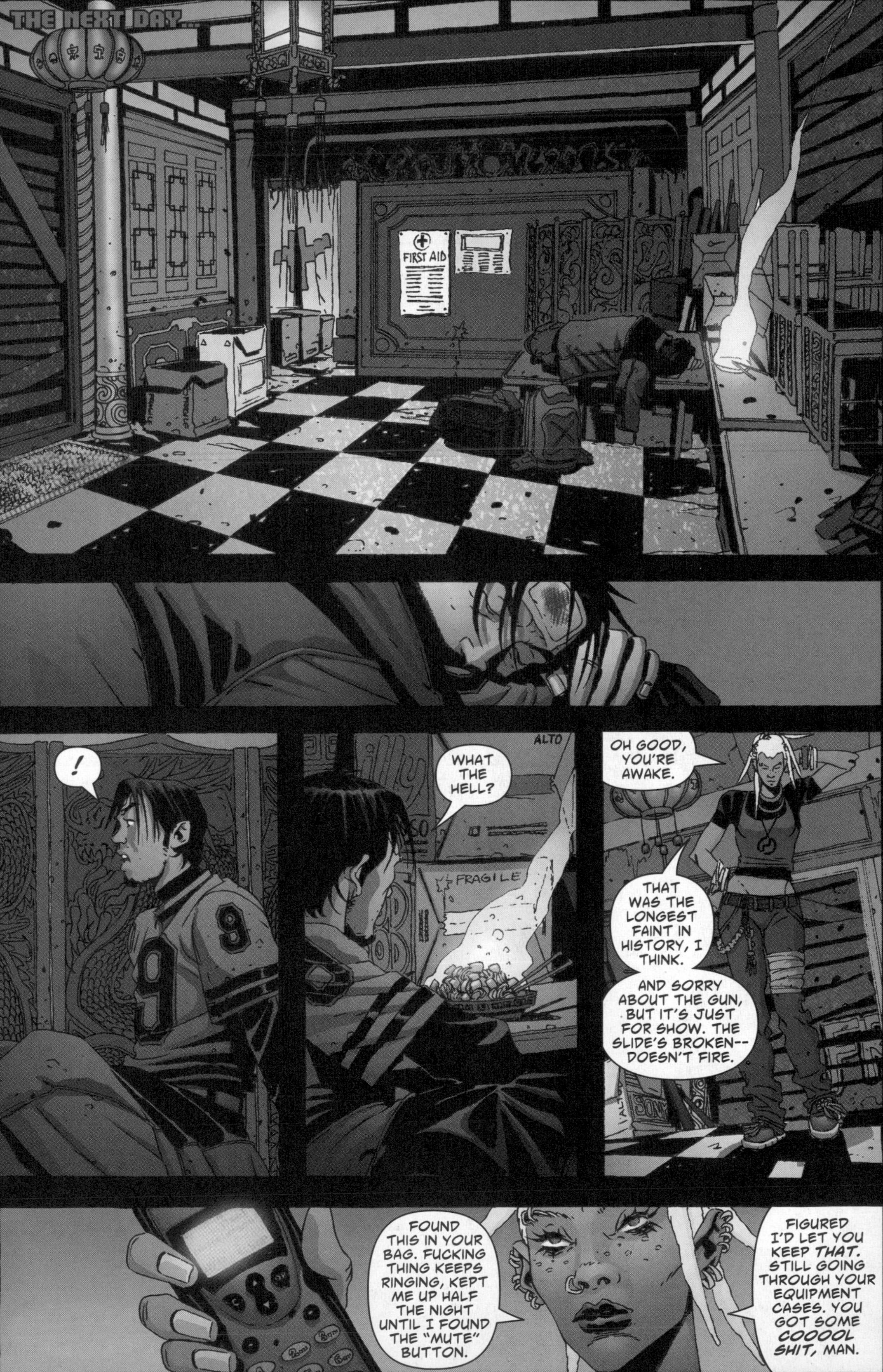
THE NEXT DAY...
FIRST AID
!
ALTO
WHAT THE HELL?
FRAGILE
OH GOOD, YOU'RE AWAKE.
THAT WAS THE LONGEST FAINT IN HISTORY, I THINK.
AND SORRY ABOUT THE GUN, BUT IT'S JUST FOR SHOW. THE SLIDE'S BROKEN-- DOESN'T FIRE.
FOUND THIS IN YOUR BAG. FUCKING THING KEEPS RINGING, KEPT ME UP HALF THE NIGHT UNTIL I FOUND THE "MUTE" BUTTON.
FIGURED I'D LET YOU KEEP *THAT*. STILL GOING THROUGH YOUR EQUIPMENT CASES. YOU GOT SOME ***COOOOL SHIT***, MAN.

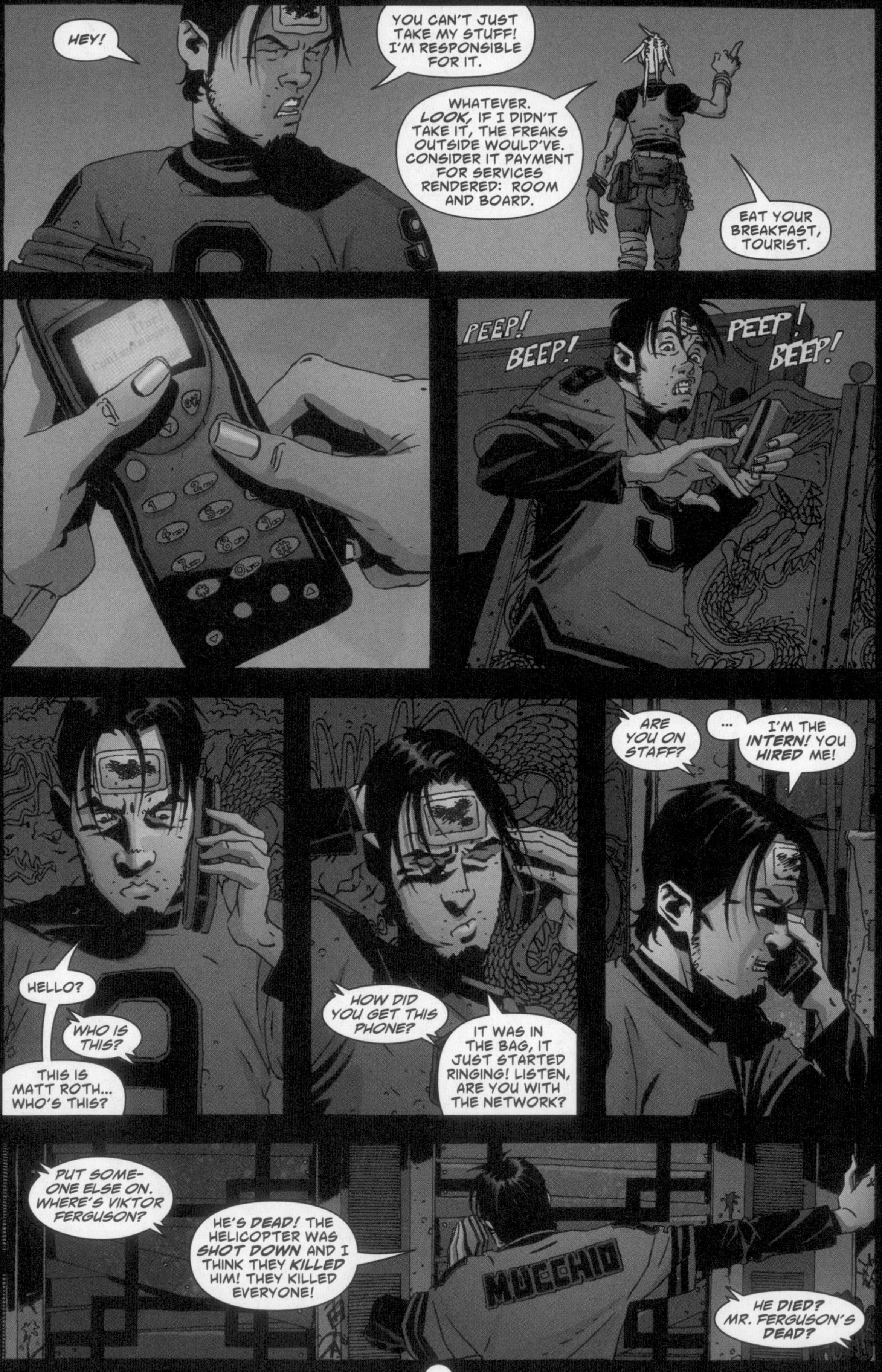
HEY!
YOU CAN'T JUST TAKE MY STUFF! I'M RESPONSIBLE FOR IT.
WHATEVER. LOOK, IF I DIDN'T TAKE IT, THE FREAKS OUTSIDE WOULD'VE. CONSIDER IT PAYMENT FOR SERVICES RENDERED: ROOM AND BOARD.
EAT YOUR BREAKFAST, TOURIST.
PEEP! BEEP!
PEEP! BEEP!
HELLO?
WHO IS THIS?
THIS IS MATT ROTH... WHO'S THIS?
HOW DID YOU GET THIS PHONE?
IT WAS IN THE BAG, IT JUST STARTED RINGING! LISTEN, ARE YOU WITH THE NETWORK?
ARE YOU ON STAFF?
... I'M THE INTERN! YOU HIRED ME!
PUT SOME-ONE ELSE ON. WHERE'S VIKTOR FERGUSON?
HE'S DEAD! THE HELICOPTER WAS SHOT DOWN AND I THINK THEY KILLED HIM! THEY KILLED EVERYONE!
MUCCHIO
HE DIED? MR. FERGUSON'S DEAD?

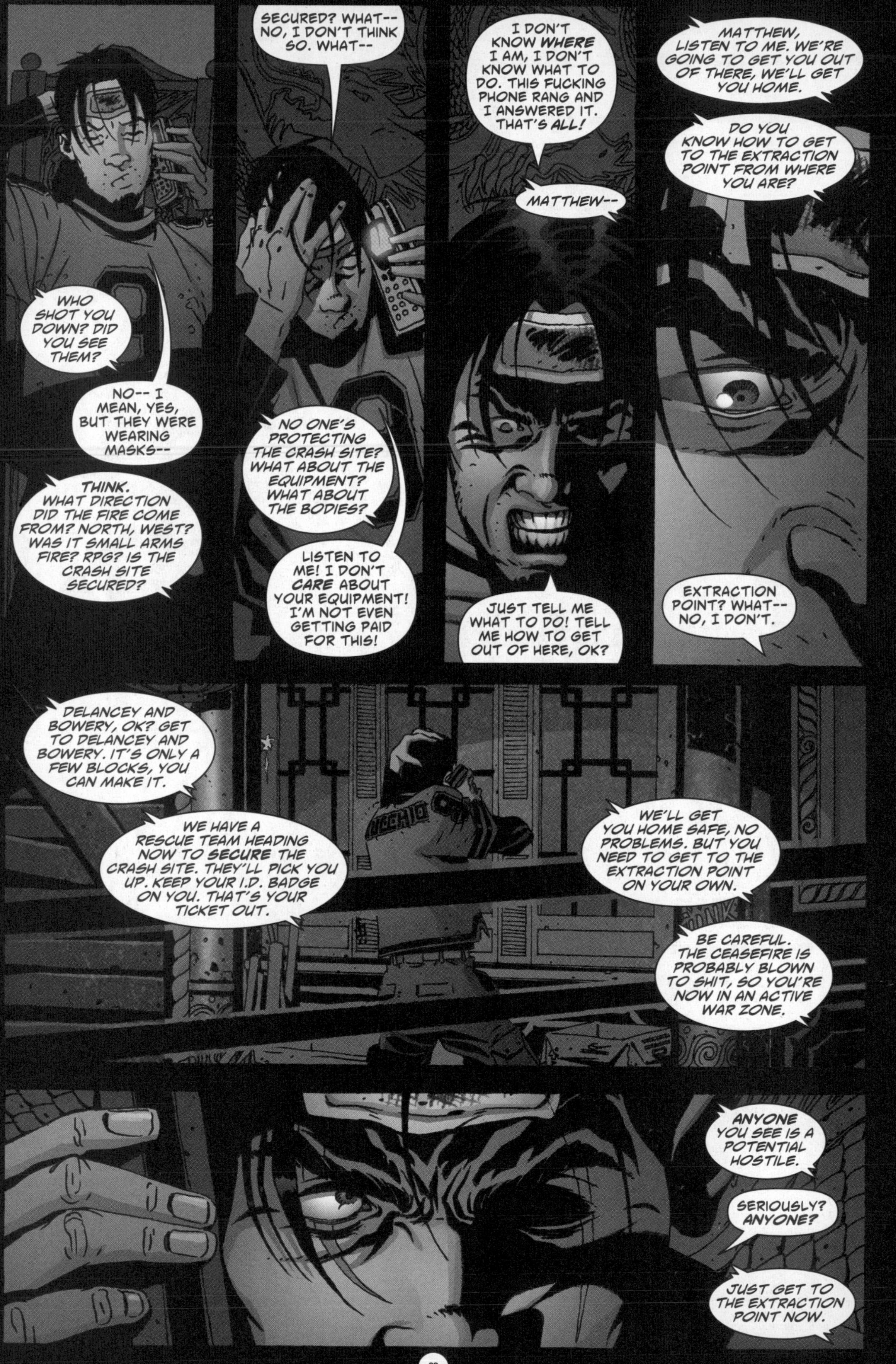

WHO SHOT YOU DOWN? DID YOU SEE THEM?
NO-- I MEAN, YES, BUT THEY WERE WEARING MASKS--
THINK. WHAT DIRECTION DID THE FIRE COME FROM? NORTH, WEST? WAS IT SMALL ARMS FIRE? RPG? IS THE CRASH SITE SECURED?
SECURED? WHAT-- NO, I DON'T THINK SO. WHAT--
NO ONE'S PROTECTING THE CRASH SITE? WHAT ABOUT THE EQUIPMENT? WHAT ABOUT THE BODIES?
LISTEN TO ME! I DON'T CARE ABOUT YOUR EQUIPMENT! I'M NOT EVEN GETTING PAID FOR THIS!
I DON'T KNOW WHERE I AM, I DON'T KNOW WHAT TO DO. THIS FUCKING PHONE RANG AND I ANSWERED IT. THAT'S ALL!
MATTHEW--
JUST TELL ME WHAT TO DO! TELL ME HOW TO GET OUT OF HERE, OK?
MATTHEW, LISTEN TO ME. WE'RE GOING TO GET YOU OUT OF THERE, WE'LL GET YOU HOME.
DO YOU KNOW HOW TO GET TO THE EXTRACTION POINT FROM WHERE YOU ARE?
EXTRACTION POINT? WHAT-- NO, I DON'T.
DELANCEY AND BOWERY, OK? GET TO DELANCEY AND BOWERY. IT'S ONLY A FEW BLOCKS, YOU CAN MAKE IT.
WE HAVE A RESCUE TEAM HEADING NOW TO SECURE THE CRASH SITE. THEY'LL PICK YOU UP. KEEP YOUR I.D. BADGE ON YOU. THAT'S YOUR TICKET OUT.
WE'LL GET YOU HOME SAFE, NO PROBLEMS. BUT YOU NEED TO GET TO THE EXTRACTION POINT ON YOUR OWN.
BE CAREFUL. THE CEASEFIRE IS PROBABLY BLOWN TO SHIT, SO YOU'RE NOW IN AN ACTIVE WAR ZONE.
ANYONE YOU SEE IS A POTENTIAL HOSTILE.
SERIOUSLY? ANYONE?
JUST GET TO THE EXTRACTION POINT NOW.

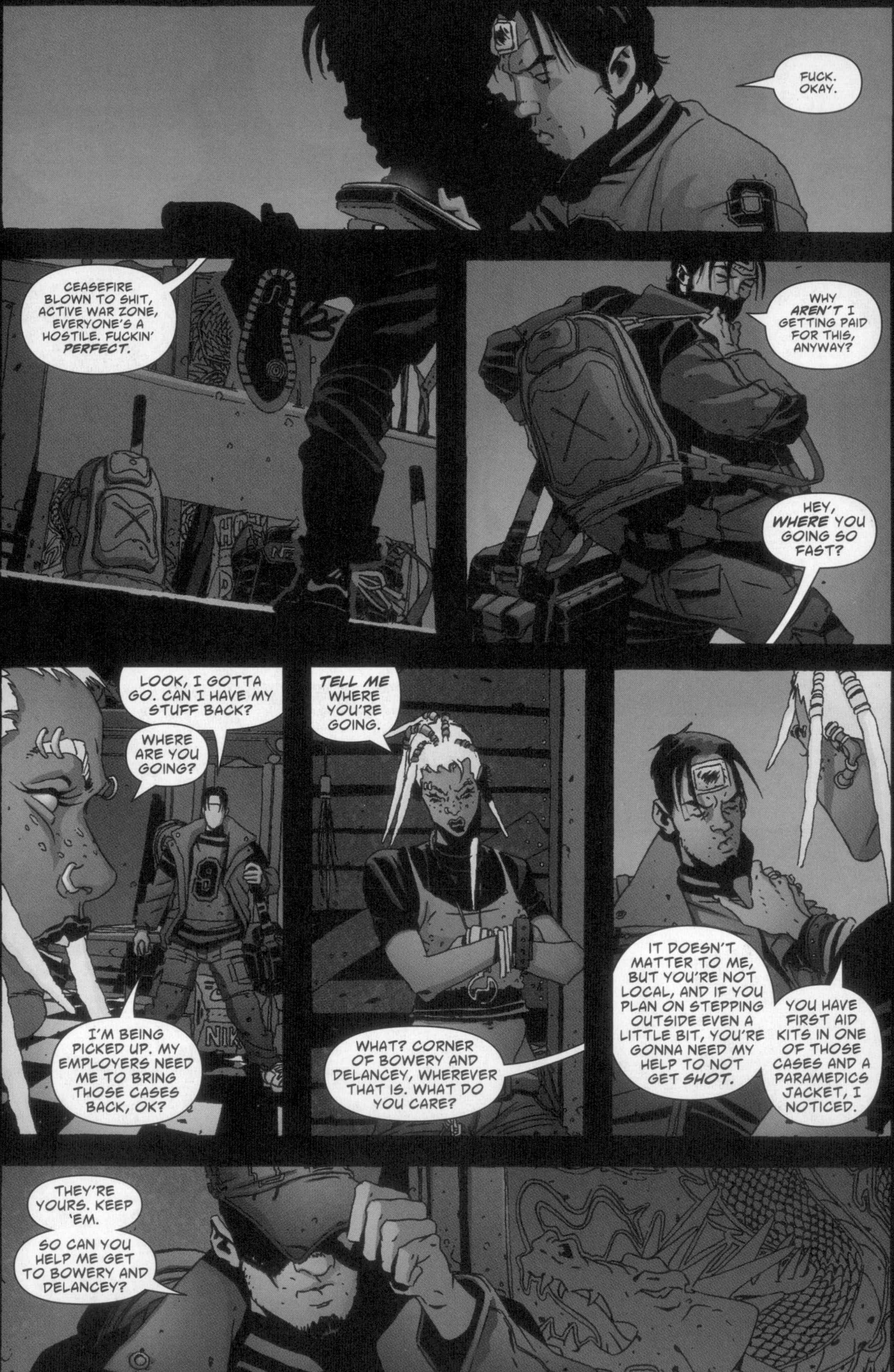
FUCK. OKAY.
CEASEFIRE BLOWN TO SHIT, ACTIVE WAR ZONE, EVERYONE'S A HOSTILE. FUCKIN' PERFECT.
WHY AREN'T I GETTING PAID FOR THIS, ANYWAY?
HEY, WHERE YOU GOING SO FAST?
LOOK, I GOTTA GO. CAN I HAVE MY STUFF BACK?
WHERE ARE YOU GOING?
I'M BEING PICKED UP. MY EMPLOYERS NEED ME TO BRING THOSE CASES BACK, OK?
TELL ME WHERE YOU'RE GOING.
WHAT? CORNER OF BOWERY AND DELANCEY, WHEREVER THAT IS. WHAT DO YOU CARE?
IT DOESN'T MATTER TO ME, BUT YOU'RE NOT LOCAL, AND IF YOU PLAN ON STEPPING OUTSIDE EVEN A LITTLE BIT, YOU'RE GONNA NEED MY HELP TO NOT GET SHOT.
YOU HAVE FIRST AID KITS IN ONE OF THOSE CASES AND A PARAMEDICS JACKET, I NOTICED.
THEY'RE YOURS. KEEP 'EM.
SO CAN YOU HELP ME GET TO BOWERY AND DELANCEY?

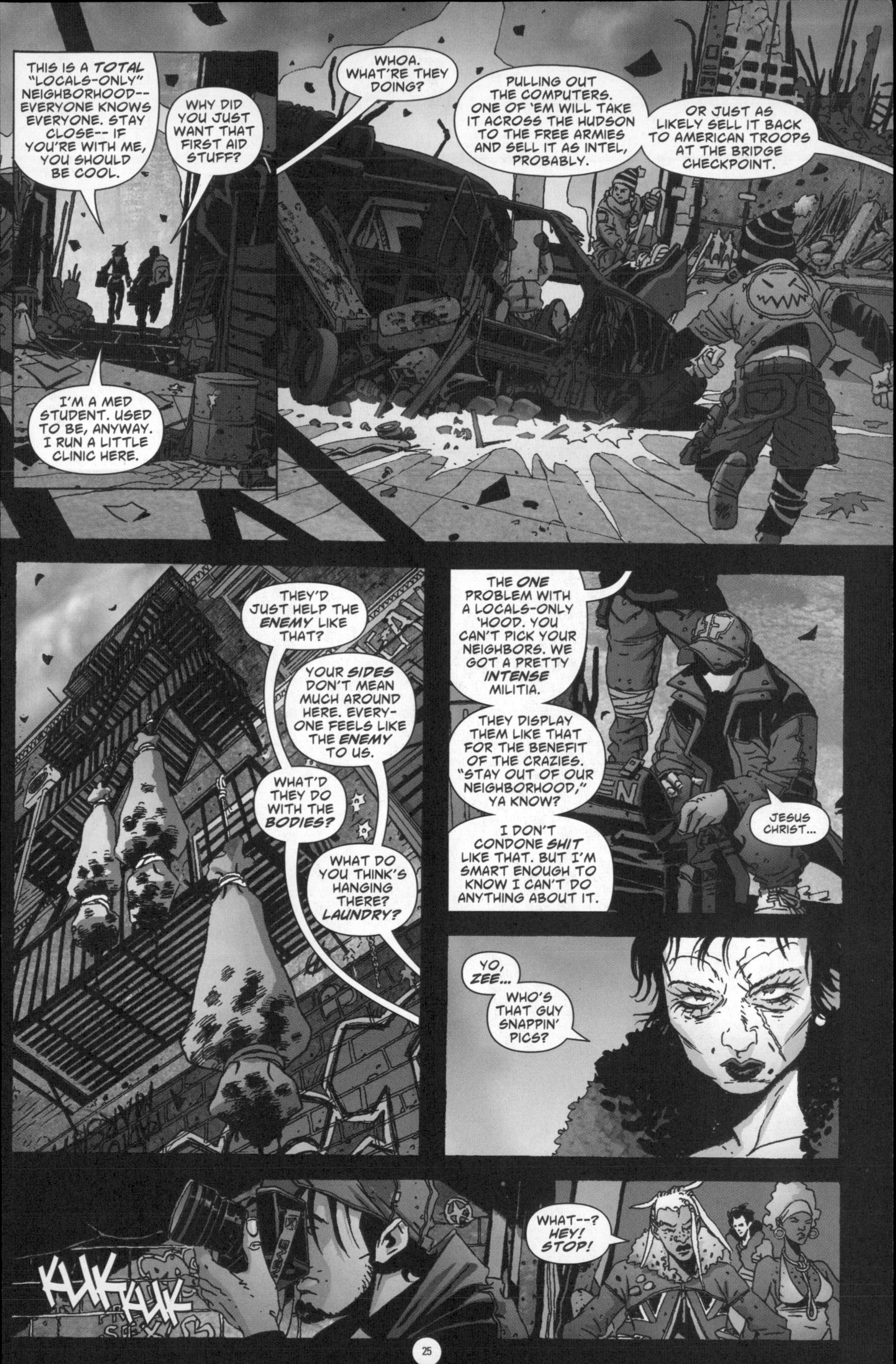
THIS IS A *TOTAL* "LOCALS-ONLY" NEIGHBORHOOD-- EVERYONE KNOWS EVERYONE. STAY CLOSE-- IF YOU'RE WITH ME, YOU SHOULD BE COOL.
WHY DID YOU JUST WANT THAT FIRST AID STUFF?
I'M A MED STUDENT. USED TO BE, ANYWAY. I RUN A LITTLE CLINIC HERE.
WHOA. WHAT'RE THEY DOING?
PULLING OUT THE COMPUTERS. ONE OF 'EM WILL TAKE IT ACROSS THE HUDSON TO THE FREE ARMIES AND SELL IT AS INTEL, PROBABLY.
OR JUST AS LIKELY SELL IT BACK TO AMERICAN TROOPS AT THE BRIDGE CHECKPOINT.
THEY'D JUST HELP THE *ENEMY* LIKE THAT?
YOUR *SIDES* DON'T MEAN MUCH AROUND HERE. EVERY-ONE FEELS LIKE THE *ENEMY* TO US.
WHAT'D THEY DO WITH THE *BODIES?*
WHAT DO YOU THINK'S HANGING THERE? *LAUNDRY?*
THE *ONE* PROBLEM WITH A LOCALS-ONLY 'HOOD. YOU CAN'T PICK YOUR NEIGHBORS. WE GOT A PRETTY *INTENSE* MILITIA.
THEY DISPLAY THEM LIKE THAT FOR THE BENEFIT OF THE CRAZIES. "STAY OUT OF OUR NEIGHBORHOOD," YA KNOW?
I DON'T CONDONE *SHIT* LIKE THAT. BUT I'M SMART ENOUGH TO KNOW I CAN'T DO ANYTHING ABOUT IT.
JESUS CHRIST...
YO, *ZEE*... WHO'S THAT GUY SNAPPIN' PICS?
KLIK KLIK
WHAT--? *HEY! STOP!*

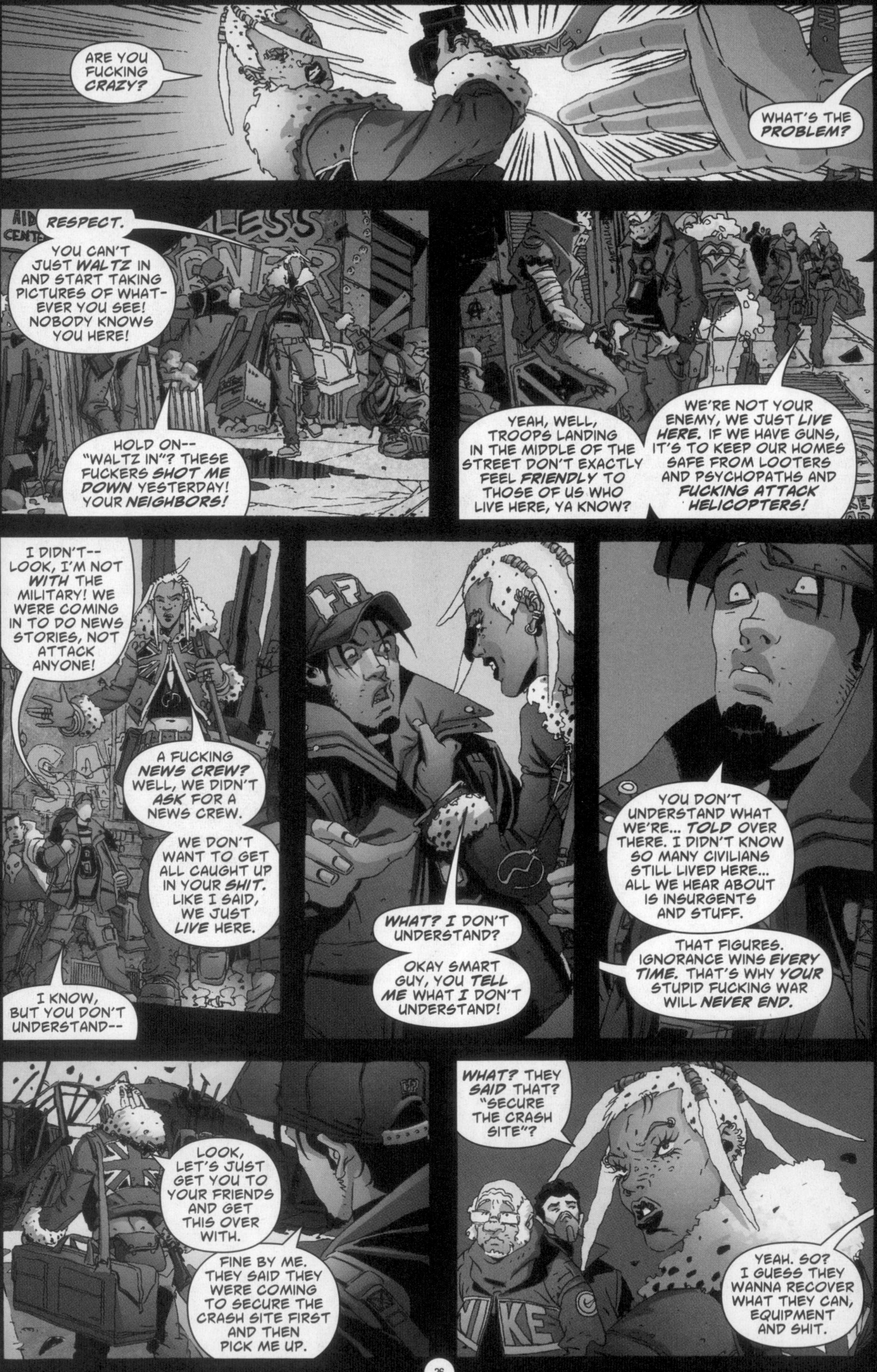
ARE YOU FUCKING CRAZY?
WHAT'S THE PROBLEM?
RESPECT.
YOU CAN'T JUST WALTZ IN AND START TAKING PICTURES OF WHAT-EVER YOU SEE! NOBODY KNOWS YOU HERE!
HOLD ON-- "WALTZ IN"? THESE FUCKERS SHOT ME DOWN YESTERDAY! YOUR NEIGHBORS!
YEAH, WELL, TROOPS LANDING IN THE MIDDLE OF THE STREET DON'T EXACTLY FEEL FRIENDLY TO THOSE OF US WHO LIVE HERE, YA KNOW?
WE'RE NOT YOUR ENEMY, WE JUST LIVE HERE. IF WE HAVE GUNS, IT'S TO KEEP OUR HOMES SAFE FROM LOOTERS AND PSYCHOPATHS AND FUCKING ATTACK HELICOPTERS!
I DIDN'T-- LOOK, I'M NOT WITH THE MILITARY! WE WERE COMING IN TO DO NEWS STORIES, NOT ATTACK ANYONE!
A FUCKING NEWS CREW? WELL, WE DIDN'T ASK FOR A NEWS CREW.
WE DON'T WANT TO GET ALL CAUGHT UP IN YOUR SHIT. LIKE I SAID, WE JUST LIVE HERE.
I KNOW, BUT YOU DON'T UNDERSTAND--
WHAT? I DON'T UNDERSTAND?
OKAY SMART GUY, YOU TELL ME WHAT I DON'T UNDERSTAND!
YOU DON'T UNDERSTAND WHAT WE'RE... TOLD OVER THERE. I DIDN'T KNOW SO MANY CIVILIANS STILL LIVED HERE... ALL WE HEAR ABOUT IS INSURGENTS AND STUFF.
THAT FIGURES. IGNORANCE WINS EVERY TIME. THAT'S WHY YOUR STUPID FUCKING WAR WILL NEVER END.
LOOK, LET'S JUST GET YOU TO YOUR FRIENDS AND GET THIS OVER WITH.
FINE BY ME. THEY SAID THEY WERE COMING TO SECURE THE CRASH SITE FIRST AND THEN PICK ME UP.
WHAT? THEY SAID THAT? "SECURE THE CRASH SITE"?
YEAH. SO? I GUESS THEY WANNA RECOVER WHAT THEY CAN, EQUIPMENT AND SHIT.

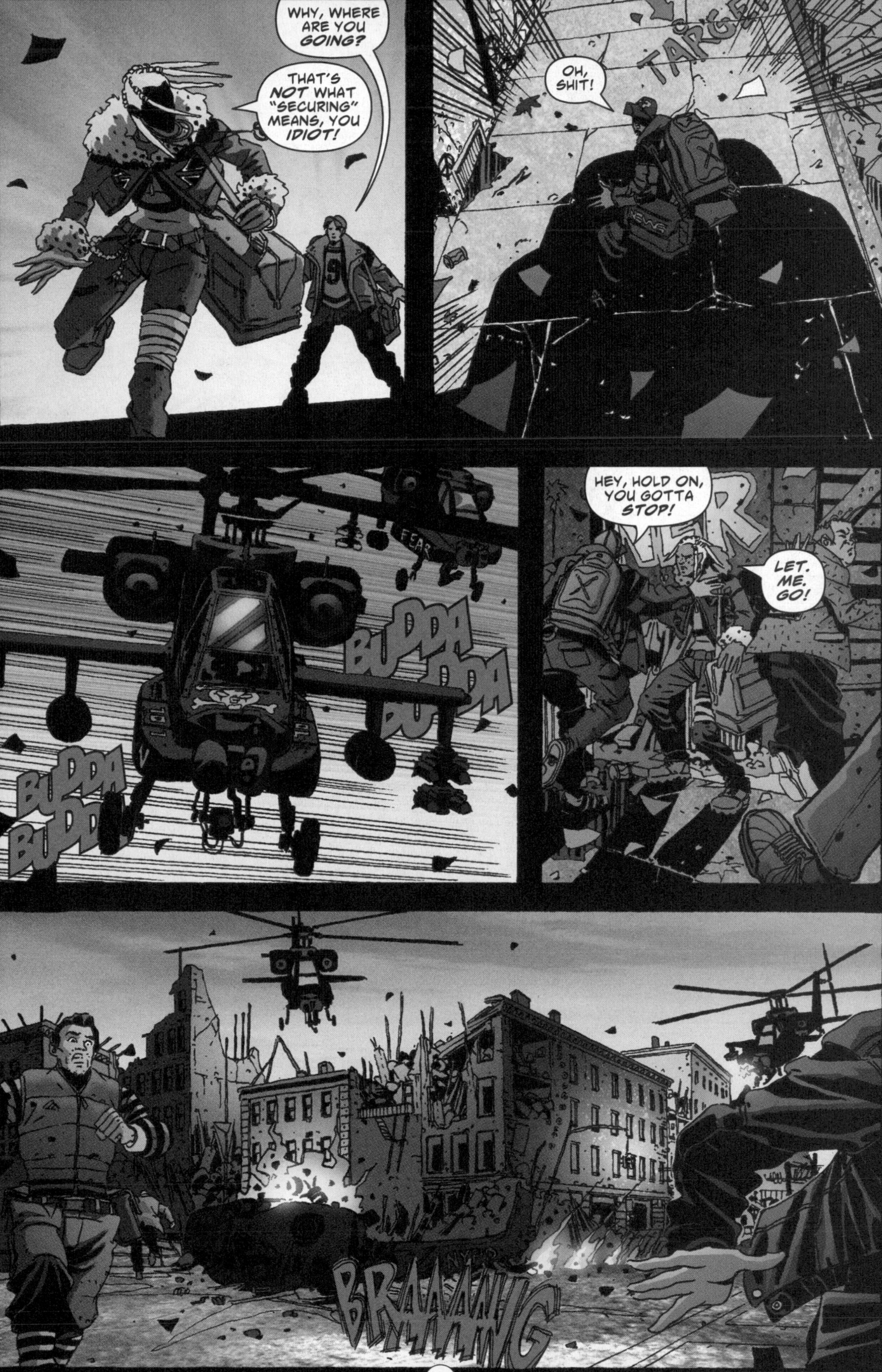
WHY, WHERE ARE YOU GOING?
THAT'S NOT WHAT "SECURING" MEANS, YOU IDIOT!
OH, SHIT!
TARGE
BUDDA BUDDA BUDDA
BUDDA BUDD
HEY, HOLD ON, YOU GOTTA STOP!
LET. ME. GO!
BRAAAAANG

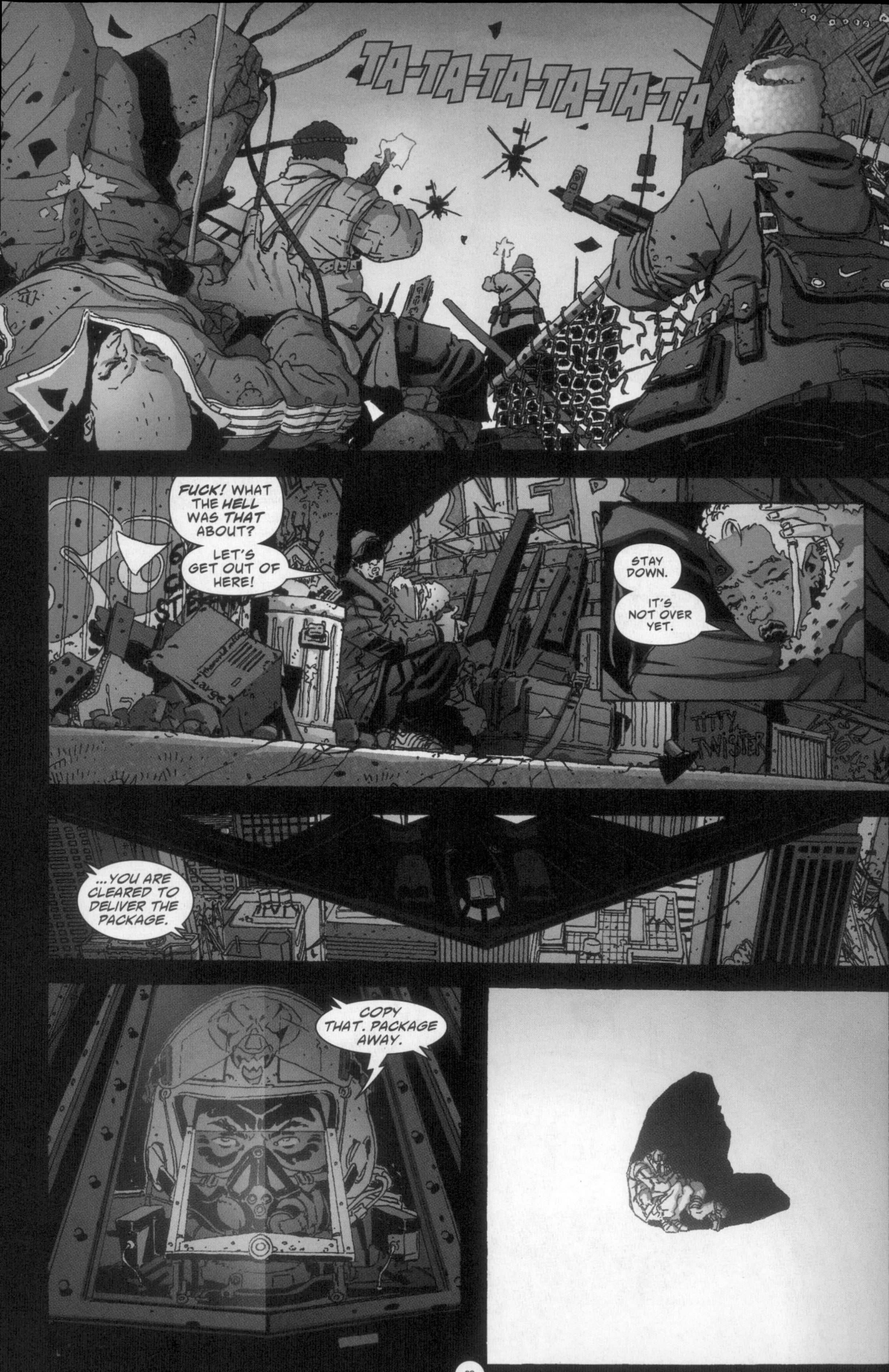
TA-TA-TA-TA-TA-TA
FUCK! WHAT THE HELL WAS THAT ABOUT?
LET'S GET OUT OF HERE!
STAY DOWN.
IT'S NOT OVER YET.
Large
TITTY TWISTER
...YOU ARE CLEARED TO DELIVER THE PACKAGE.
COPY THAT. PACKAGE AWAY.

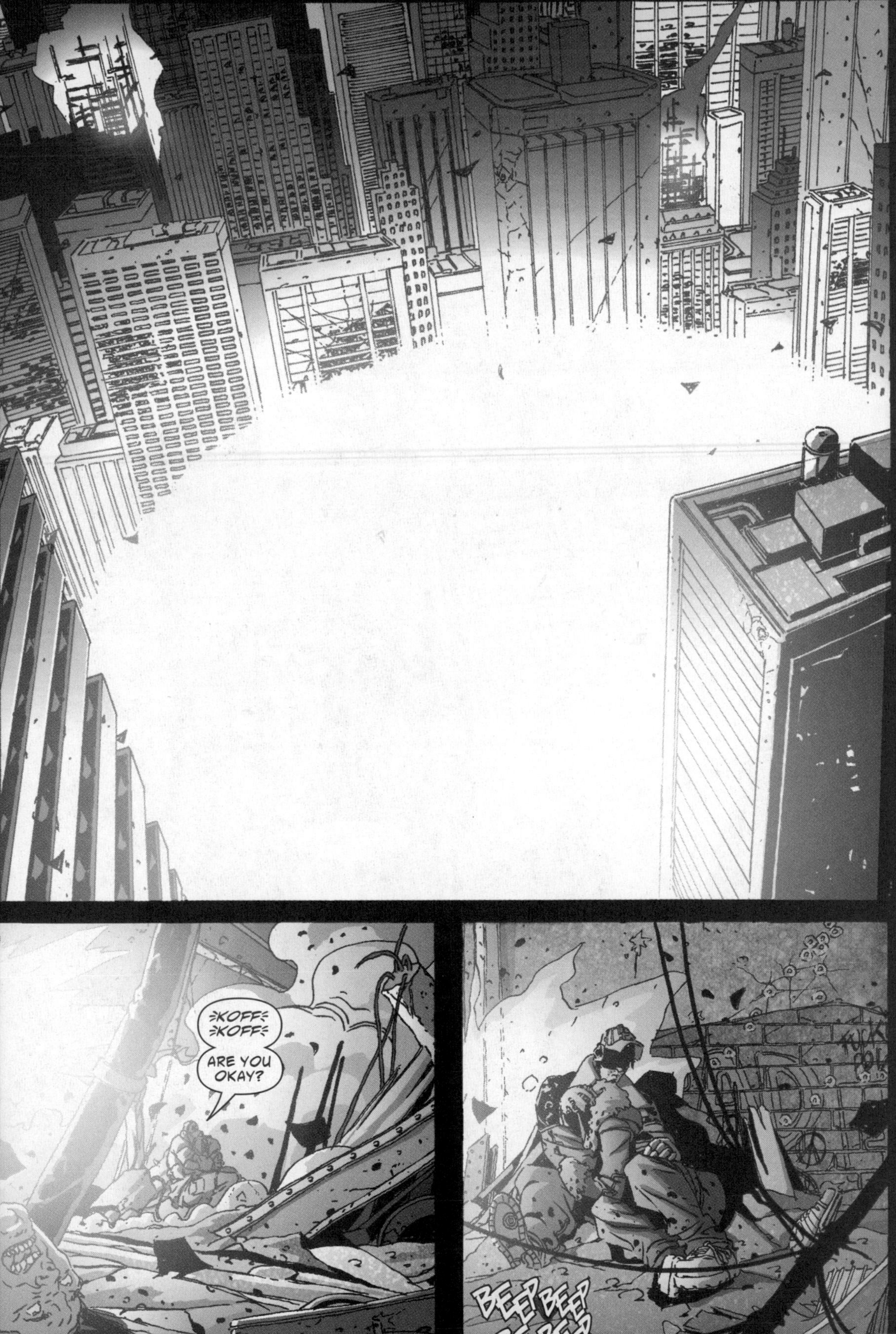
KOFF KOFF
ARE YOU OKAY?
BEEP BEEP BE-BEEP

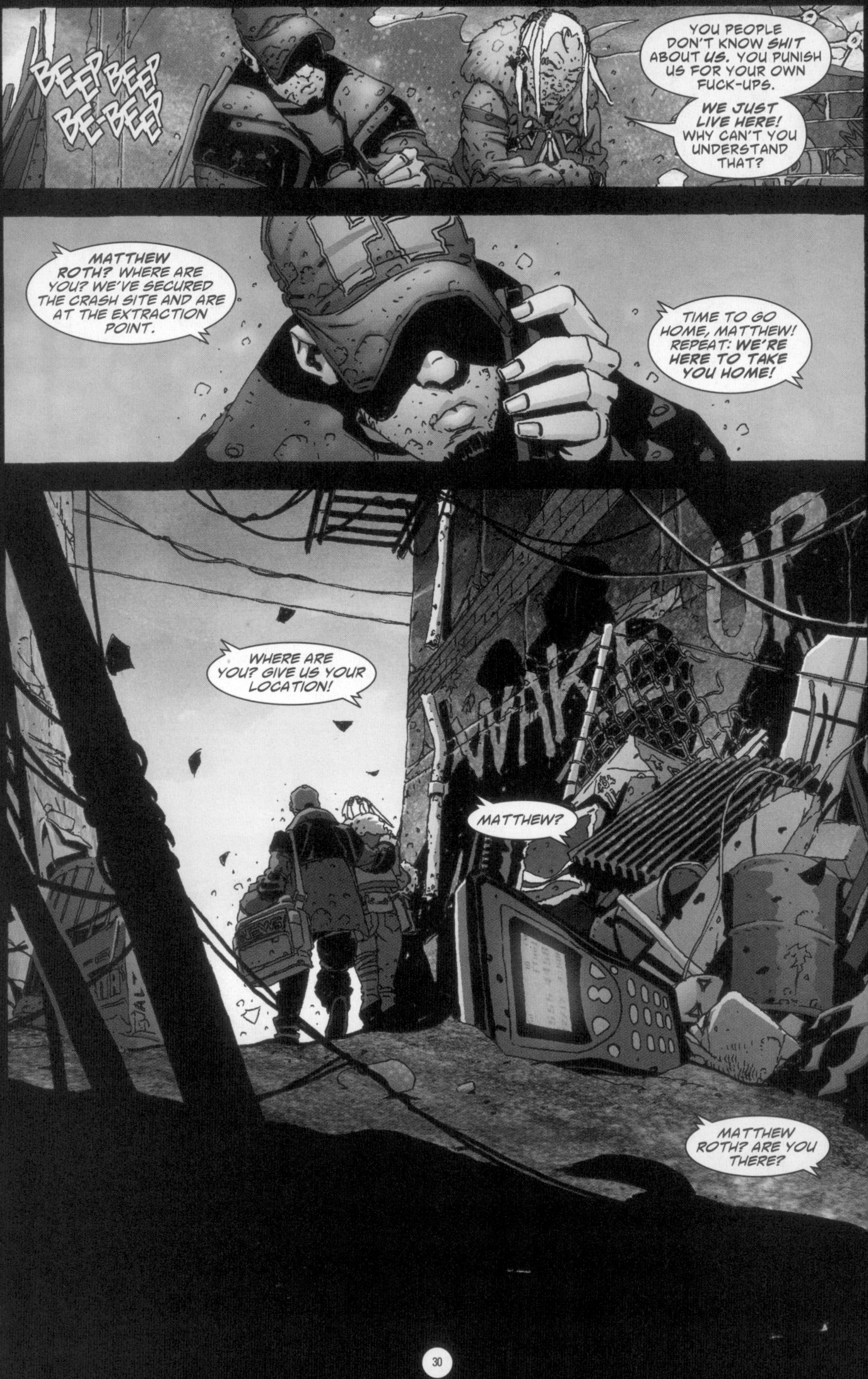
BEEP BEEP BE-BEEP
YOU PEOPLE DON'T KNOW SHIT ABOUT US. YOU PUNISH US FOR YOUR OWN FUCK-UPS.
WE JUST LIVE HERE! WHY CAN'T YOU UNDERSTAND THAT?
MATTHEW ROTH? WHERE ARE YOU? WE'VE SECURED THE CRASH SITE AND ARE AT THE EXTRACTION POINT.
TIME TO GO HOME, MATTHEW! REPEAT: WE'RE HERE TO TAKE YOU HOME!
WHERE ARE YOU? GIVE US YOUR LOCATION!
MATTHEW?
MATTHEW ROTH? ARE YOU THERE?

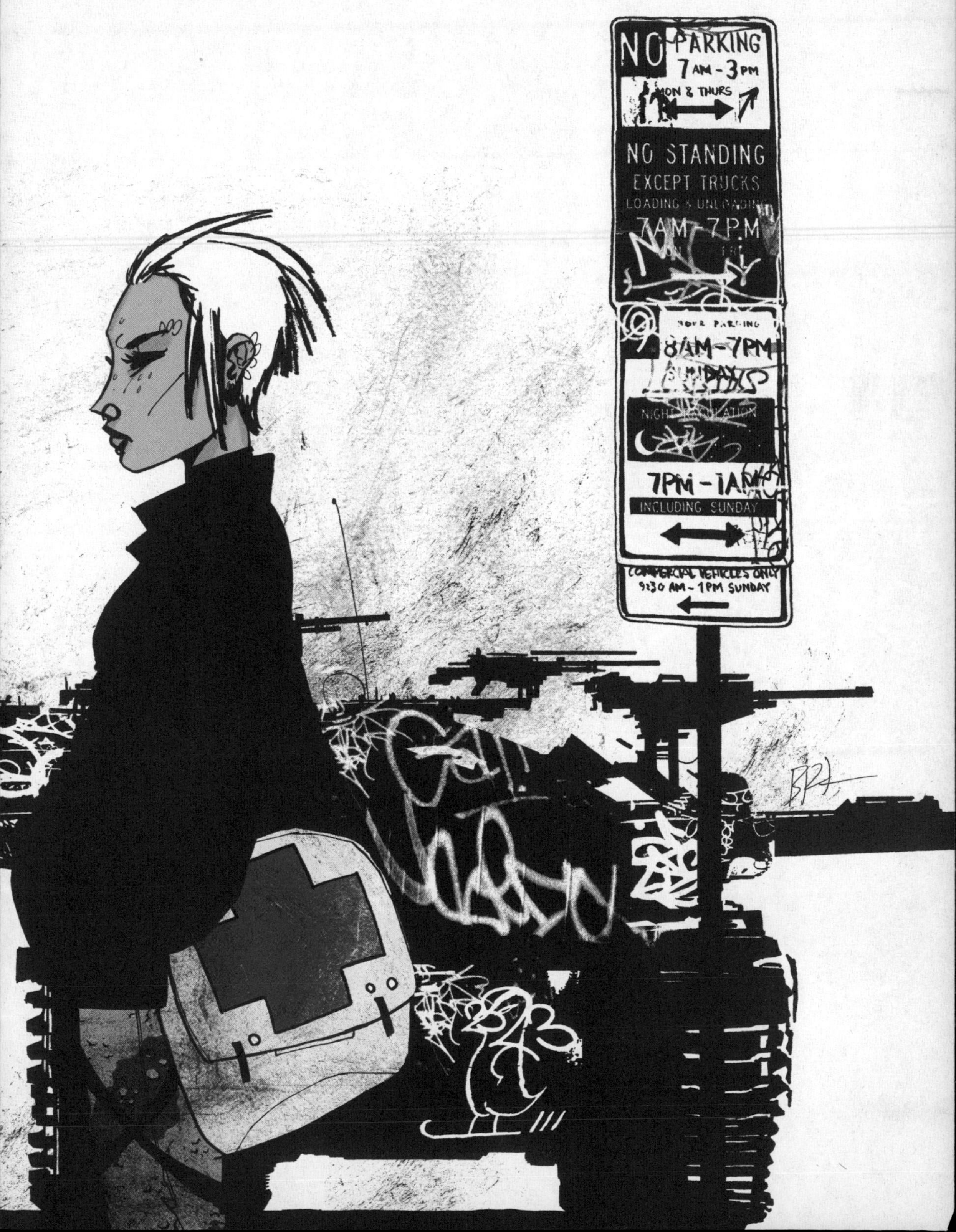
NO PARKING
7AM - 3PM
MON & THURS
NO STANDING
EXCEPT TRUCKS
8AM-7PM
7PM - 1AM
INCLUDING SUNDAY
COMMERCIAL VEHICLES ONLY
9:30 AM - 1PM SUNDAY

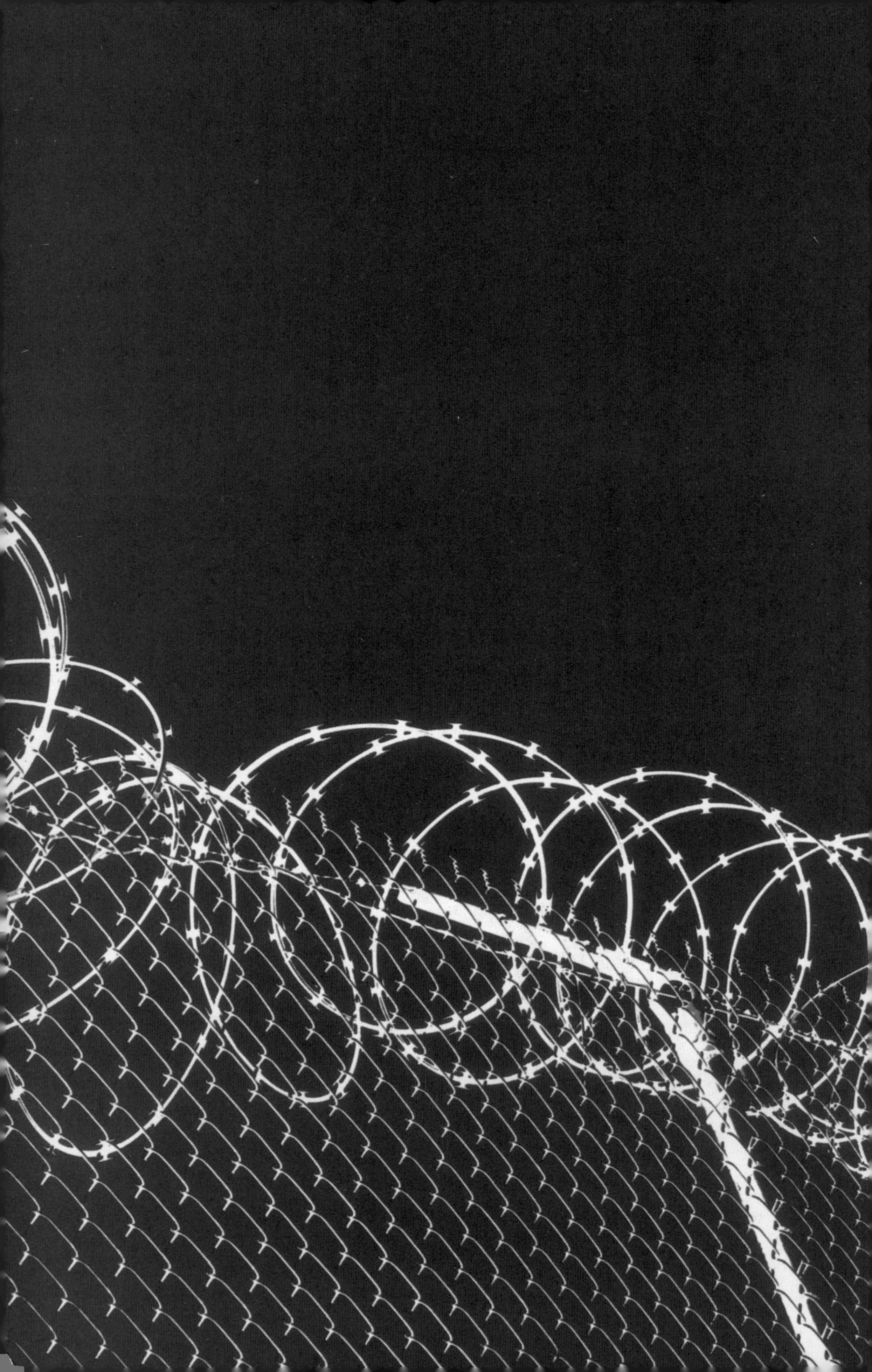

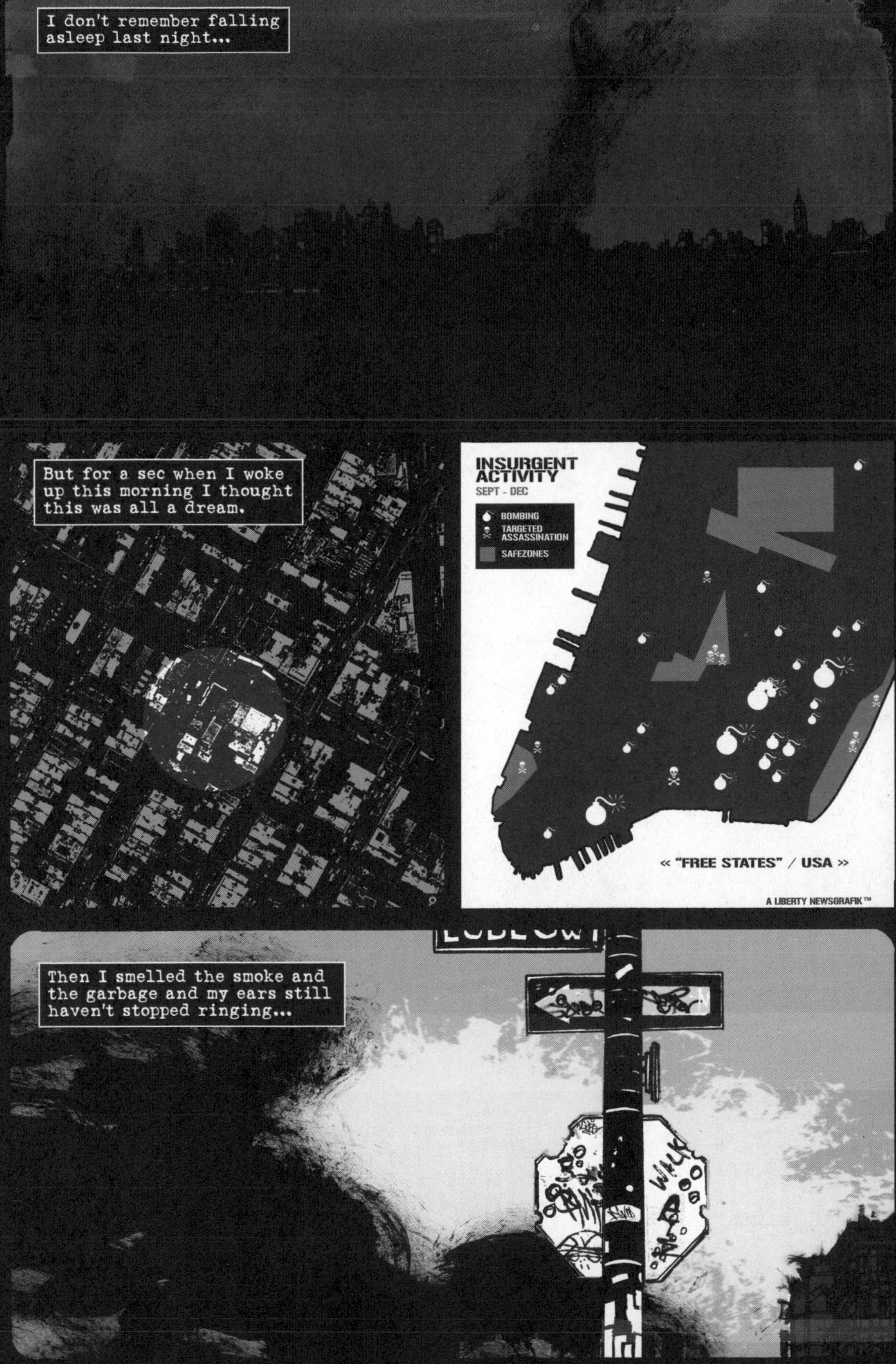
I don't remember falling asleep last night...
But for a sec when I woke up this morning I thought this was all a dream.
INSURGENT ACTIVITY
SEPT - DEC
BOMBING
TARGETED ASSASSINATION
SAFEZONES
« "FREE STATES" / USA »
A LIBERTY NEWSGRAFIK ™
Then I smelled the smoke and the garbage and my ears still haven't stopped ringing...
WALK

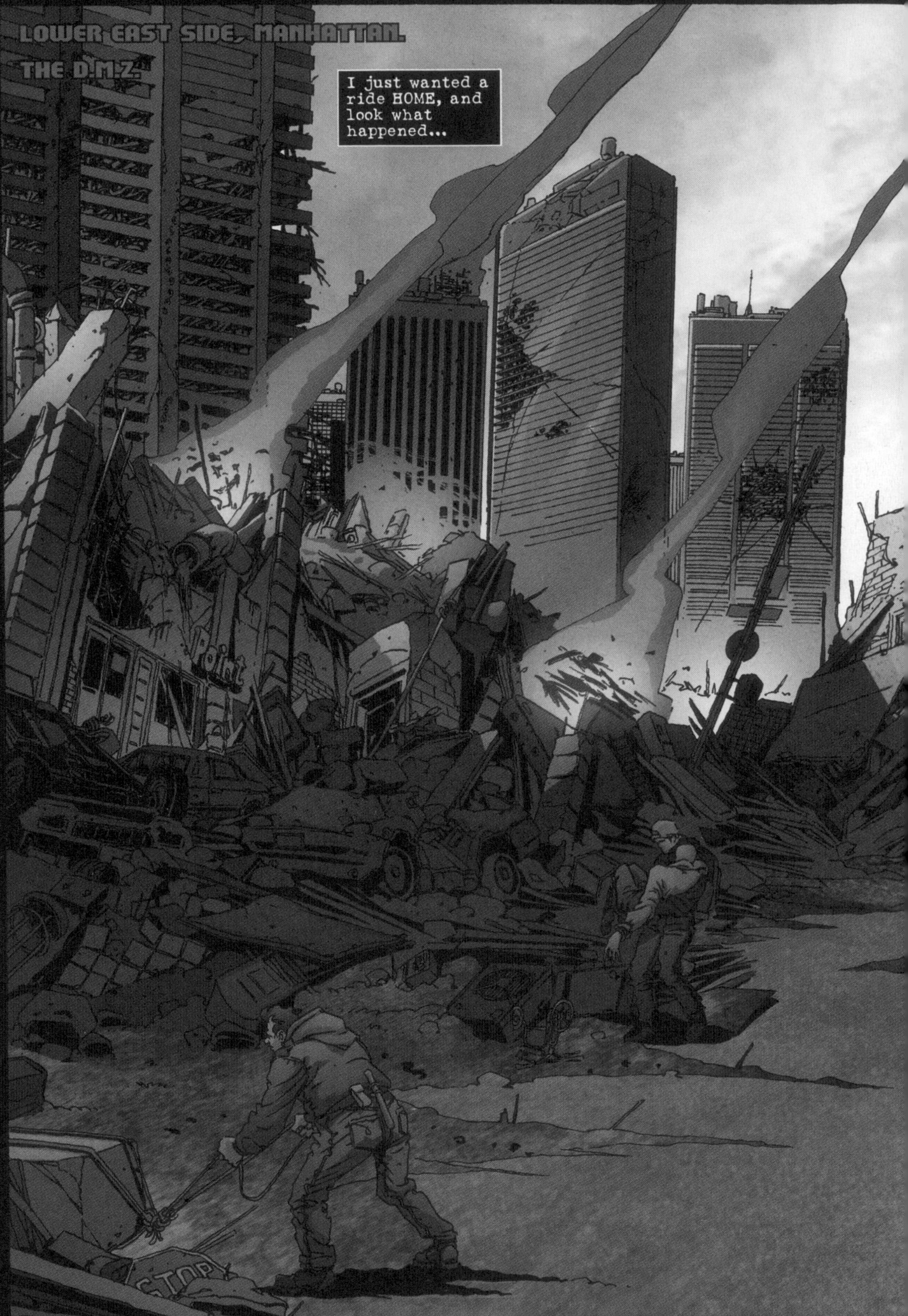
LOWER EAST SIDE, MANHATTAN.
THE D.M.Z.
I just wanted a ride HOME, and look what happened...
STOP

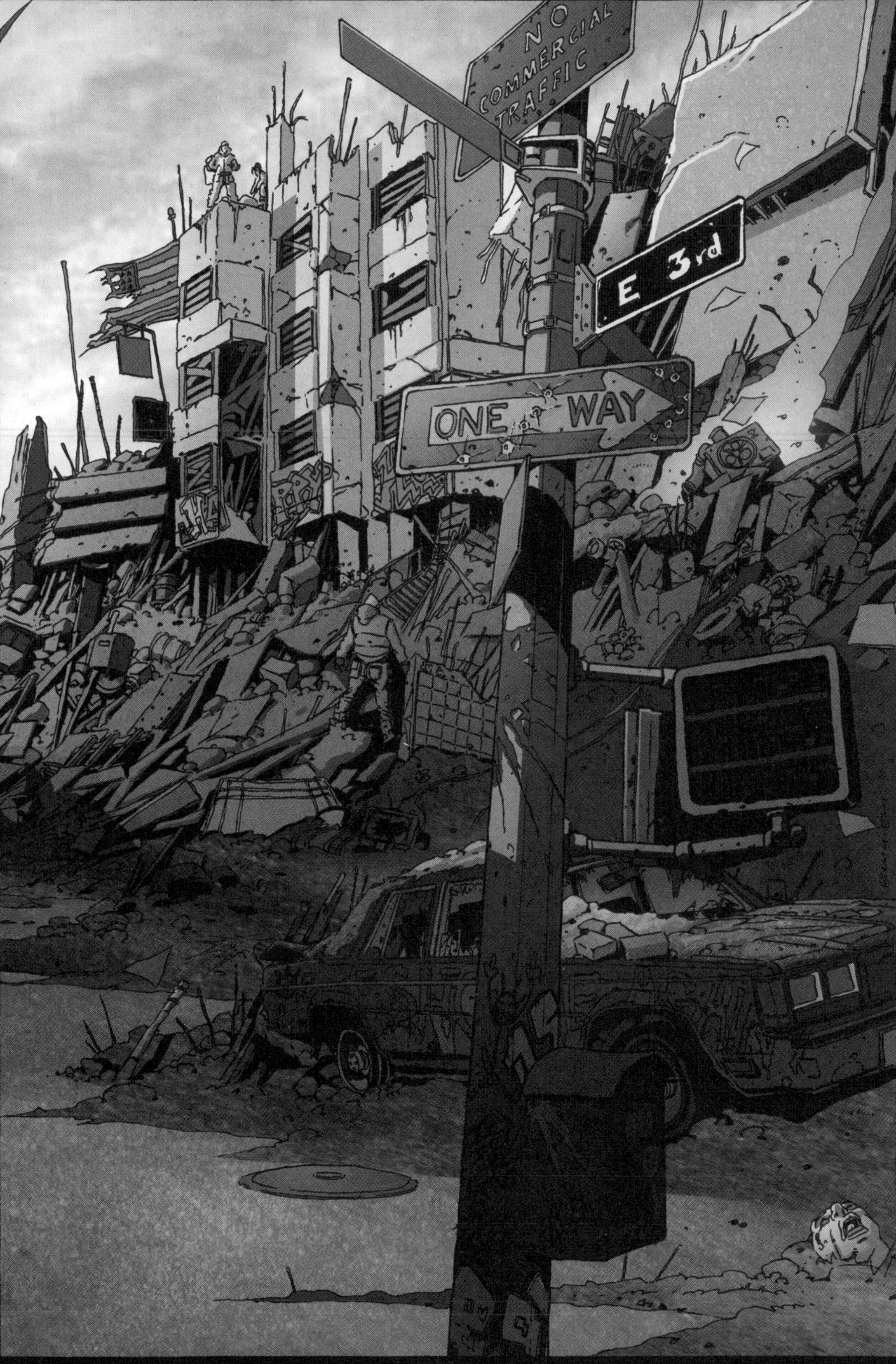
NO COMMERCIAL TRAFFIC
E 3rd
ONE WAY

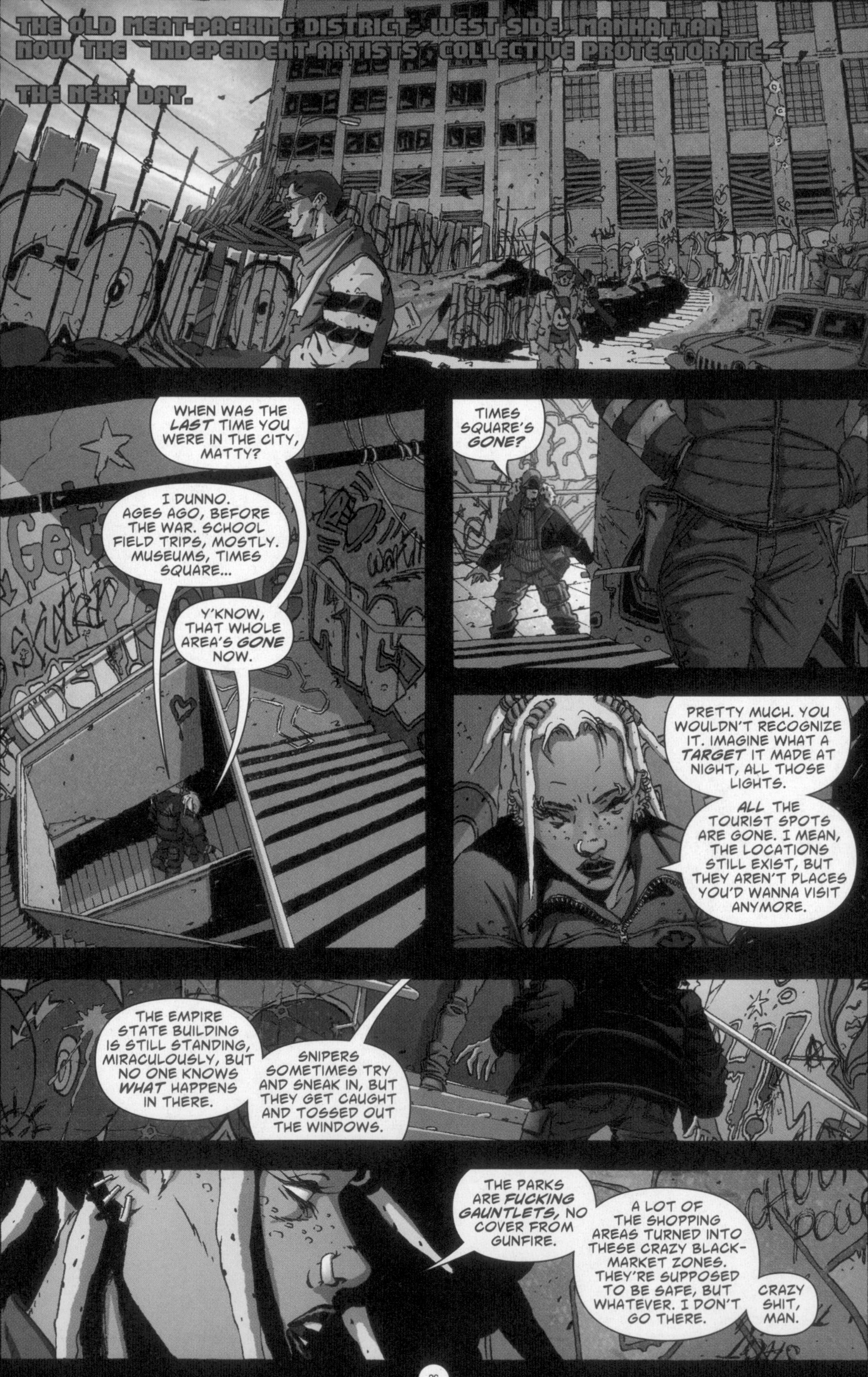

THE OLD MEAT-PACKING DISTRICT, WEST SIDE, MANHATTAN, NOW THE "INDEPENDENT ARTISTS' COLLECTIVE PROTECTORATE."
THE NEXT DAY.
WHEN WAS THE LAST TIME YOU WERE IN THE CITY, MATTY?
I DUNNO. AGES AGO, BEFORE THE WAR. SCHOOL FIELD TRIPS, MOSTLY. MUSEUMS, TIMES SQUARE...
Y'KNOW, THAT WHOLE AREA'S GONE NOW.
TIMES SQUARE'S GONE?
PRETTY MUCH. YOU WOULDN'T RECOGNIZE IT. IMAGINE WHAT A TARGET IT MADE AT NIGHT, ALL THOSE LIGHTS.
ALL THE TOURIST SPOTS ARE GONE. I MEAN, THE LOCATIONS STILL EXIST, BUT THEY AREN'T PLACES YOU'D WANNA VISIT ANYMORE.
THE EMPIRE STATE BUILDING IS STILL STANDING, MIRACULOUSLY, BUT NO ONE KNOWS WHAT HAPPENS IN THERE.
SNIPERS SOMETIMES TRY AND SNEAK IN, BUT THEY GET CAUGHT AND TOSSED OUT THE WINDOWS.
THE PARKS ARE FUCKING GAUNTLETS, NO COVER FROM GUNFIRE.
A LOT OF THE SHOPPING AREAS TURNED INTO THESE CRAZY BLACK-MARKET ZONES. THEY'RE SUPPOSED TO BE SAFE, BUT WHATEVER. I DON'T GO THERE.
CRAZY SHIT, MAN.

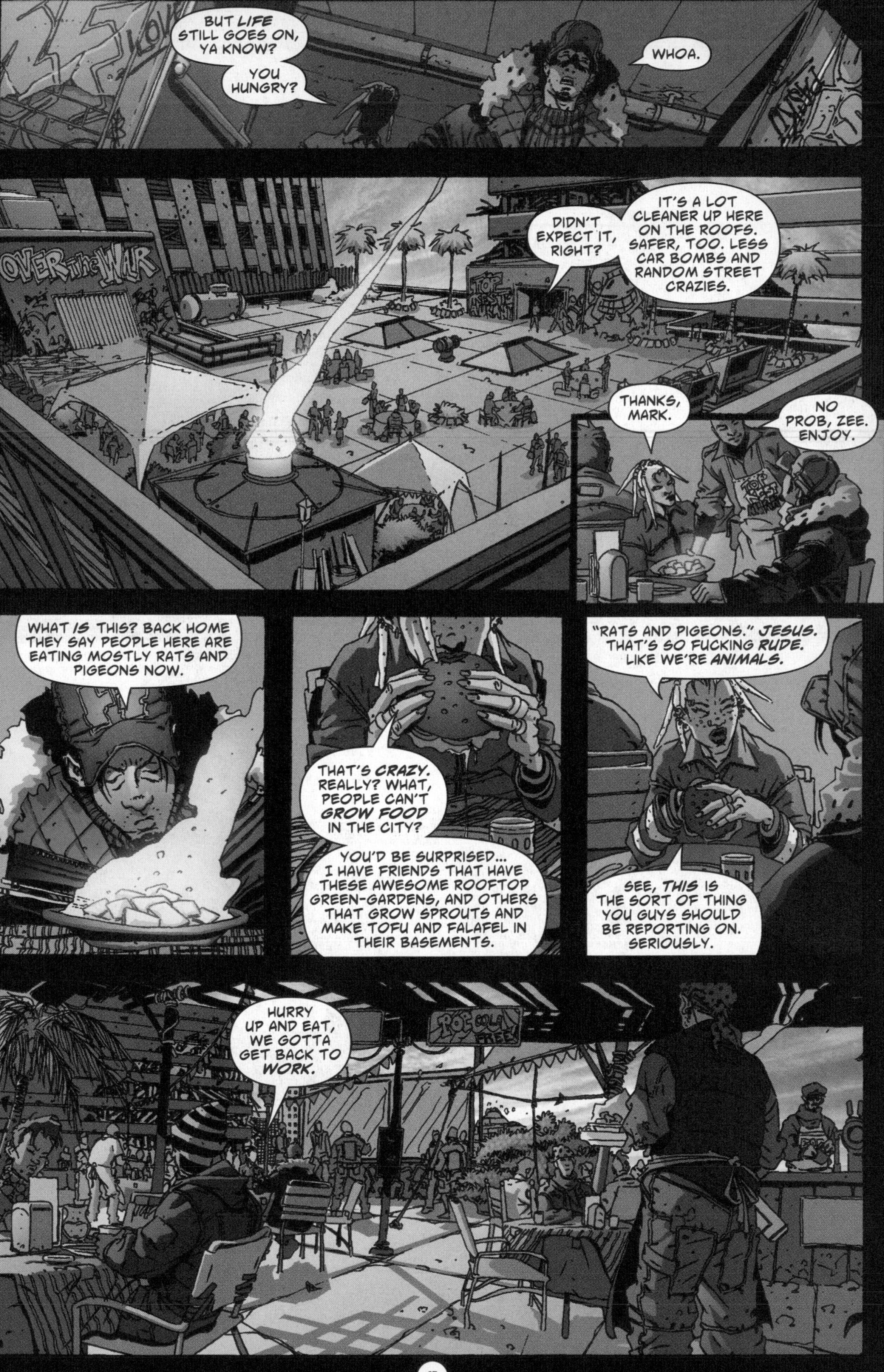
BUT LIFE STILL GOES ON, YA KNOW?
YOU HUNGRY?
WHOA.
OVER the WAR
DIDN'T EXPECT IT, RIGHT?
IT'S A LOT CLEANER UP HERE ON THE ROOFS. SAFER, TOO. LESS CAR BOMBS AND RANDOM STREET CRAZIES.
THANKS, MARK.
NO PROB, ZEE. ENJOY.
WHAT IS THIS? BACK HOME THEY SAY PEOPLE HERE ARE EATING MOSTLY RATS AND PIGEONS NOW.
THAT'S CRAZY. REALLY? WHAT, PEOPLE CAN'T GROW FOOD IN THE CITY?
YOU'D BE SURPRISED... I HAVE FRIENDS THAT HAVE THESE AWESOME ROOFTOP GREEN-GARDENS, AND OTHERS THAT GROW SPROUTS AND MAKE TOFU AND FALAFEL IN THEIR BASEMENTS.
"RATS AND PIGEONS." JESUS. THAT'S SO FUCKING RUDE. LIKE WE'RE ANIMALS.
SEE, THIS IS THE SORT OF THING YOU GUYS SHOULD BE REPORTING ON. SERIOUSLY.
HURRY UP AND EAT, WE GOTTA GET BACK TO WORK.

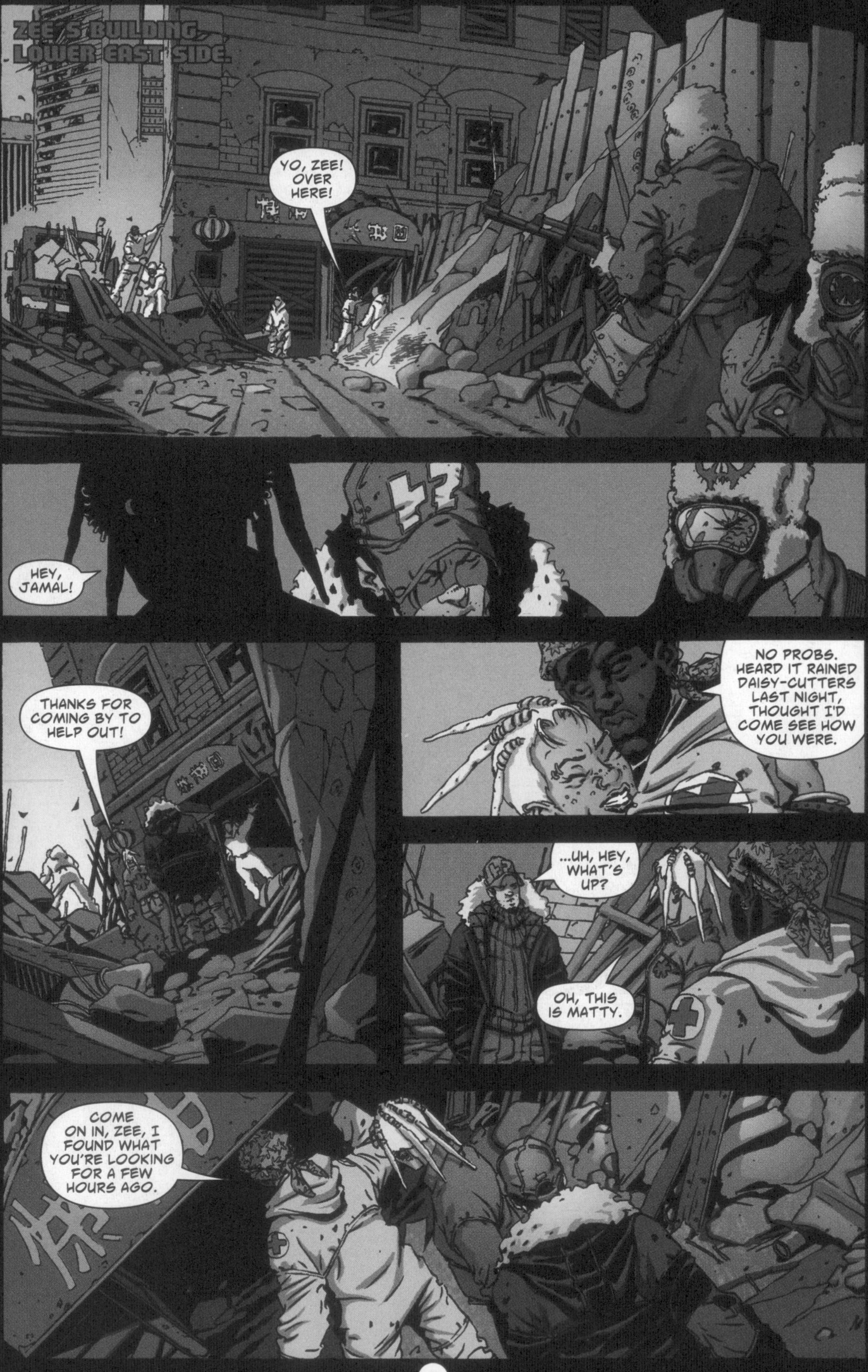
ZEE'S BUILDING, LOWER EAST SIDE.
YO, ZEE! OVER HERE!
HEY, JAMAL!
THANKS FOR COMING BY TO HELP OUT!
NO PROBS. HEARD IT RAINED DAISY-CUTTERS LAST NIGHT, THOUGHT I'D COME SEE HOW YOU WERE.
...UH, HEY, WHAT'S UP?
OH, THIS IS MATTY.
COME ON IN, ZEE, I FOUND WHAT YOU'RE LOOKING FOR A FEW HOURS AGO.

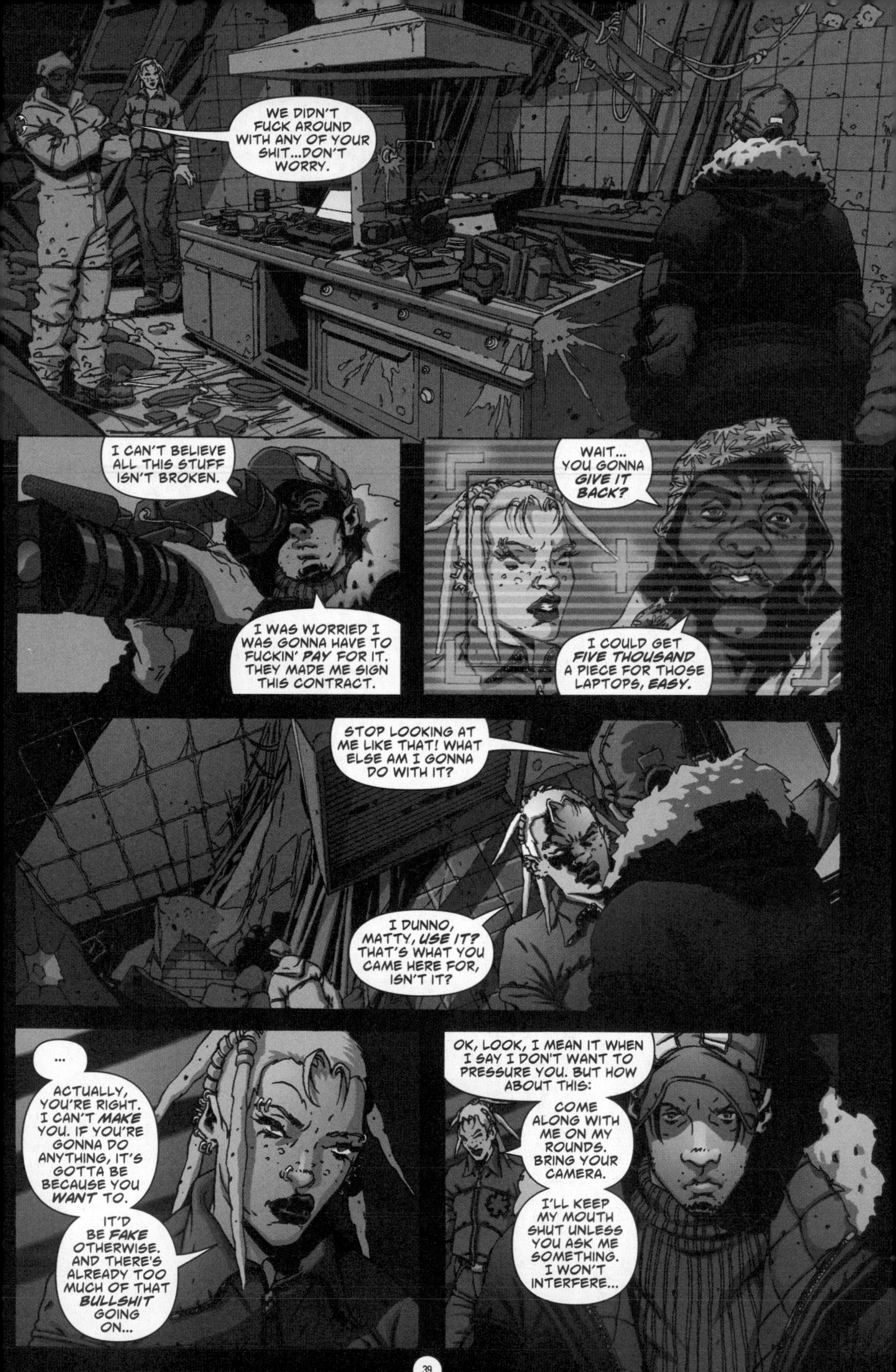
WE DIDN'T FUCK AROUND WITH ANY OF YOUR SHIT...DON'T WORRY.
I CAN'T BELIEVE ALL THIS STUFF ISN'T BROKEN.
I WAS WORRIED I WAS GONNA HAVE TO FUCKIN' *PAY* FOR IT. THEY MADE ME SIGN THIS CONTRACT.
WAIT... YOU GONNA *GIVE IT BACK?*
I COULD GET *FIVE THOUSAND* A PIECE FOR THOSE LAPTOPS, *EASY.*
STOP LOOKING AT ME LIKE THAT! WHAT ELSE AM I GONNA DO WITH IT?
I DUNNO, MATTY, *USE IT?* THAT'S WHAT YOU CAME HERE FOR, ISN'T IT?
...
ACTUALLY, YOU'RE RIGHT. I CAN'T *MAKE* YOU. IF YOU'RE GONNA DO ANYTHING, IT'S GOTTA BE BECAUSE YOU *WANT* TO.
IT'D BE *FAKE* OTHERWISE. AND THERE'S ALREADY TOO MUCH OF THAT *BULLSHIT* GOING ON...
OK, LOOK, I MEAN IT WHEN I SAY I DON'T WANT TO PRESSURE YOU. BUT HOW ABOUT THIS:
COME ALONG WITH ME ON MY ROUNDS. BRING YOUR CAMERA.
I'LL KEEP MY MOUTH SHUT UNLESS YOU ASK ME SOMETHING. I WON'T INTERFERE...

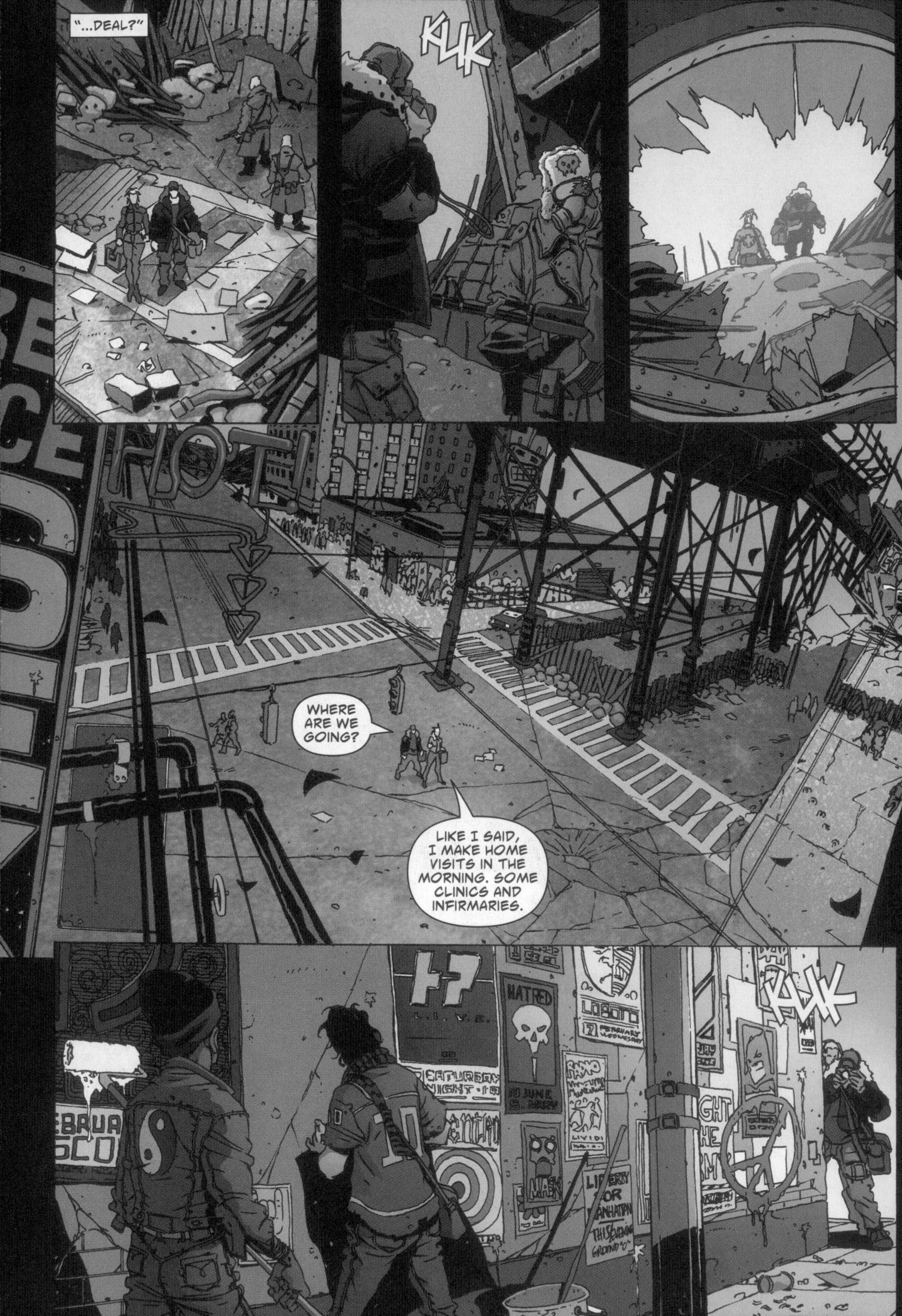
"...DEAL?"
KLIK
WHERE ARE WE GOING?
LIKE I SAID, I MAKE HOME VISITS IN THE MORNING. SOME CLINICS AND INFIRMARIES.
KLIK

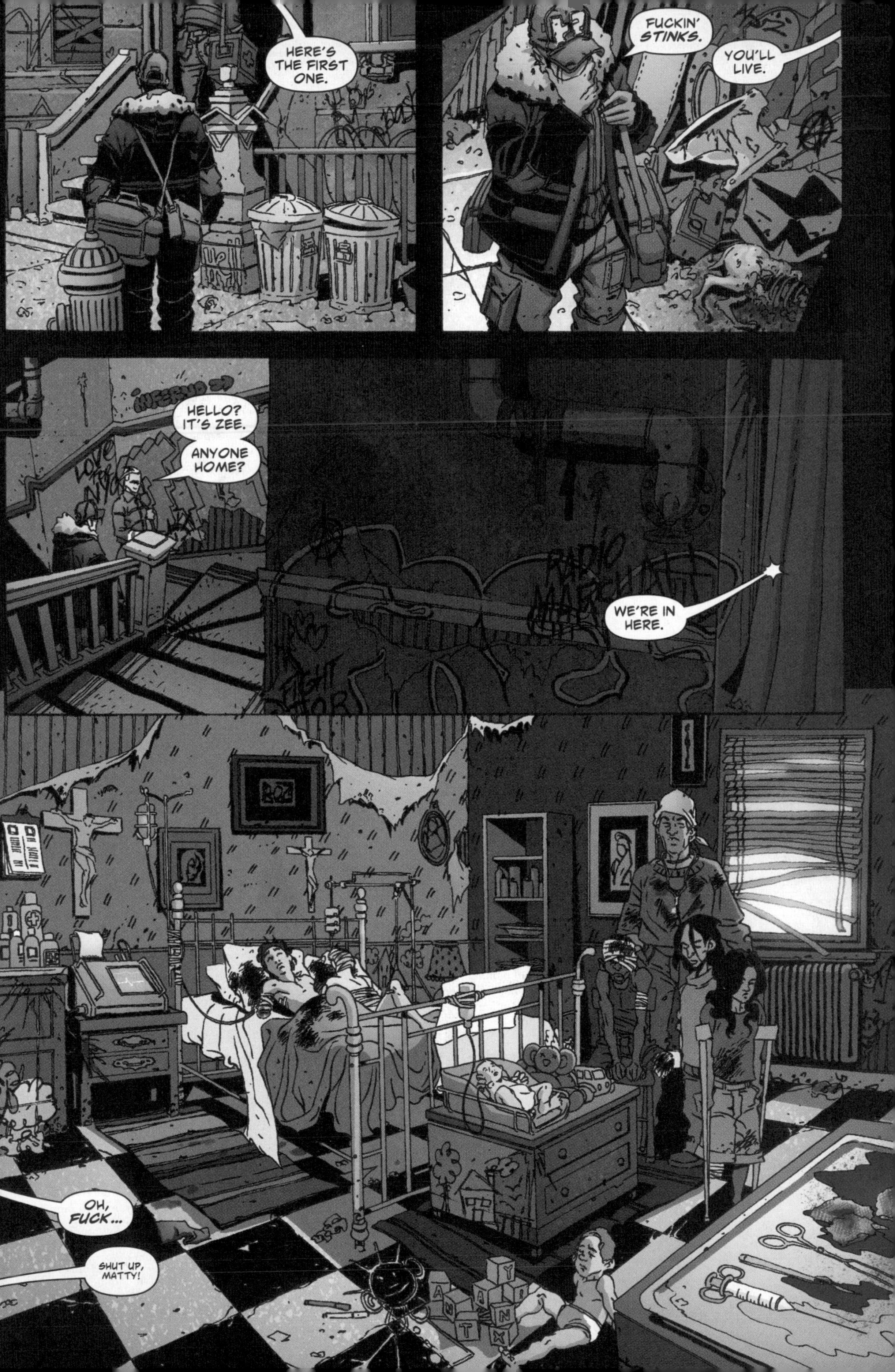
HERE'S THE FIRST ONE.
FUCKIN' STINKS.
YOU'LL LIVE.
HELLO? IT'S ZEE.
ANYONE HOME?
WE'RE IN HERE.
OH, FUCK...
SHUT UP, MATTY!

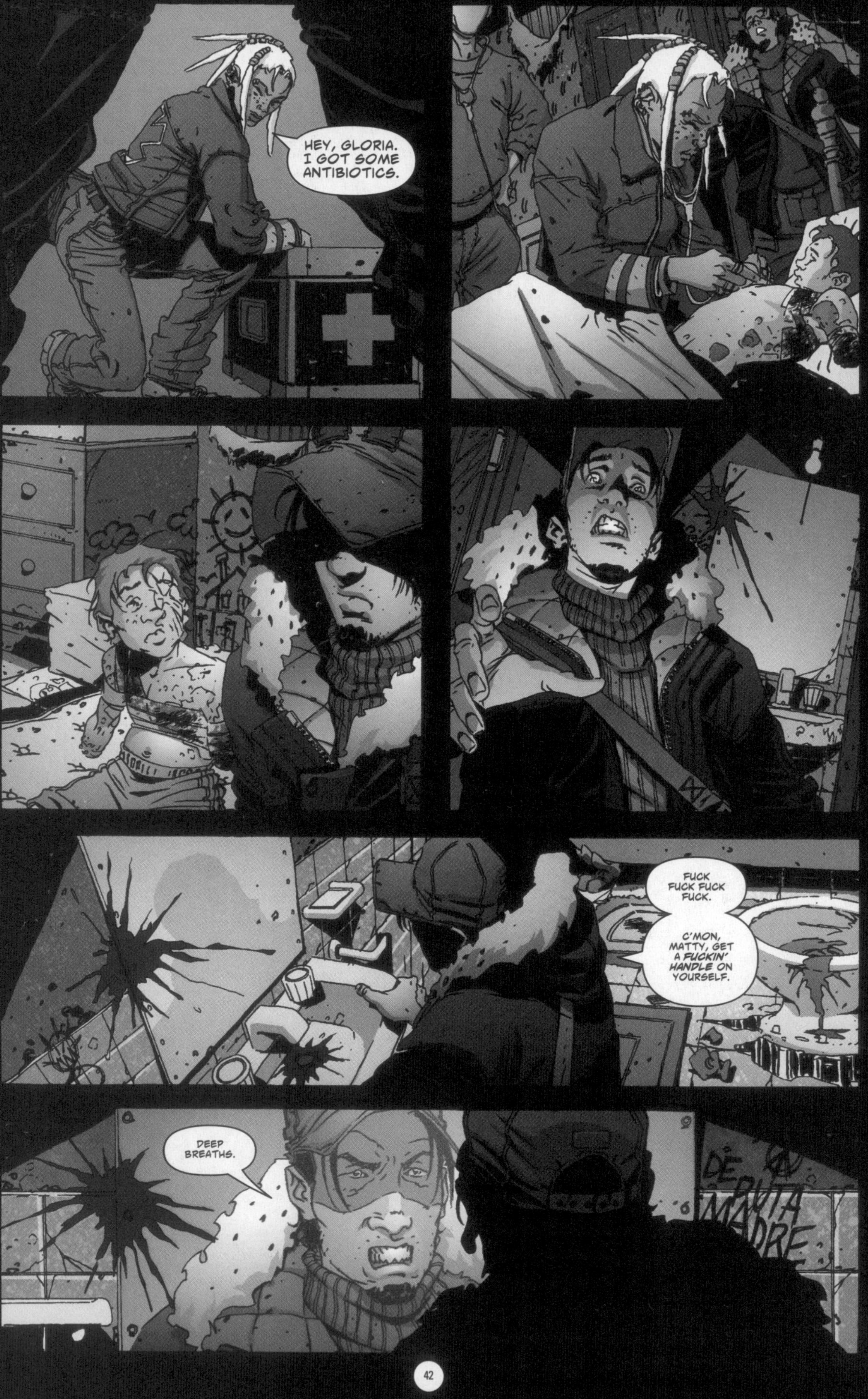
HEY, GLORIA. I GOT SOME ANTIBIOTICS.
FUCK FUCK FUCK FUCK.
C'MON, MATTY, GET A *FUCKIN'* *HANDLE* ON YOURSELF.
DEEP BREATHS.
DE PUTA MADRE

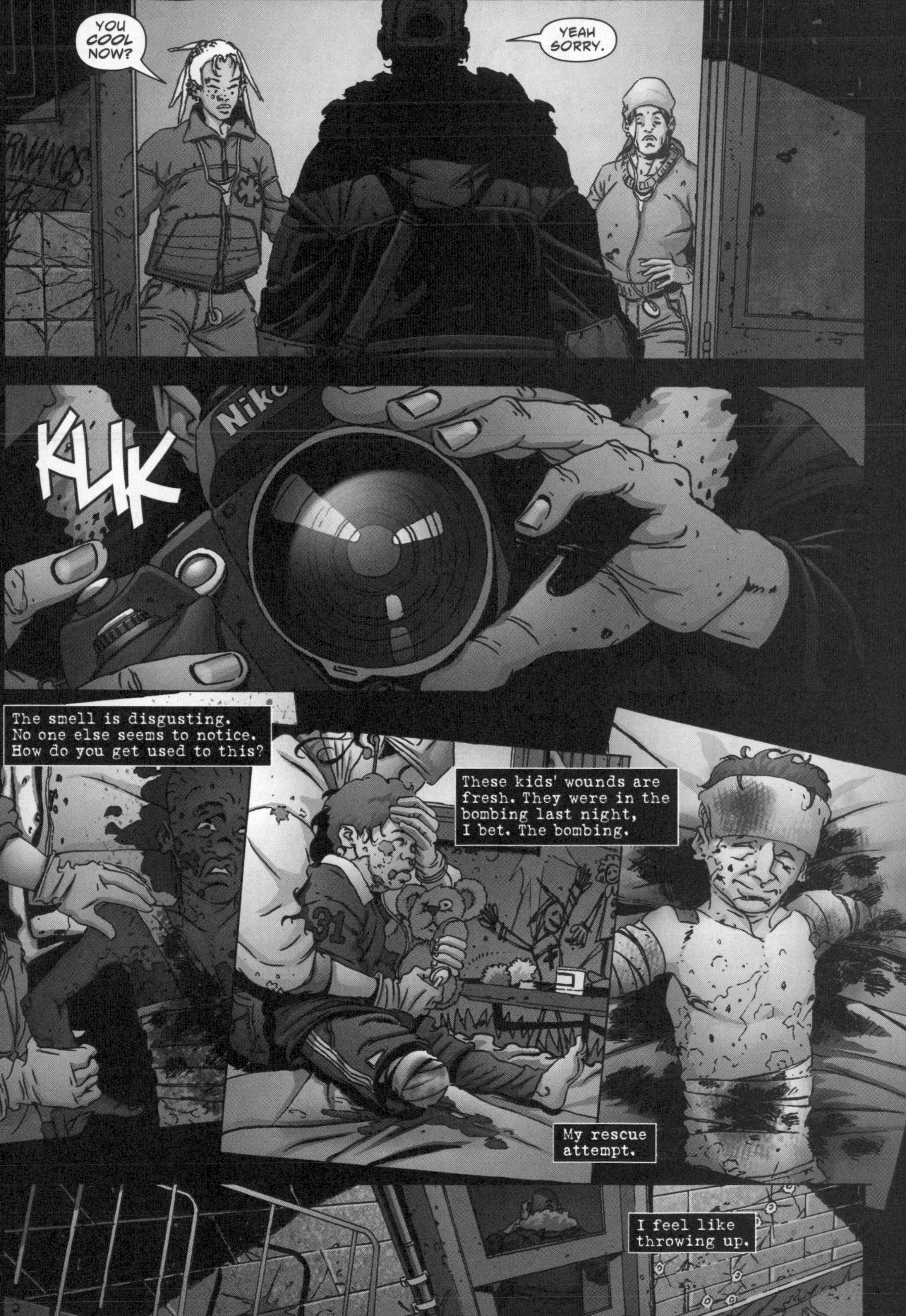

YOU COOL NOW?
YEAH SORRY.
KLIK
Niko
The smell is disgusting. No one else seems to notice. How do you get used to this?
These kids' wounds are fresh. They were in the bombing last night, I bet. The bombing.
My rescue attempt.
I feel like throwing up.

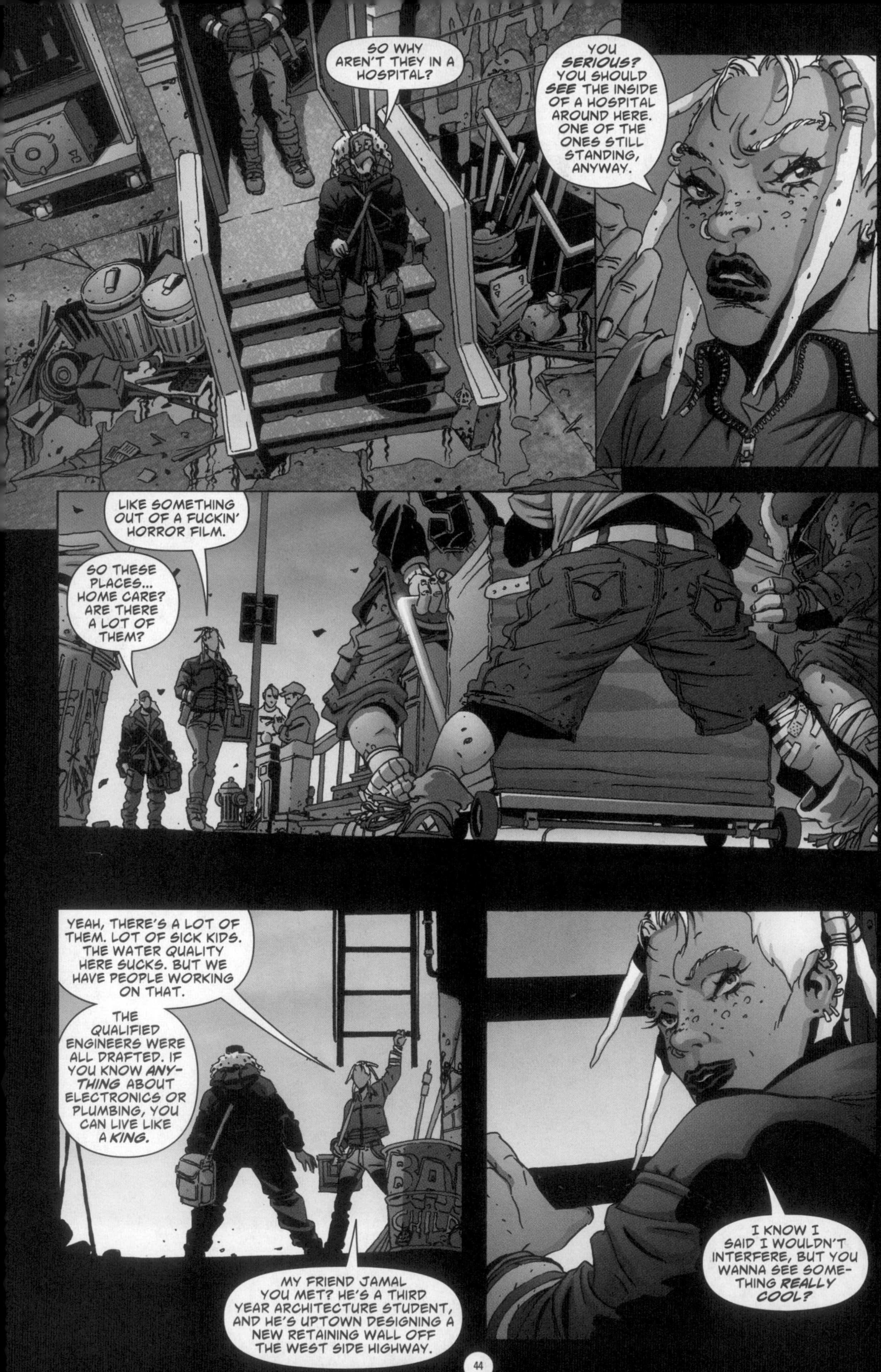

SO WHY AREN'T THEY IN A HOSPITAL?
YOU *SERIOUS?* YOU SHOULD *SEE* THE INSIDE OF A HOSPITAL AROUND HERE. ONE OF THE ONES STILL STANDING, ANYWAY.
LIKE SOMETHING OUT OF A FUCKIN' HORROR FILM.
SO THESE PLACES... HOME CARE? ARE THERE A LOT OF THEM?
YEAH, THERE'S A LOT OF THEM. LOT OF SICK KIDS. THE WATER QUALITY HERE SUCKS. BUT WE HAVE PEOPLE WORKING ON THAT.
THE QUALIFIED ENGINEERS WERE ALL DRAFTED. IF YOU KNOW *ANY-THING* ABOUT ELECTRONICS OR PLUMBING, YOU CAN LIVE LIKE A *KING*.
MY FRIEND JAMAL YOU MET? HE'S A THIRD YEAR ARCHITECTURE STUDENT, AND HE'S UPTOWN DESIGNING A NEW RETAINING WALL OFF THE WEST SIDE HIGHWAY.
I KNOW I SAID I WOULDN'T INTERFERE, BUT YOU WANNA SEE SOME-THING *REALLY COOL?*

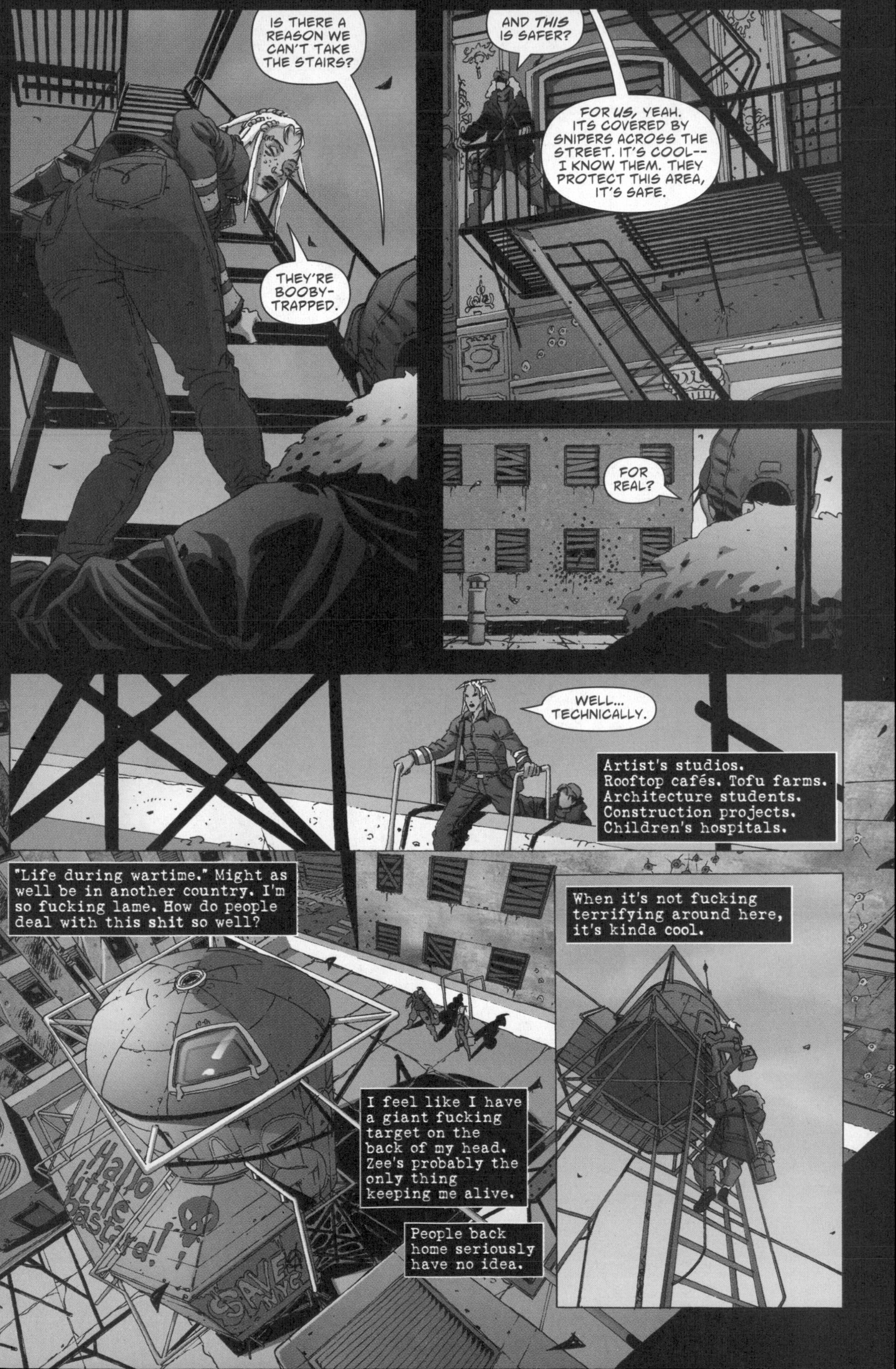
IS THERE A REASON WE CAN'T TAKE THE STAIRS?
THEY'RE BOOBY-TRAPPED.
AND THIS IS SAFER?
FOR US, YEAH. ITS COVERED BY SNIPERS ACROSS THE STREET. IT'S COOL-- I KNOW THEM. THEY PROTECT THIS AREA, IT'S SAFE.
FOR REAL?
WELL... TECHNICALLY.
Artist's studios. Rooftop cafés. Tofu farms. Architecture students. Construction projects. Children's hospitals.
"Life during wartime." Might as well be in another country. I'm so fucking lame. How do people deal with this shit so well?
When it's not fucking terrifying around here, it's kinda cool.
I feel like I have a giant fucking target on the back of my head. Zee's probably the only thing keeping me alive.
People back home seriously have no idea.
Hallo little bastard!
SAVE NYC

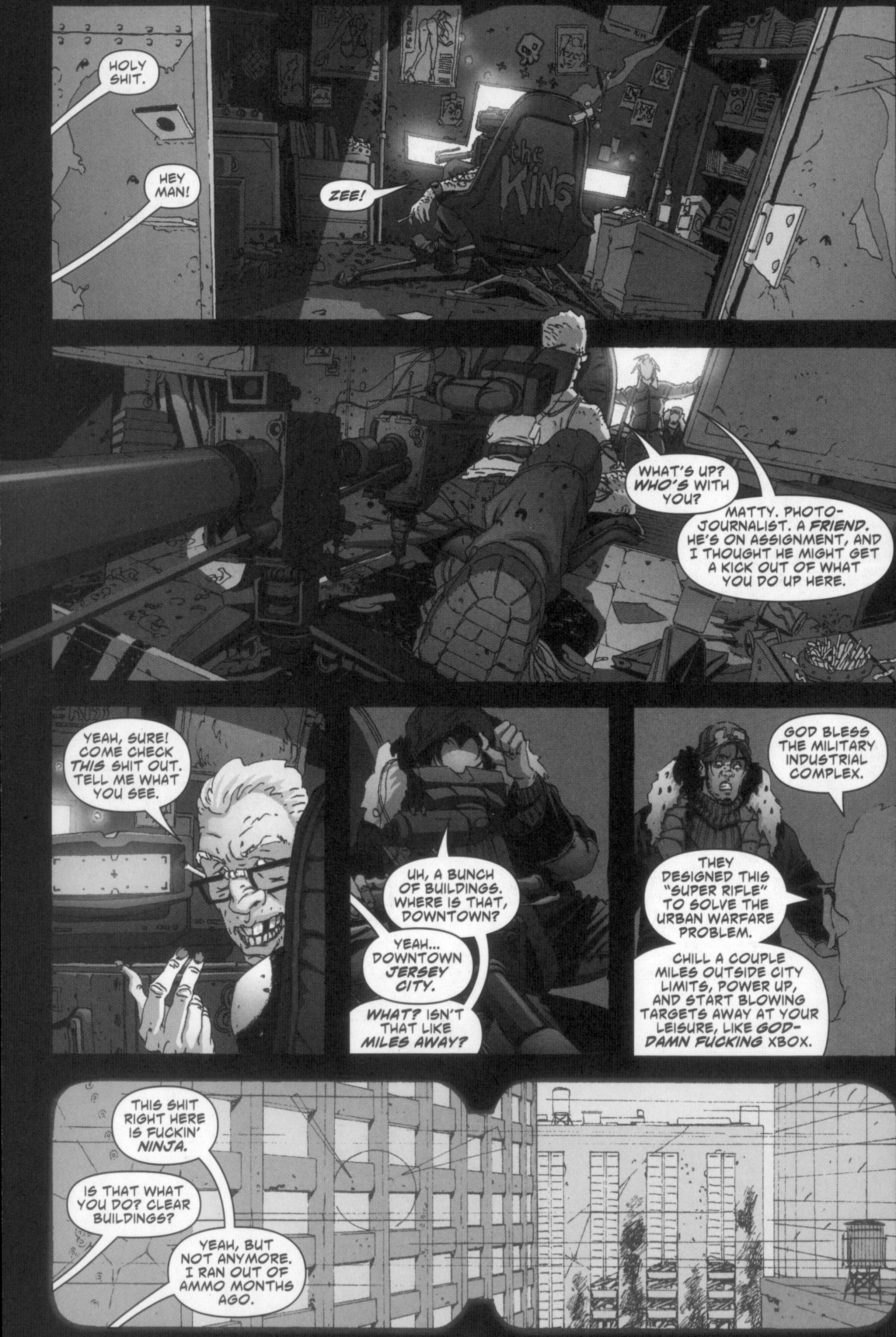
HOLY SHIT.
HEY MAN!
ZEE!
WHAT'S UP? WHO'S WITH YOU?
MATTY. PHOTO-JOURNALIST. A FRIEND. HE'S ON ASSIGNMENT, AND I THOUGHT HE MIGHT GET A KICK OUT OF WHAT YOU DO UP HERE.
YEAH, SURE! COME CHECK THIS SHIT OUT. TELL ME WHAT YOU SEE.
UH, A BUNCH OF BUILDINGS. WHERE IS THAT, DOWNTOWN?
YEAH... DOWNTOWN JERSEY CITY.
WHAT? ISN'T THAT LIKE MILES AWAY?
GOD BLESS THE MILITARY INDUSTRIAL COMPLEX.
THEY DESIGNED THIS "SUPER RIFLE" TO SOLVE THE URBAN WARFARE PROBLEM.
CHILL A COUPLE MILES OUTSIDE CITY LIMITS, POWER UP, AND START BLOWING TARGETS AWAY AT YOUR LEISURE, LIKE GOD-DAMN FUCKING XBOX.
THIS SHIT RIGHT HERE IS FUCKIN' NINJA.
IS THAT WHAT YOU DO? CLEAR BUILDINGS?
YEAH, BUT NOT ANYMORE. I RAN OUT OF AMMO MONTHS AGO.

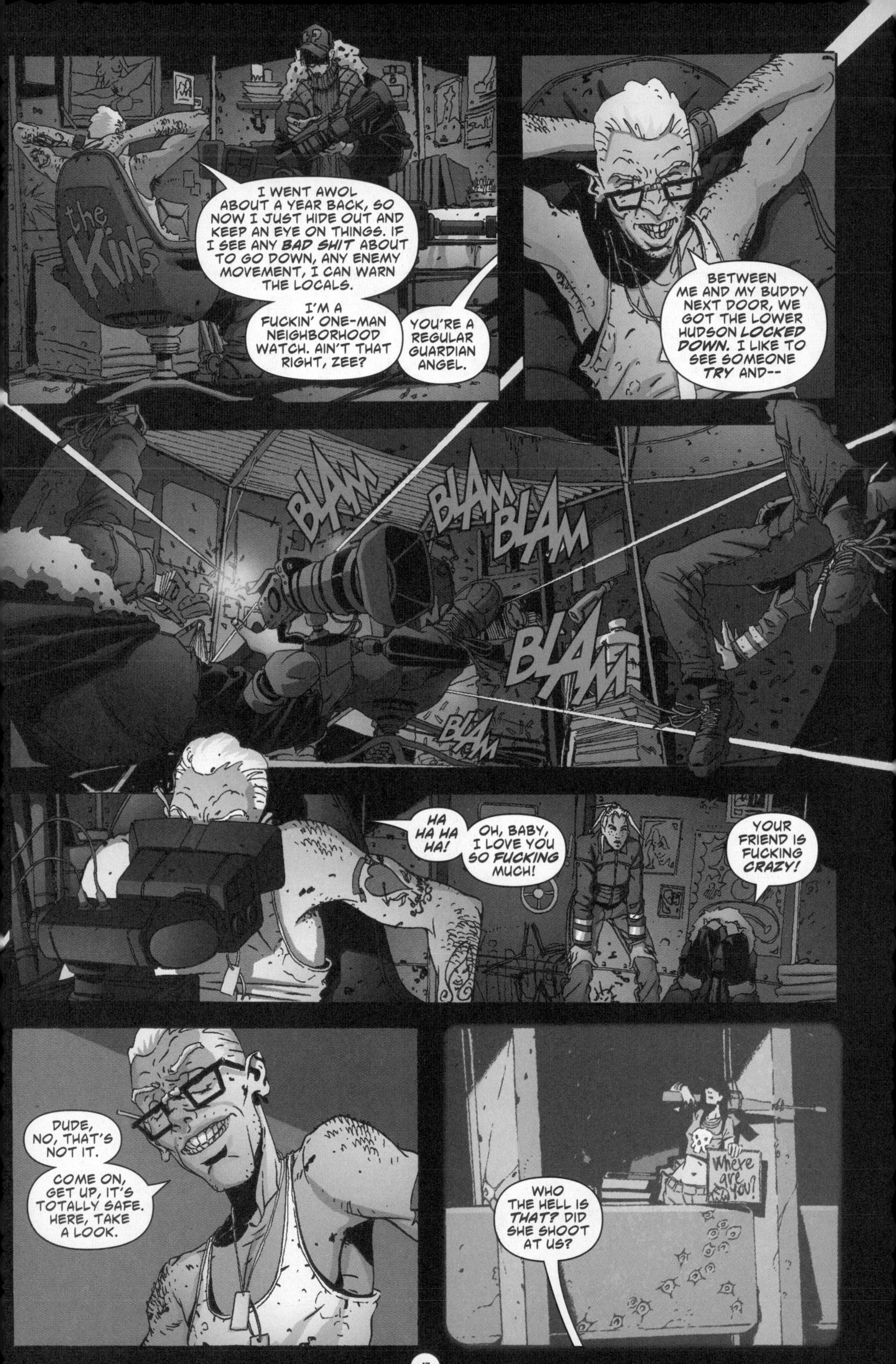
I WENT AWOL ABOUT A YEAR BACK, SO NOW I JUST HIDE OUT AND KEEP AN EYE ON THINGS. IF I SEE ANY BAD SHIT ABOUT TO GO DOWN, ANY ENEMY MOVEMENT, I CAN WARN THE LOCALS.
I'M A FUCKIN' ONE-MAN NEIGHBORHOOD WATCH. AIN'T THAT RIGHT, ZEE?
YOU'RE A REGULAR GUARDIAN ANGEL.
the KING
BETWEEN ME AND MY BUDDY NEXT DOOR, WE GOT THE LOWER HUDSON LOCKED DOWN. I LIKE TO SEE SOMEONE TRY AND--
BLAM
BLAM BLAM
BLAM
BLAM
HA HA HA HA!
OH, BABY, I LOVE YOU SO FUCKING MUCH!
YOUR FRIEND IS FUCKING CRAZY!
DUDE, NO, THAT'S NOT IT.
COME ON, GET UP, IT'S TOTALLY SAFE. HERE, TAKE A LOOK.
Where are you?
WHO THE HELL IS THAT? DID SHE SHOOT AT US?

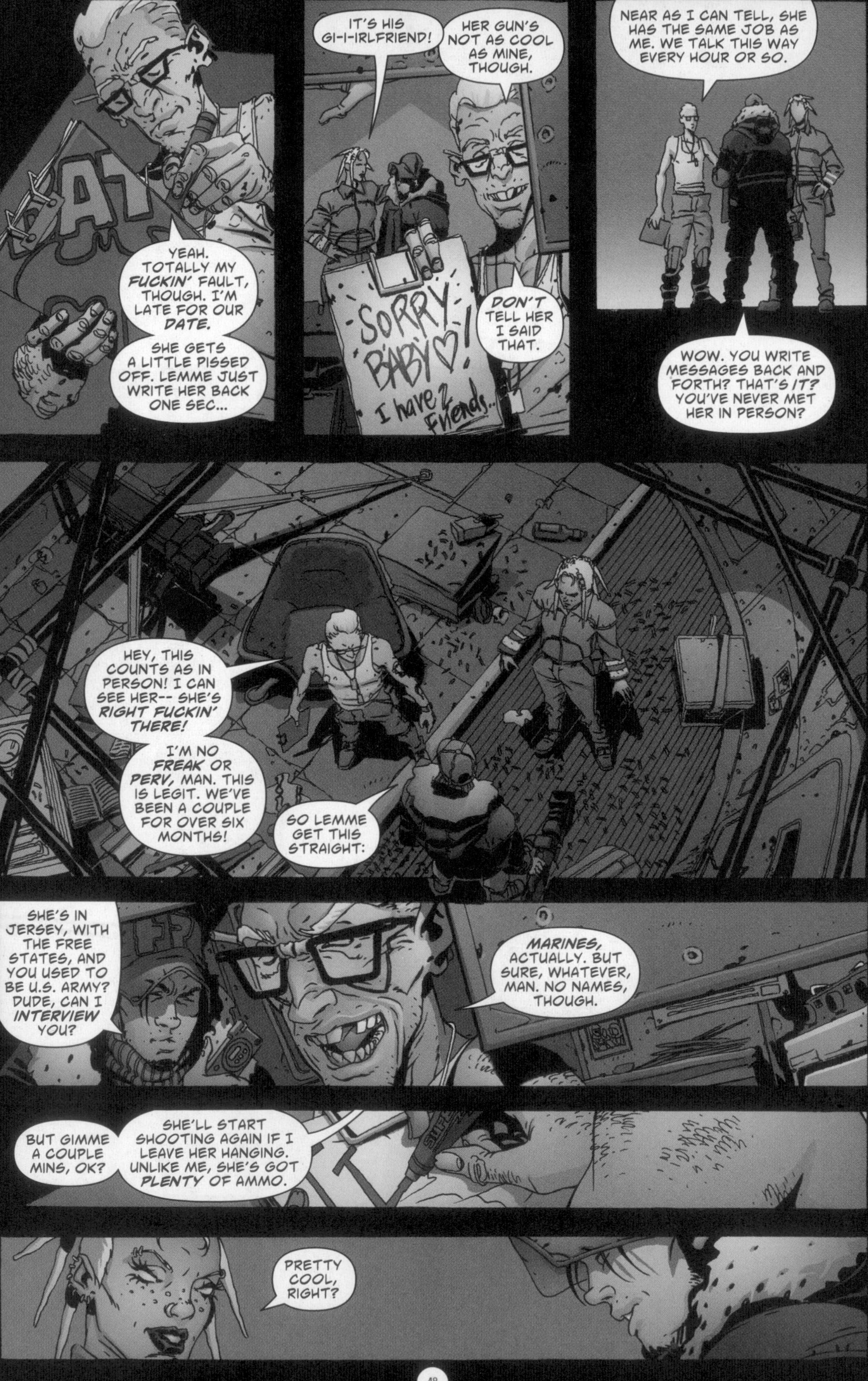
YEAH. TOTALLY MY FUCKIN' FAULT, THOUGH. I'M LATE FOR OUR DATE.
SHE GETS A LITTLE PISSED OFF. LEMME JUST WRITE HER BACK ONE SEC...
IT'S HIS GI-I-IRLFRIEND!
HER GUN'S NOT AS COOL AS MINE, THOUGH.
SORRY BABY♡! I have 2 Friends...
DON'T TELL HER I SAID THAT.
NEAR AS I CAN TELL, SHE HAS THE SAME JOB AS ME. WE TALK THIS WAY EVERY HOUR OR SO.
WOW. YOU WRITE MESSAGES BACK AND FORTH? THAT'S IT? YOU'VE NEVER MET HER IN PERSON?
HEY, THIS COUNTS AS IN PERSON! I CAN SEE HER-- SHE'S RIGHT FUCKIN' THERE!
I'M NO FREAK OR PERV, MAN. THIS IS LEGIT. WE'VE BEEN A COUPLE FOR OVER SIX MONTHS!
SO LEMME GET THIS STRAIGHT:
SHE'S IN JERSEY, WITH THE FREE STATES, AND YOU USED TO BE U.S. ARMY? DUDE, CAN I INTERVIEW YOU?
MARINES, ACTUALLY. BUT SURE, WHATEVER, MAN. NO NAMES, THOUGH.
BUT GIMME A COUPLE MINS, OK?
SHE'LL START SHOOTING AGAIN IF I LEAVE HER HANGING. UNLIKE ME, SHE'S GOT PLENTY OF AMMO.
PRETTY COOL, RIGHT?

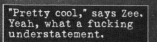

"Pretty cool," says Zee. Yeah, what a fucking understatement.

I know it makes me sound like an asshole, but as sad as those injured kids were, it's this sniper that makes me want to stay and file stories.

This couple, on opposite sides of a civil war, literally looking down the barrels of their guns at each other, writing love notes. Both of them traitors. Neither of them cares.

If you can really call them that. "Love bridging the gaps of war." It would be such a fucking cliché if it wasn't so sincere.

I've only been here two days. What else is out there?

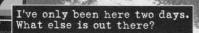

And what's that information worth?

The real question is, will the network accept what I send them?

Or will they just call in another air strike?

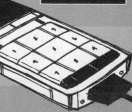

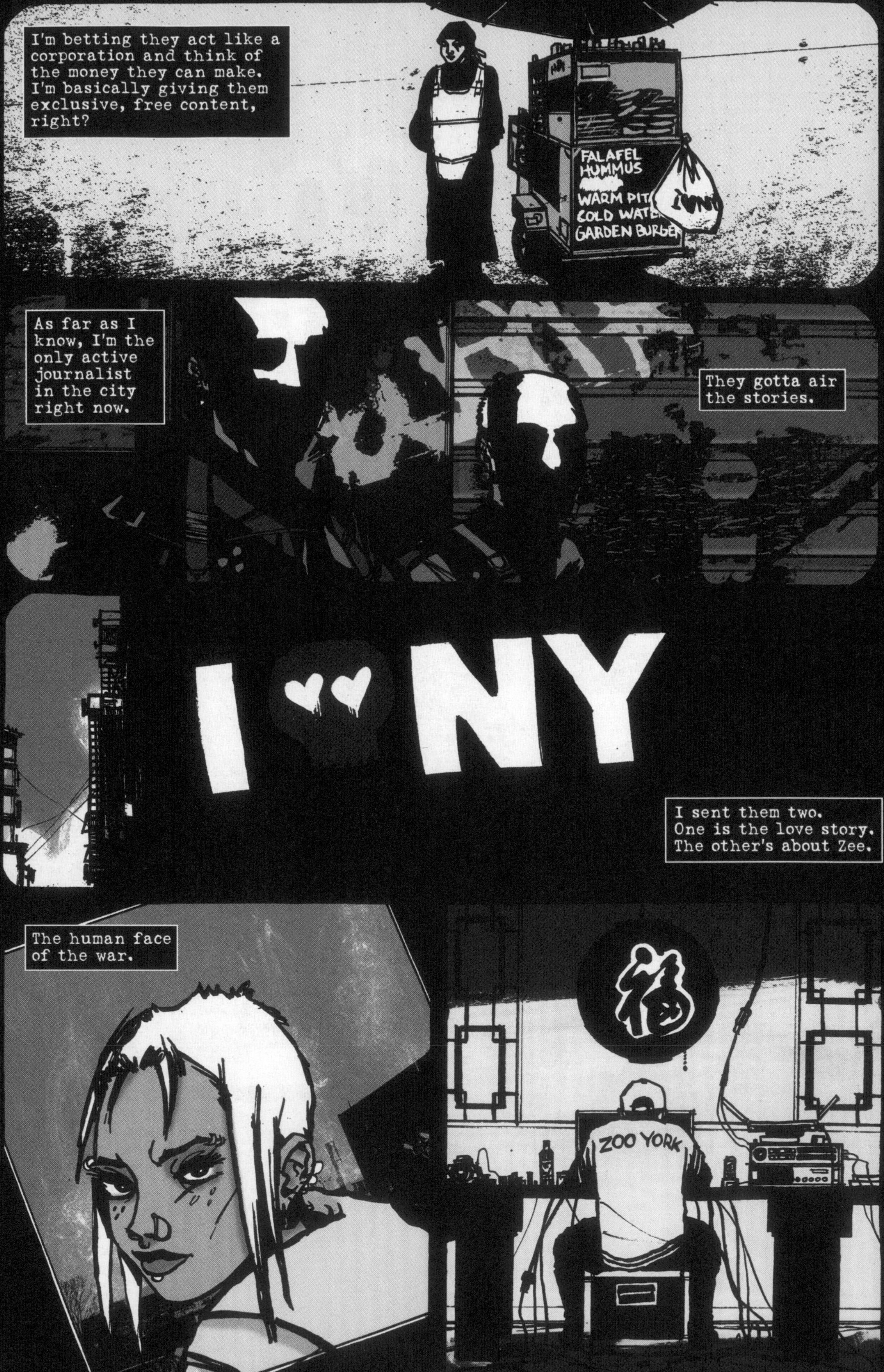
I'm betting they act like a corporation and think of the money they can make. I'm basically giving them exclusive, free content, right?
FALAFEL
HUMMUS
WARM PITA
COLD WATER
GARDEN BURGER
As far as I know, I'm the only active journalist in the city right now.
They gotta air the stories.
I NY
I sent them two. One is the love story. The other's about Zee.
The human face of the war.
ZOO YORK

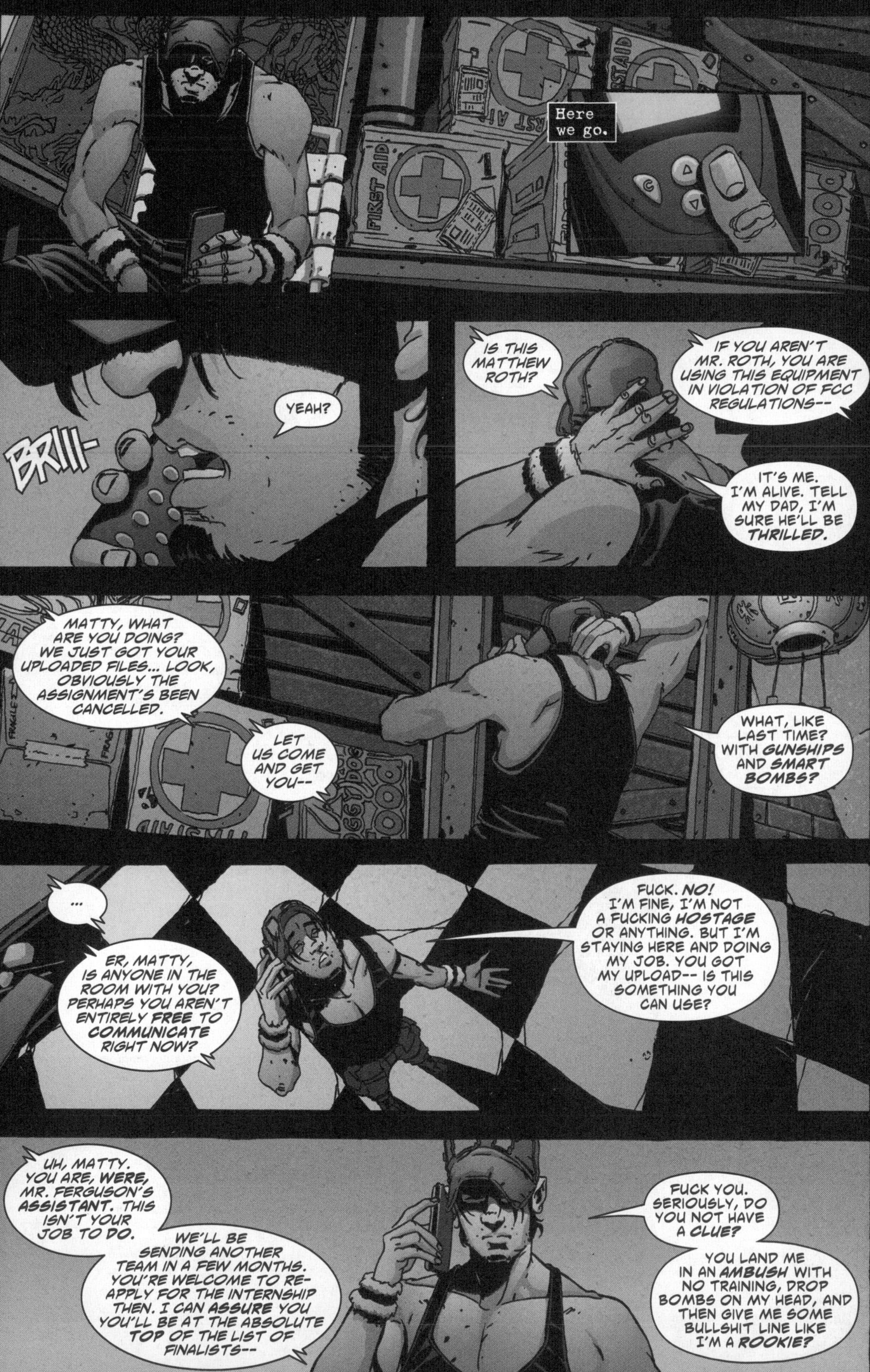
Here we go.
FIRST AID
YEAH?
BRIII-
IS THIS MATTHEW ROTH?
IF YOU AREN'T MR. ROTH, YOU ARE USING THIS EQUIPMENT IN VIOLATION OF FCC REGULATIONS--
IT'S ME. I'M ALIVE. TELL MY DAD, I'M SURE HE'LL BE THRILLED.
MATTY, WHAT ARE YOU DOING? WE JUST GOT YOUR UPLOADED FILES... LOOK, OBVIOUSLY THE ASSIGNMENT'S BEEN CANCELLED.
LET US COME AND GET YOU--
WHAT, LIKE LAST TIME? WITH GUNSHIPS AND SMART BOMBS?
...
ER, MATTY, IS ANYONE IN THE ROOM WITH YOU? PERHAPS YOU AREN'T ENTIRELY FREE TO COMMUNICATE RIGHT NOW?
FUCK. NO! I'M FINE, I'M NOT A FUCKING HOSTAGE OR ANYTHING. BUT I'M STAYING HERE AND DOING MY JOB. YOU GOT MY UPLOAD-- IS THIS SOMETHING YOU CAN USE?
UH, MATTY. YOU ARE, WERE, MR. FERGUSON'S ASSISTANT. THIS ISN'T YOUR JOB TO DO.
WE'LL BE SENDING ANOTHER TEAM IN A FEW MONTHS. YOU'RE WELCOME TO RE-APPLY FOR THE INTERNSHIP THEN. I CAN ASSURE YOU YOU'LL BE AT THE ABSOLUTE TOP OF THE LIST OF FINALISTS--
FUCK YOU. SERIOUSLY, DO YOU NOT HAVE A CLUE?
YOU LAND ME IN AN AMBUSH WITH NO TRAINING, DROP BOMBS ON MY HEAD, AND THEN GIVE ME SOME BULLSHIT LINE LIKE I'M A ROOKIE?

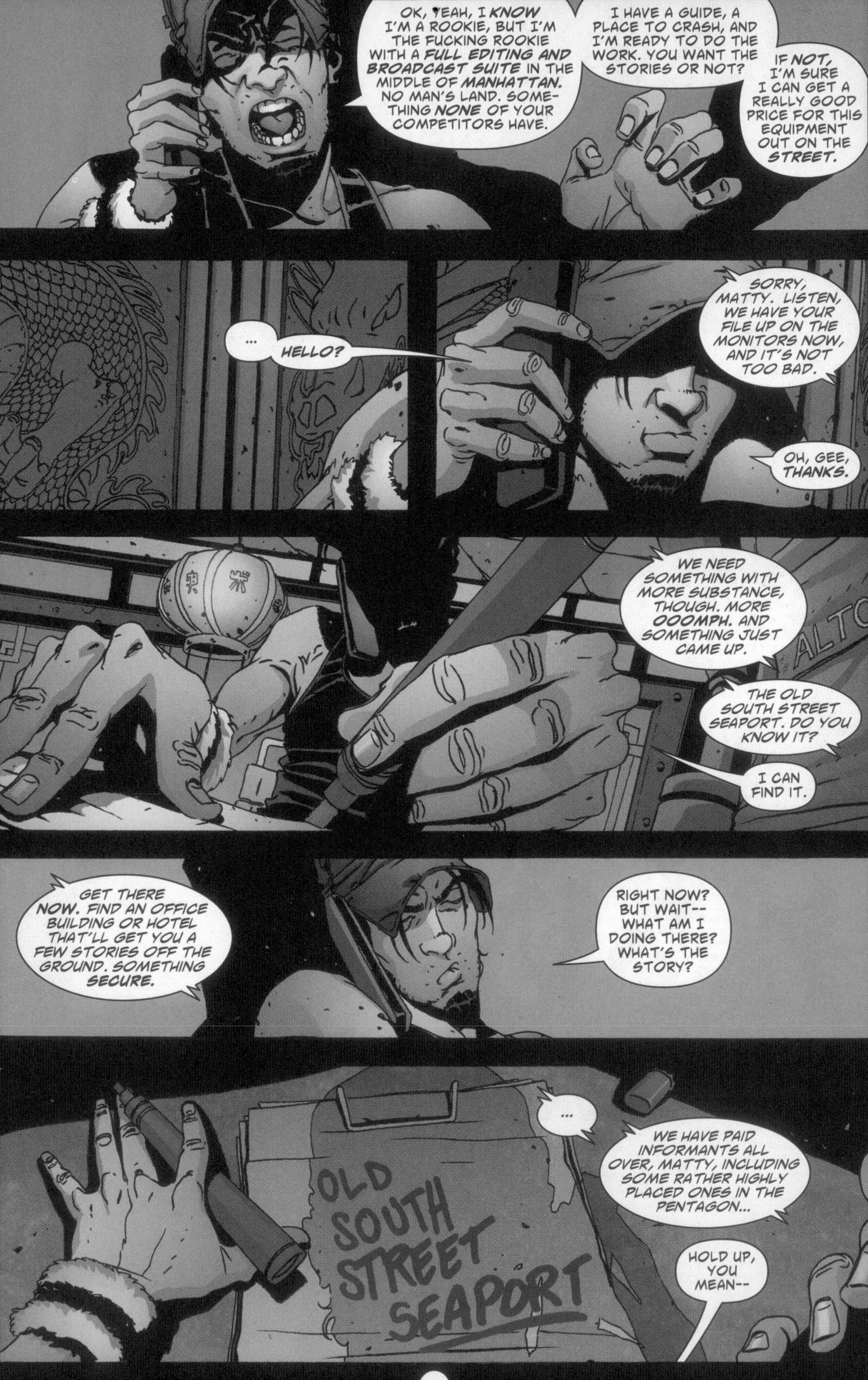
OK, YEAH, I KNOW I'M A ROOKIE, BUT I'M THE FUCKING ROOKIE WITH A FULL EDITING AND BROADCAST SUITE IN THE MIDDLE OF MANHATTAN. NO MAN'S LAND. SOMETHING NONE OF YOUR COMPETITORS HAVE.
I HAVE A GUIDE, A PLACE TO CRASH, AND I'M READY TO DO THE WORK. YOU WANT THE STORIES OR NOT?
IF NOT, I'M SURE I CAN GET A REALLY GOOD PRICE FOR THIS EQUIPMENT OUT ON THE STREET.
... HELLO?
SORRY, MATTY. LISTEN, WE HAVE YOUR FILE UP ON THE MONITORS NOW, AND IT'S NOT TOO BAD.
OH, GEE, THANKS.
WE NEED SOMETHING WITH MORE SUBSTANCE, THOUGH. MORE OOOMPH. AND SOMETHING JUST CAME UP.
ALTO
THE OLD SOUTH STREET SEAPORT. DO YOU KNOW IT?
I CAN FIND IT.
GET THERE NOW. FIND AN OFFICE BUILDING OR HOTEL THAT'LL GET YOU A FEW STORIES OFF THE GROUND. SOMETHING SECURE.
RIGHT NOW? BUT WAIT-- WHAT AM I DOING THERE? WHAT'S THE STORY?
...
OLD SOUTH STREET SEAPORT
WE HAVE PAID INFORMANTS ALL OVER, MATTY, INCLUDING SOME RATHER HIGHLY PLACED ONES IN THE PENTAGON...
HOLD UP, YOU MEAN--

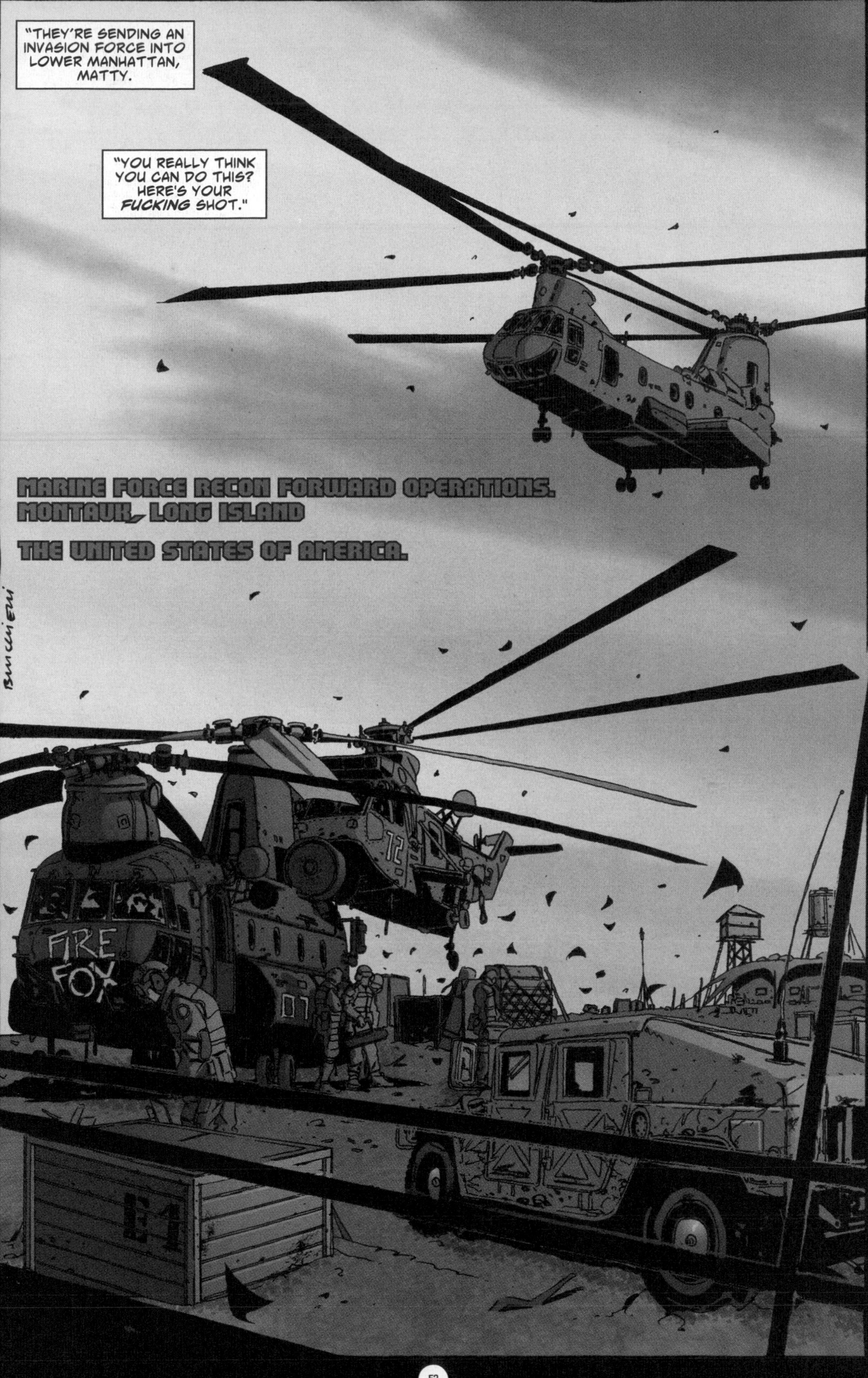
"THEY'RE SENDING AN INVASION FORCE INTO LOWER MANHATTAN, MATTY.
"YOU REALLY THINK YOU CAN DO THIS? HERE'S YOUR FUCKING SHOT."
MARINE FORCE RECON FORWARD OPERATIONS. MONTAUK, LONG ISLAND
THE UNITED STATES OF AMERICA.
FIRE FOX
72
07
E1

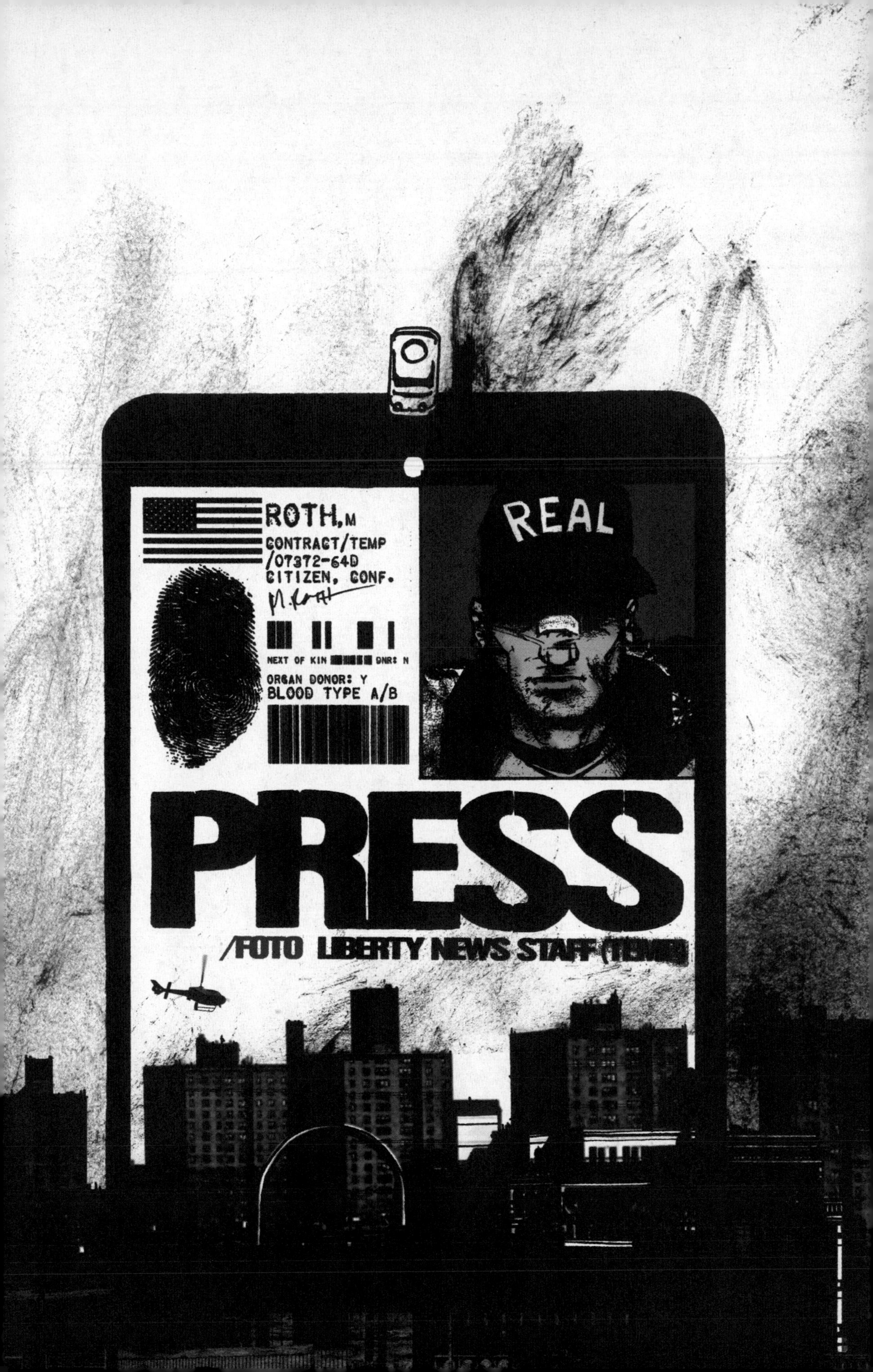
ROTH, M
CONTRACT/TEMP
/07372-64D
CITIZEN, CONF.
NEXT OF KIN [redacted] DNR: N
ORGAN DONOR: Y
BLOOD TYPE A/B
REAL
PRESS
/FOTO LIBERTY NEWS STAFF

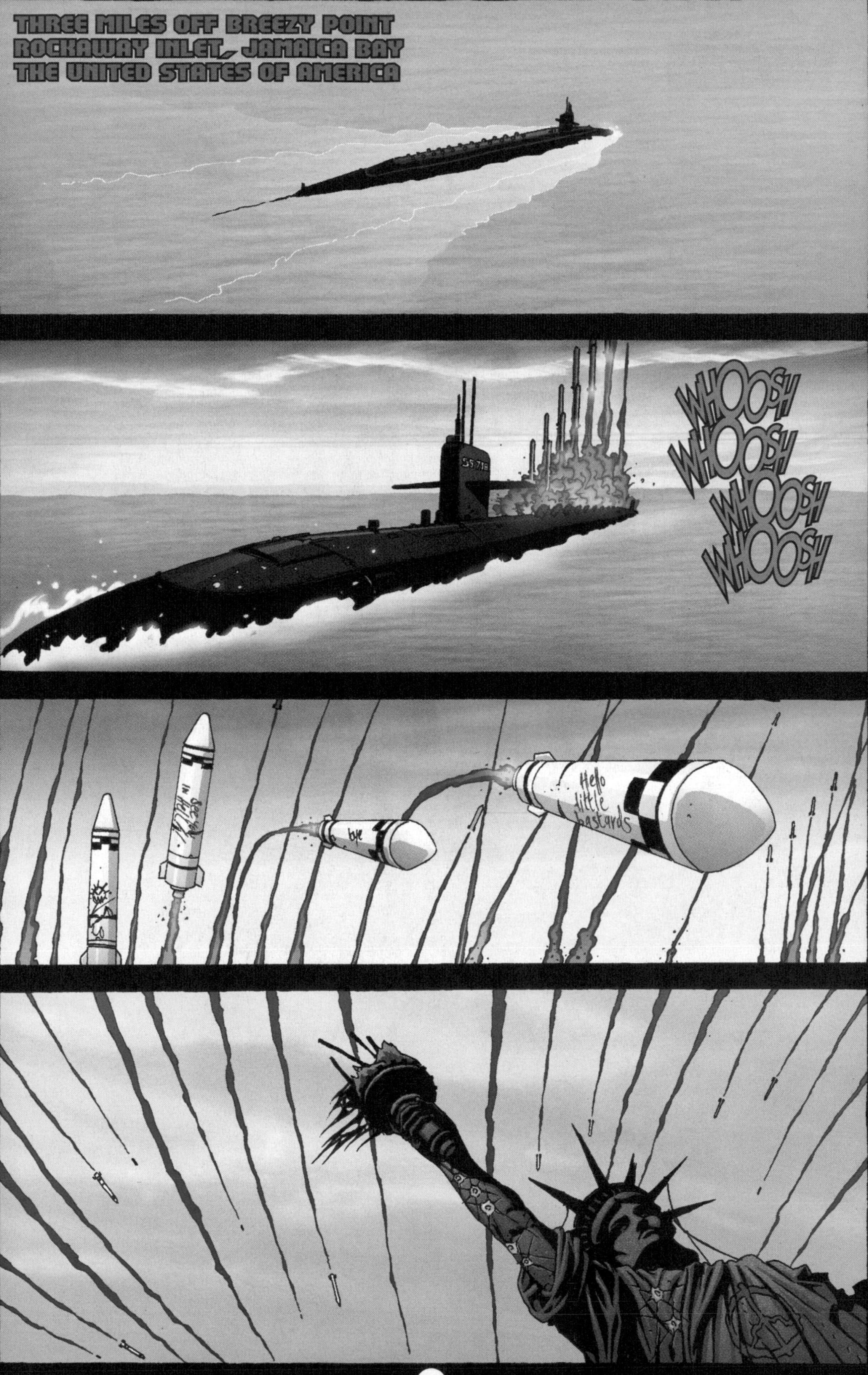
THREE MILES OFF BREEZY POINT
ROCKAWAY INLET, JAMAICA BAY
THE UNITED STATES OF AMERICA
WHOOSH
WHOOSH
WHOOSH
WHOOSH
bye
Hello little bastards

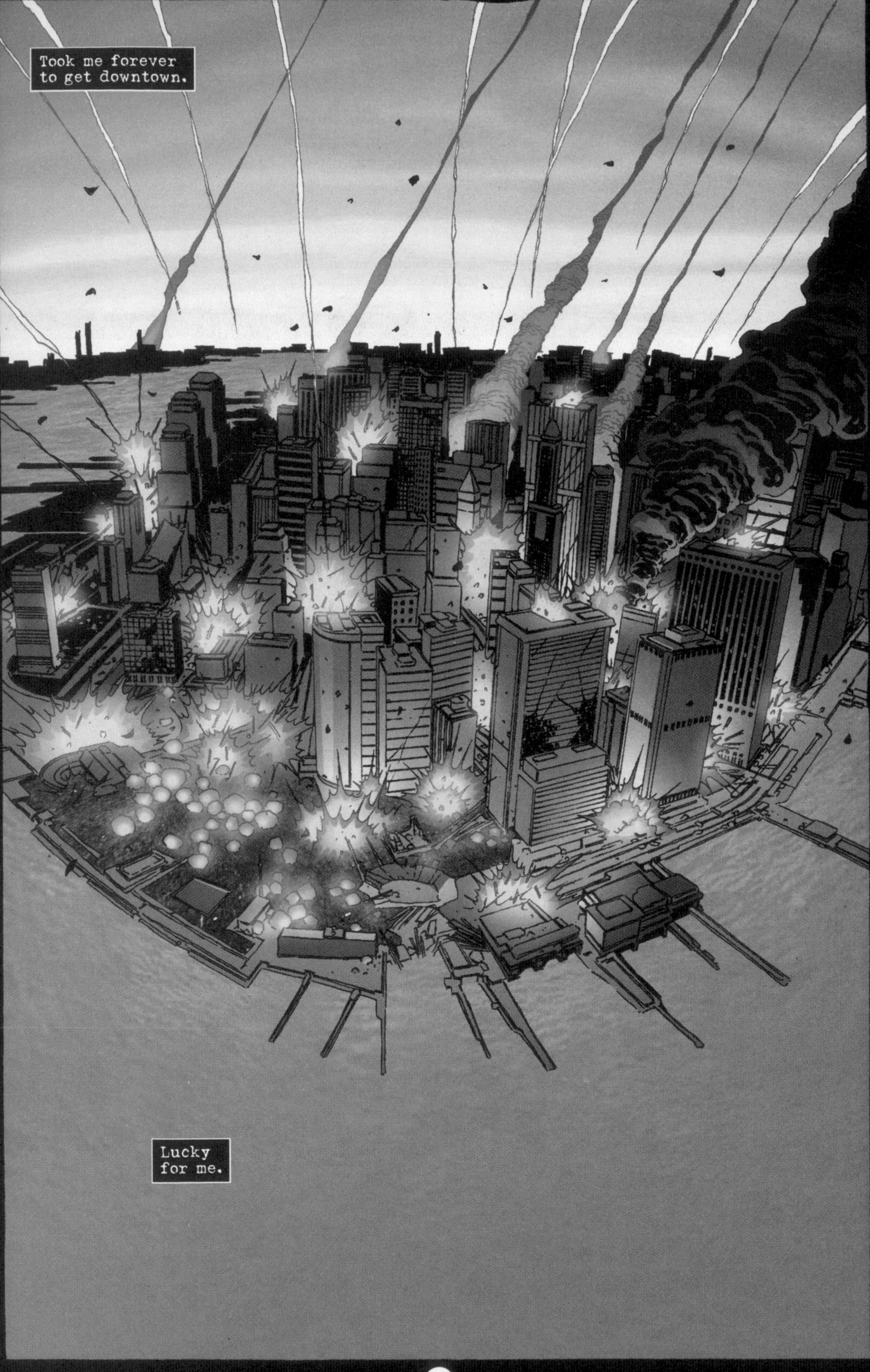
Took me forever to get downtown.
Lucky for me.

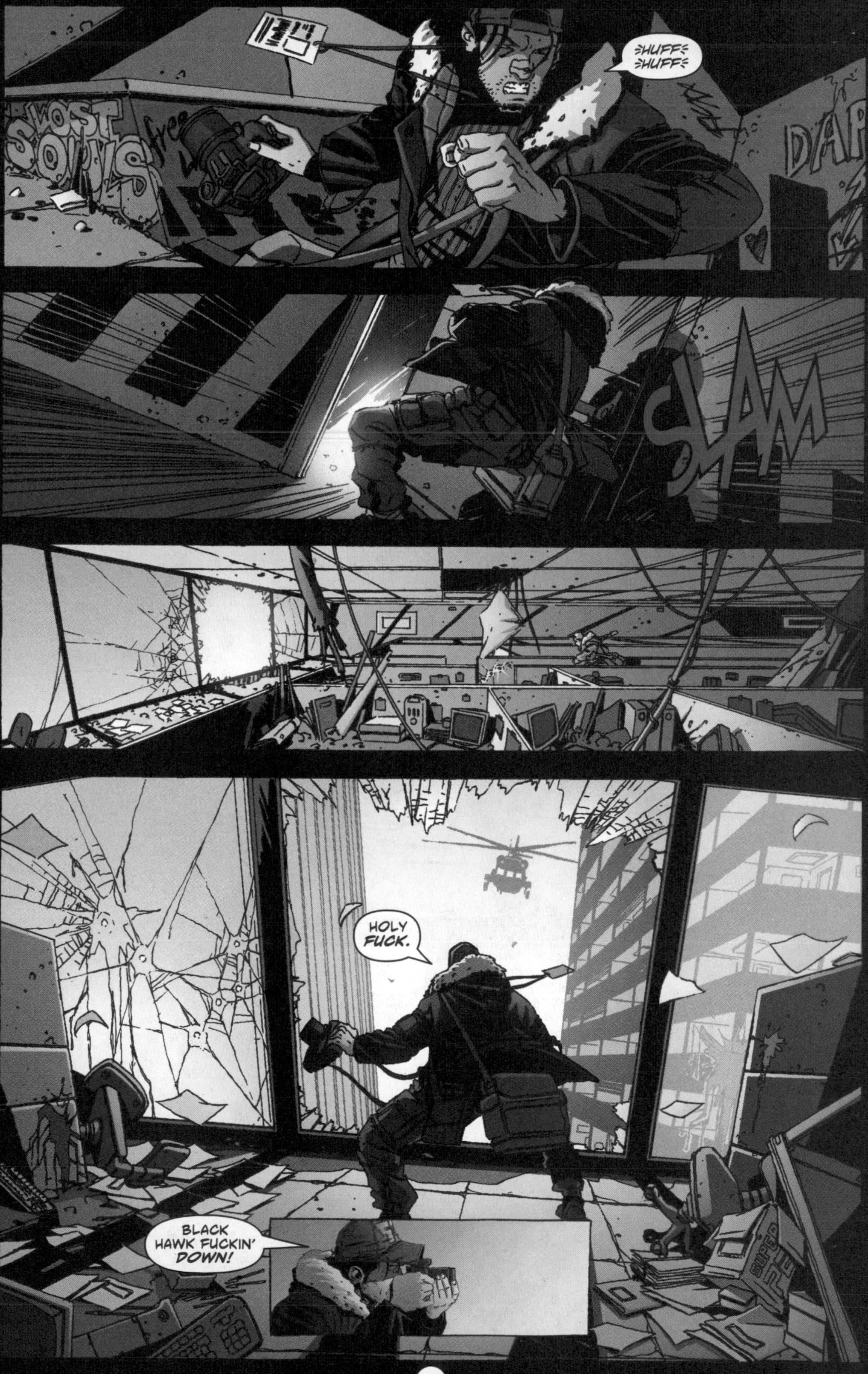
HUFF HUFF
LOST SOULS
free
SLAM
HOLY FUCK.
BLACK HAWK FUCKIN' DOWN!

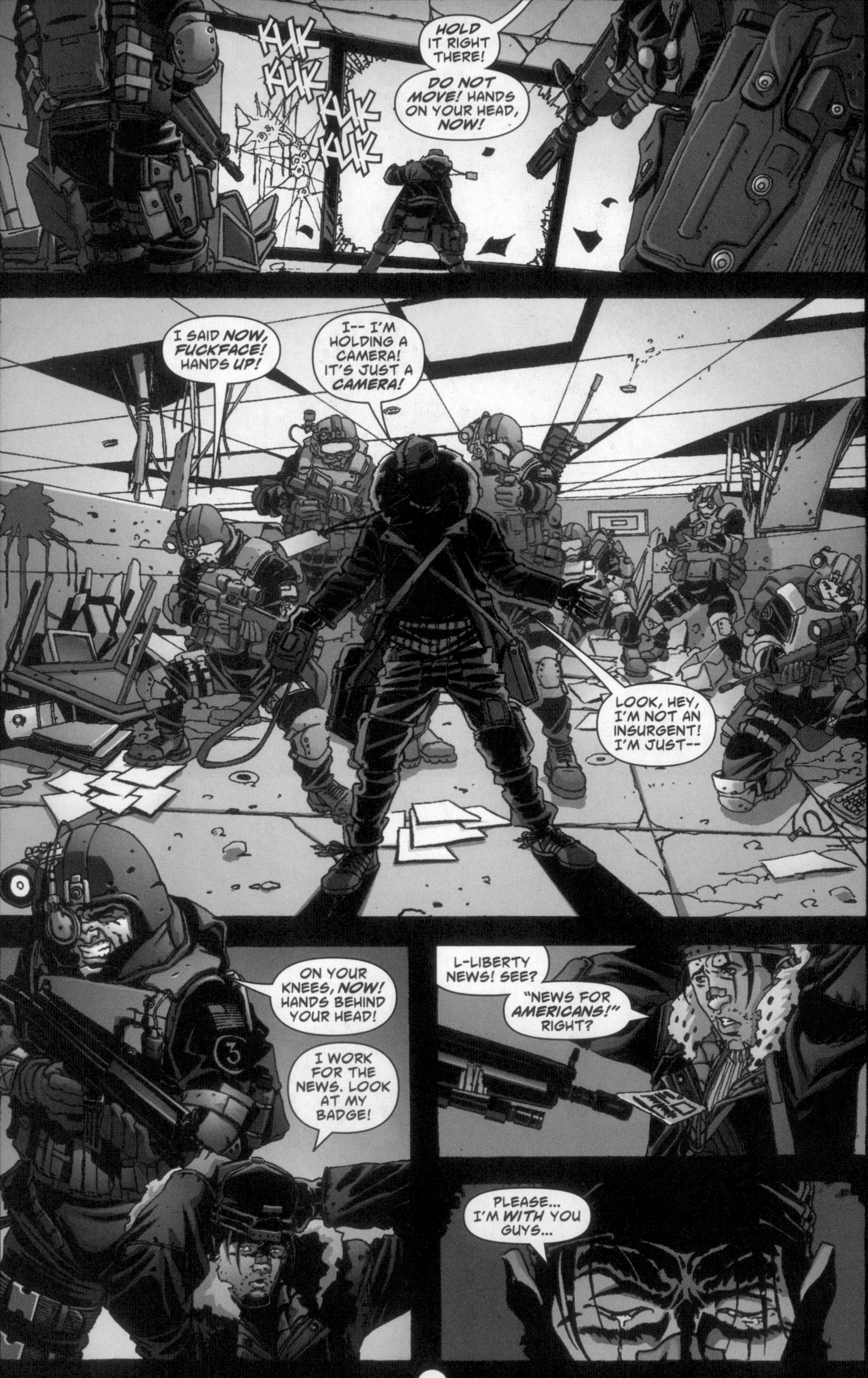
KUK KUK KUK KUK
HOLD IT RIGHT THERE!
DO NOT MOVE! HANDS ON YOUR HEAD, NOW!
I SAID NOW, FUCKFACE! HANDS UP!
I-- I'M HOLDING A CAMERA! IT'S JUST A CAMERA!
LOOK, HEY, I'M NOT AN INSURGENT! I'M JUST--
ON YOUR KNEES, NOW! HANDS BEHIND YOUR HEAD!
I WORK FOR THE NEWS. LOOK AT MY BADGE!
L-LIBERTY NEWS! SEE?
"NEWS FOR AMERICANS!" RIGHT?
PLEASE... I'M WITH YOU GUYS...

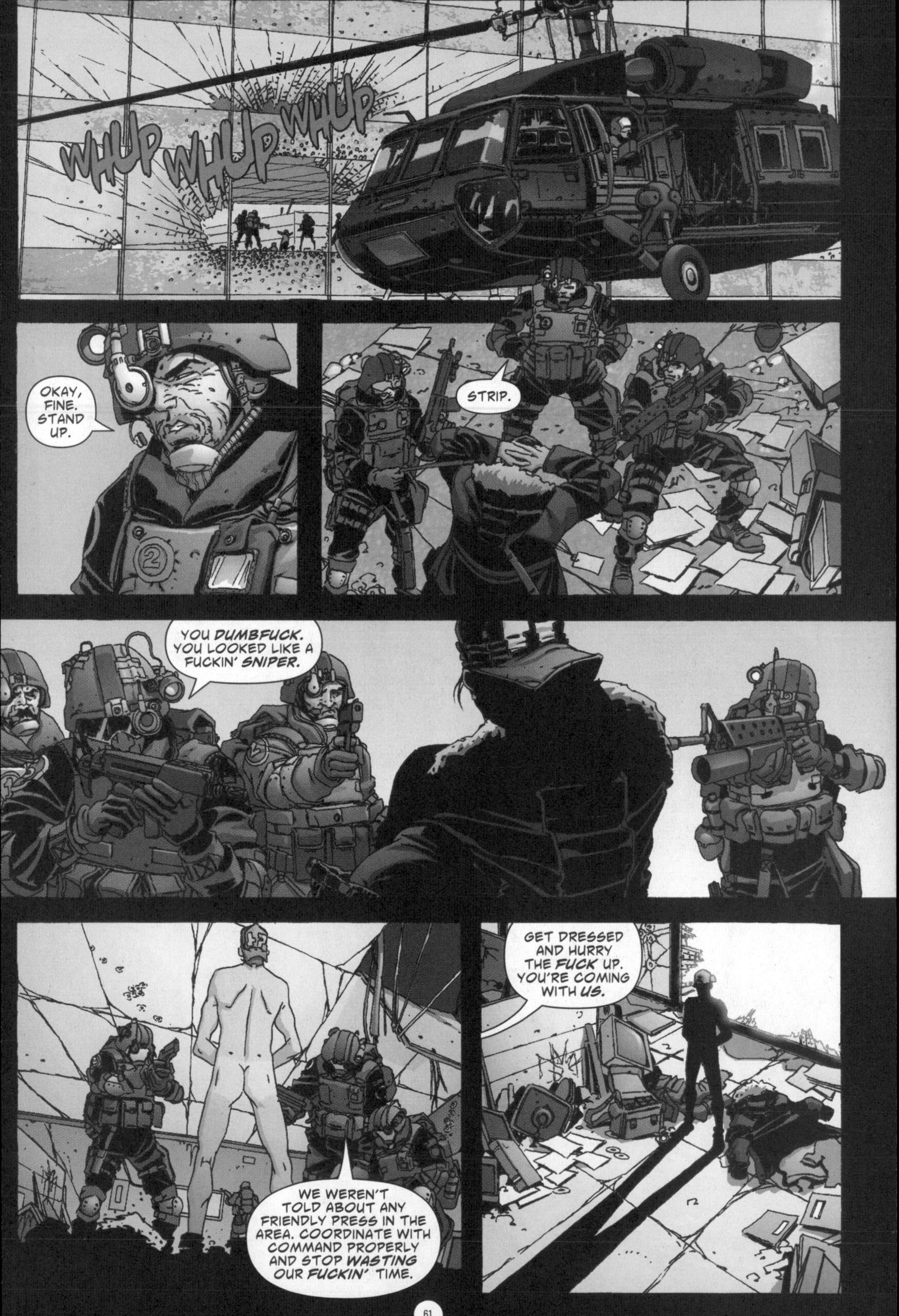
WHUP WHUP WHUP
OKAY, FINE. STAND UP.
STRIP.
YOU DUMBFUCK. YOU LOOKED LIKE A FUCKIN' SNIPER.
WE WEREN'T TOLD ABOUT ANY FRIENDLY PRESS IN THE AREA. COORDINATE WITH COMMAND PROPERLY AND STOP WASTING OUR FUCKIN' TIME.
GET DRESSED AND HURRY THE FUCK UP. YOU'RE COMING WITH US.

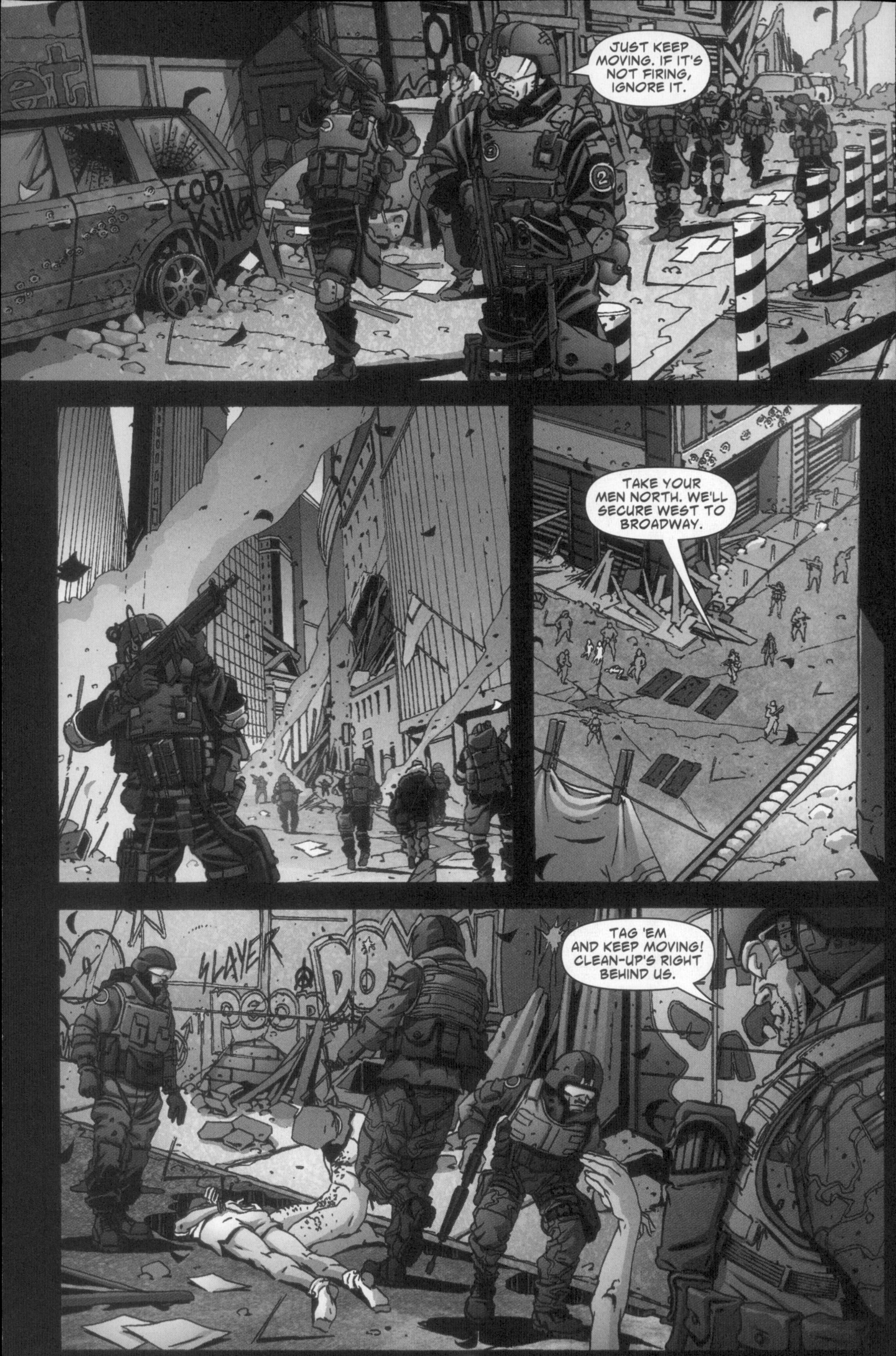
JUST KEEP MOVING. IF IT'S NOT FIRING, IGNORE IT.
TAKE YOUR MEN NORTH. WE'LL SECURE WEST TO BROADWAY.
SLAYER
TAG 'EM AND KEEP MOVING! CLEAN-UP'S RIGHT BEHIND US.

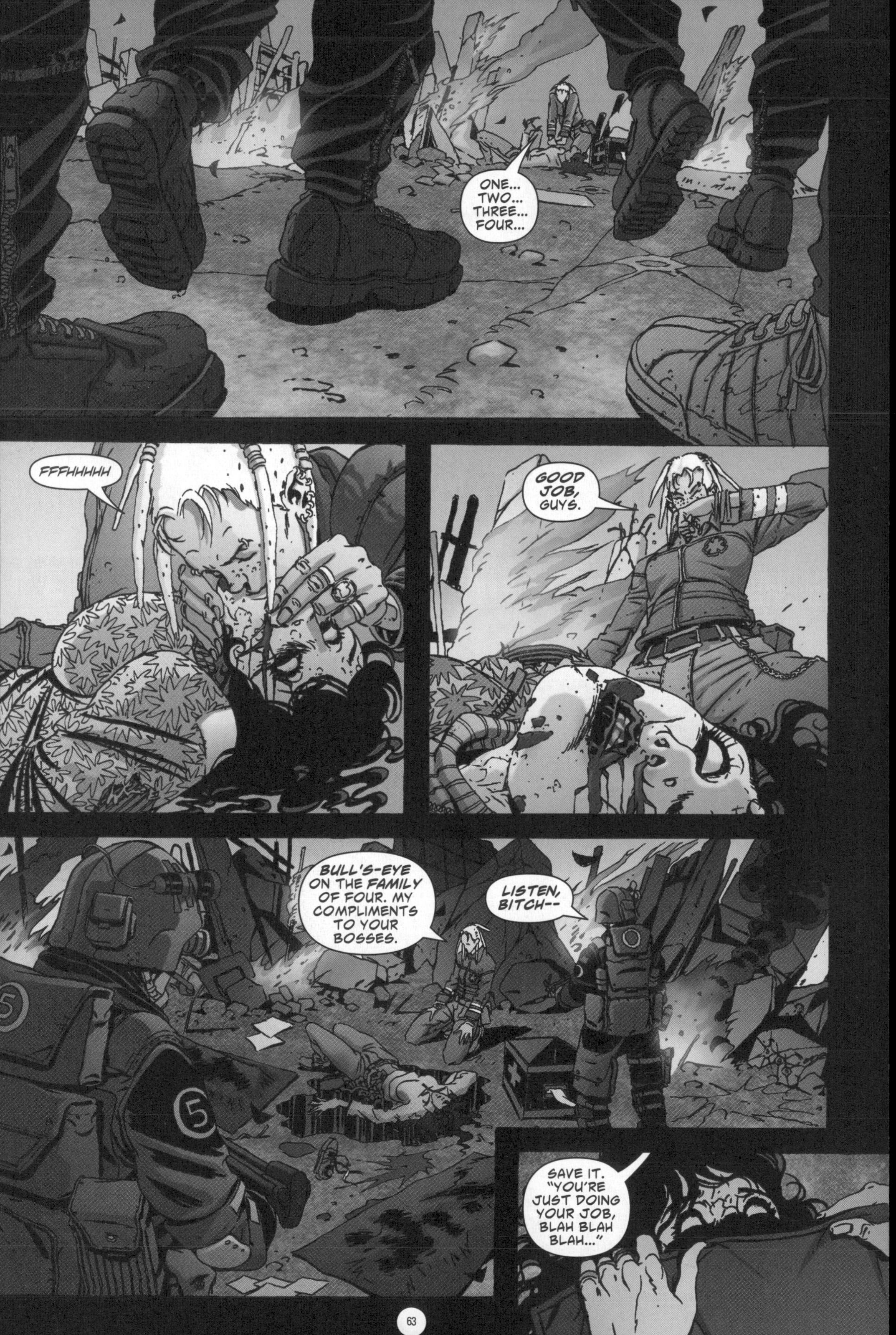
ONE... TWO... THREE... FOUR...
FFFHHHHH
GOOD JOB, GUYS.
BULL'S-EYE ON THE FAMILY OF FOUR. MY COMPLIMENTS TO YOUR BOSSES.
LISTEN, BITCH--
SAVE IT. "YOU'RE JUST DOING YOUR JOB, BLAH BLAH BLAH..."

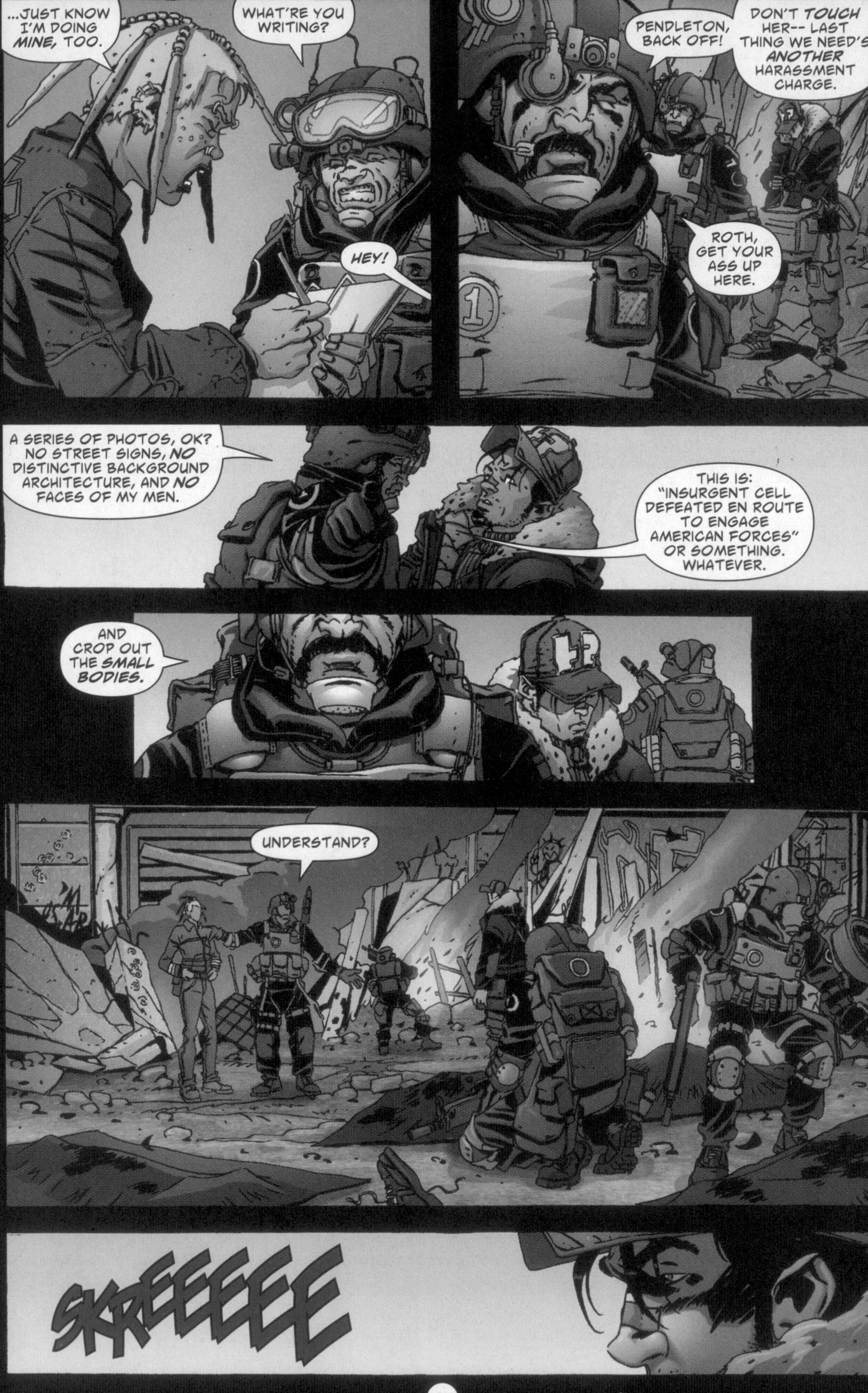
...JUST KNOW I'M DOING *MINE,* TOO.
WHAT'RE YOU WRITING?
HEY!
PENDLETON, BACK OFF!
DON'T *TOUCH* HER-- LAST THING WE NEED'S *ANOTHER* HARASSMENT CHARGE.
ROTH, GET YOUR ASS UP HERE.
A SERIES OF PHOTOS, OK? NO STREET SIGNS, *NO* DISTINCTIVE BACKGROUND ARCHITECTURE, AND *NO* FACES OF MY MEN.
THIS IS: "INSURGENT CELL DEFEATED EN ROUTE TO ENGAGE AMERICAN FORCES" OR SOMETHING. WHATEVER.
AND CROP OUT THE *SMALL BODIES.*
UNDERSTAND?
SKREEEEEE

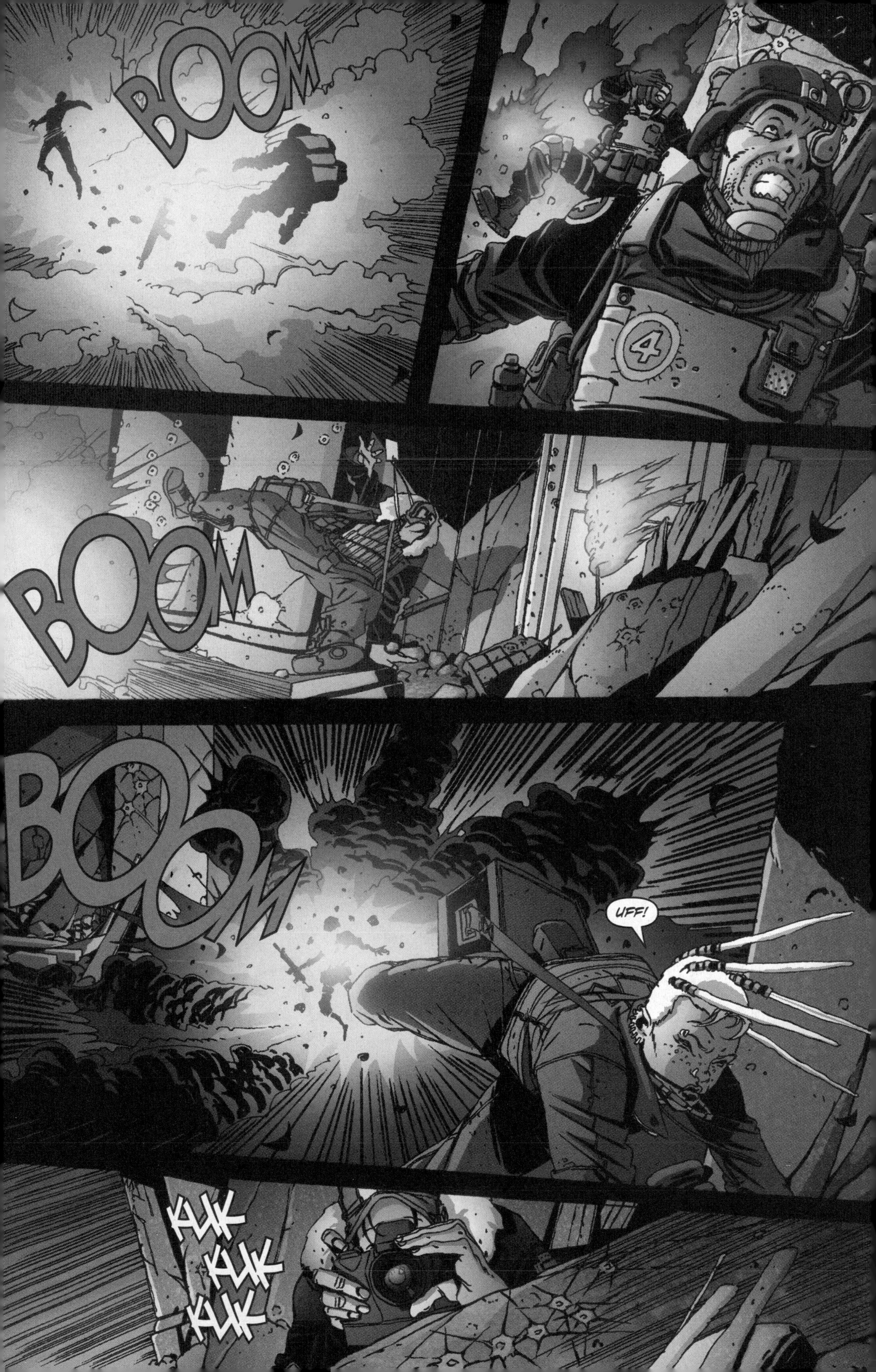
BOOM
BOOM
BOOM
UFF!
KUK
KUK
KUK

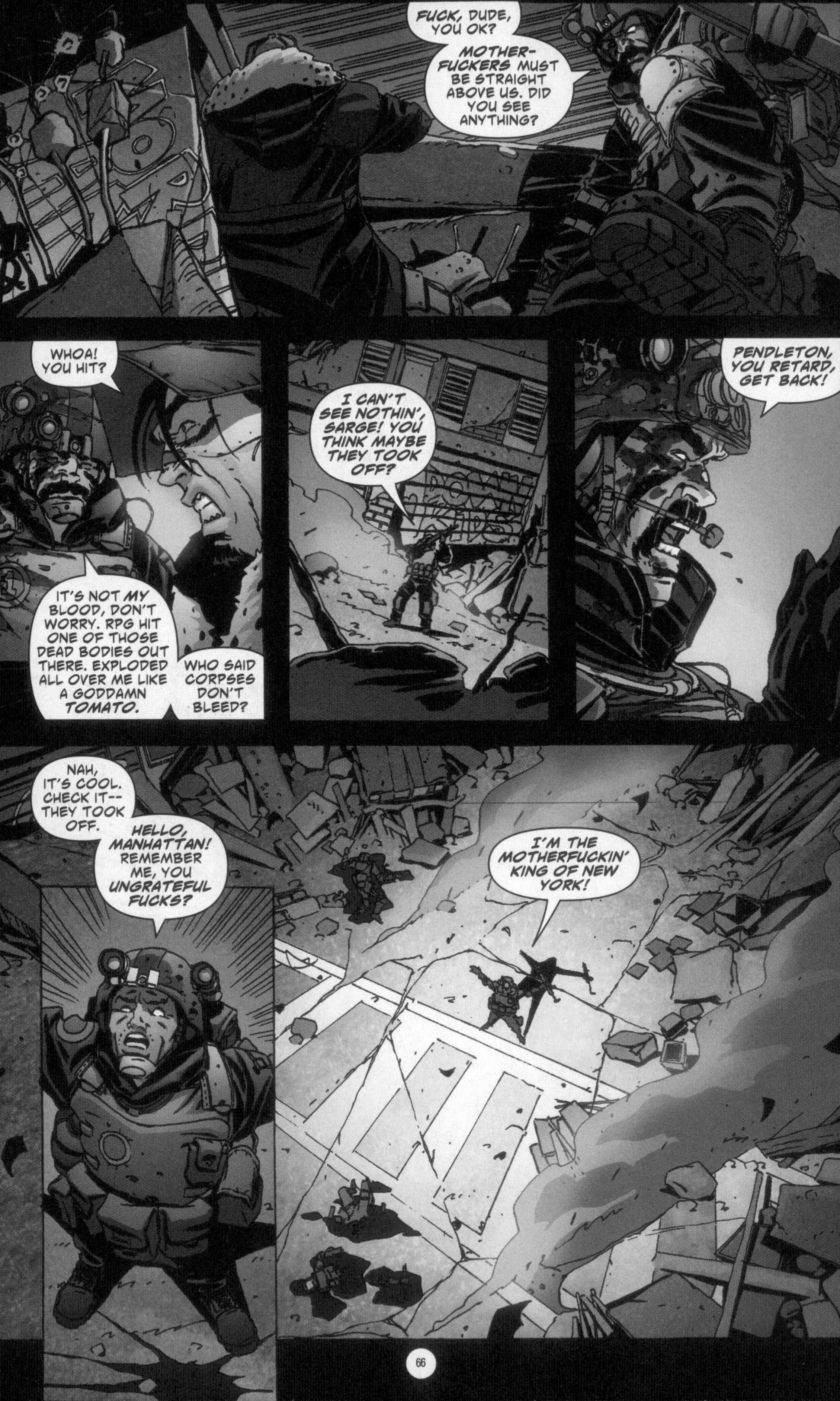

FUCK, DUDE, YOU OK?
MOTHER-FUCKERS MUST BE STRAIGHT ABOVE US. DID YOU SEE ANYTHING?
WHOA! YOU HIT?
IT'S NOT MY BLOOD, DON'T WORRY. RPG HIT ONE OF THOSE DEAD BODIES OUT THERE. EXPLODED ALL OVER ME LIKE A GODDAMN TOMATO.
WHO SAID CORPSES DON'T BLEED?
I CAN'T SEE NOTHIN', SARGE! YOU THINK MAYBE THEY TOOK OFF?
PENDLETON, YOU RETARD, GET BACK!
NAH, IT'S COOL. CHECK IT-- THEY TOOK OFF.
HELLO, MANHATTAN! REMEMBER ME, YOU UNGRATEFUL FUCKS?
I'M THE MOTHERFUCKIN' KING OF NEW YORK!

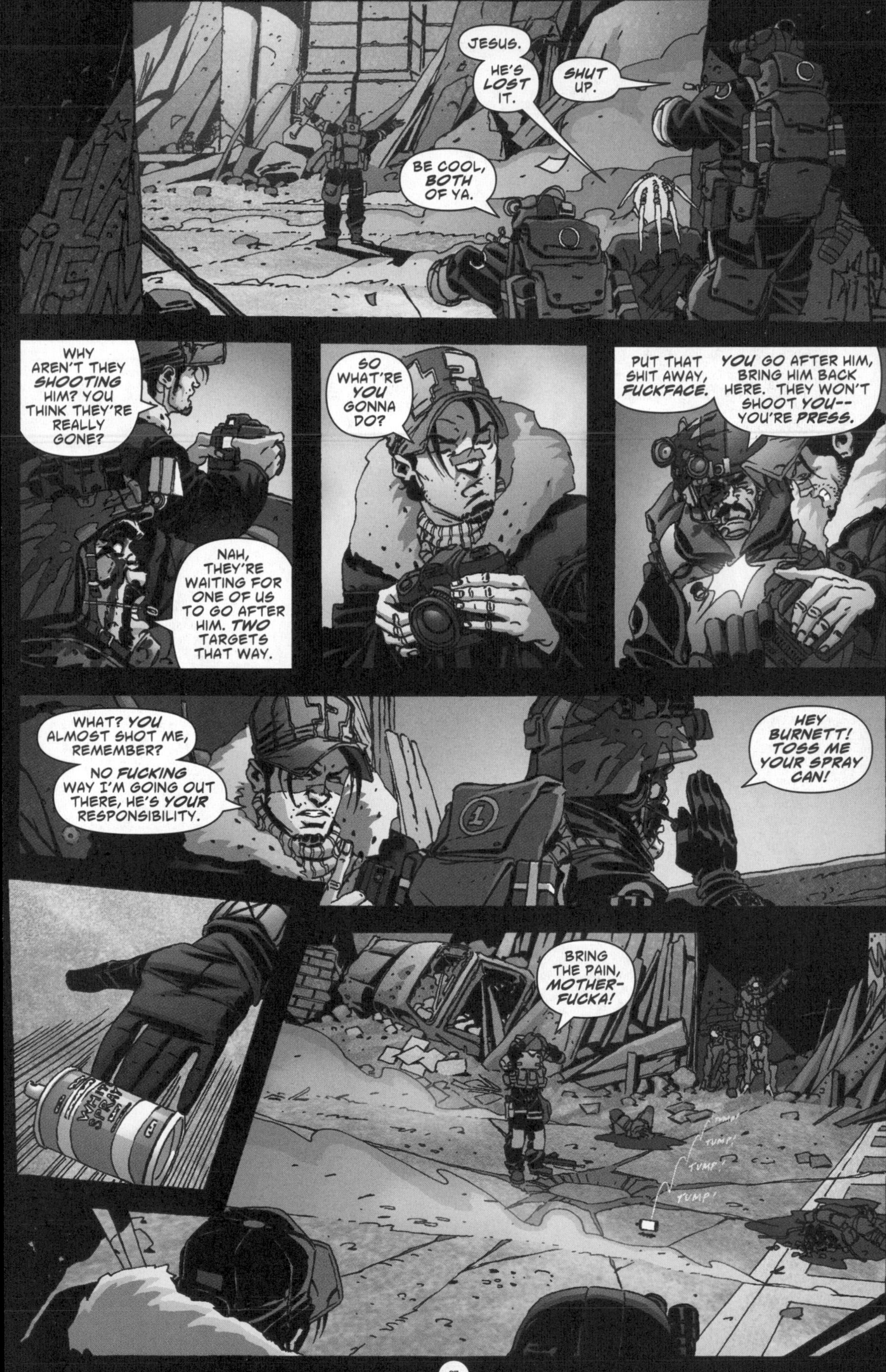
JESUS.
HE'S LOST IT.
SHUT UP.
BE COOL, BOTH OF YA.
WHY AREN'T THEY SHOOTING HIM? YOU THINK THEY'RE REALLY GONE?
NAH, THEY'RE WAITING FOR ONE OF US TO GO AFTER HIM. TWO TARGETS THAT WAY.
SO WHAT'RE YOU GONNA DO?
PUT THAT SHIT AWAY, FUCKFACE.
YOU GO AFTER HIM, BRING HIM BACK HERE. THEY WON'T SHOOT YOU-- YOU'RE PRESS.
WHAT? YOU ALMOST SHOT ME, REMEMBER?
NO FUCKING WAY I'M GOING OUT THERE, HE'S YOUR RESPONSIBILITY.
HEY BURNETT! TOSS ME YOUR SPRAY CAN!
BRING THE PAIN, MOTHER-FUCKA!
TUMP!
TUMP!
TUMP!
TUMP!

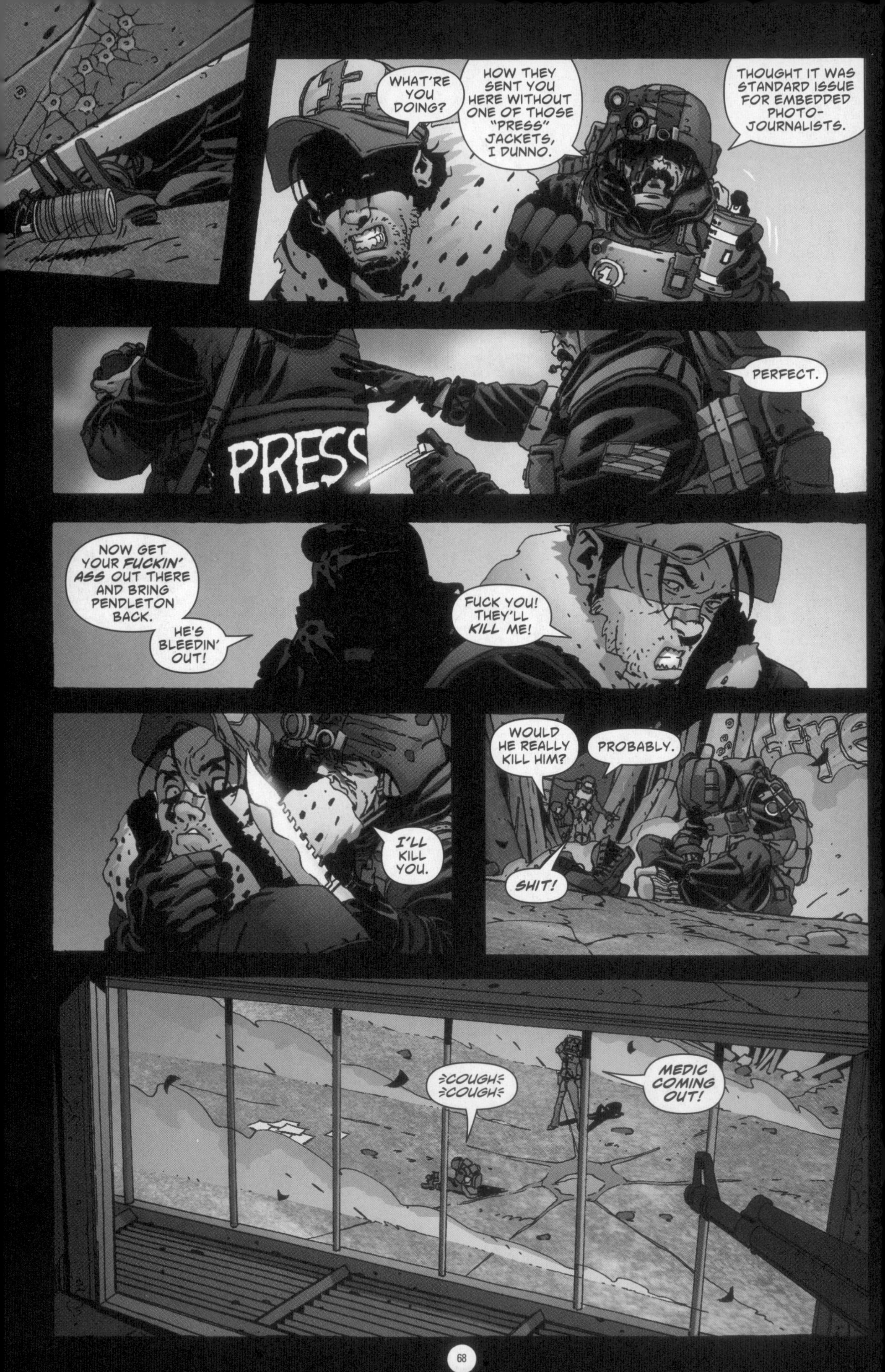
WHAT'RE YOU DOING?
HOW THEY SENT YOU HERE WITHOUT ONE OF THOSE "PRESS" JACKETS, I DUNNO.
THOUGHT IT WAS STANDARD ISSUE FOR EMBEDDED PHOTO-JOURNALISTS.
PRESS
PERFECT.
NOW GET YOUR FUCKIN' ASS OUT THERE AND BRING PENDLETON BACK.
HE'S BLEEDIN' OUT!
FUCK YOU! THEY'LL KILL ME!
I'LL KILL YOU.
WOULD HE REALLY KILL HIM?
PROBABLY.
SHIT!
COUGH COUGH
MEDIC COMING OUT!

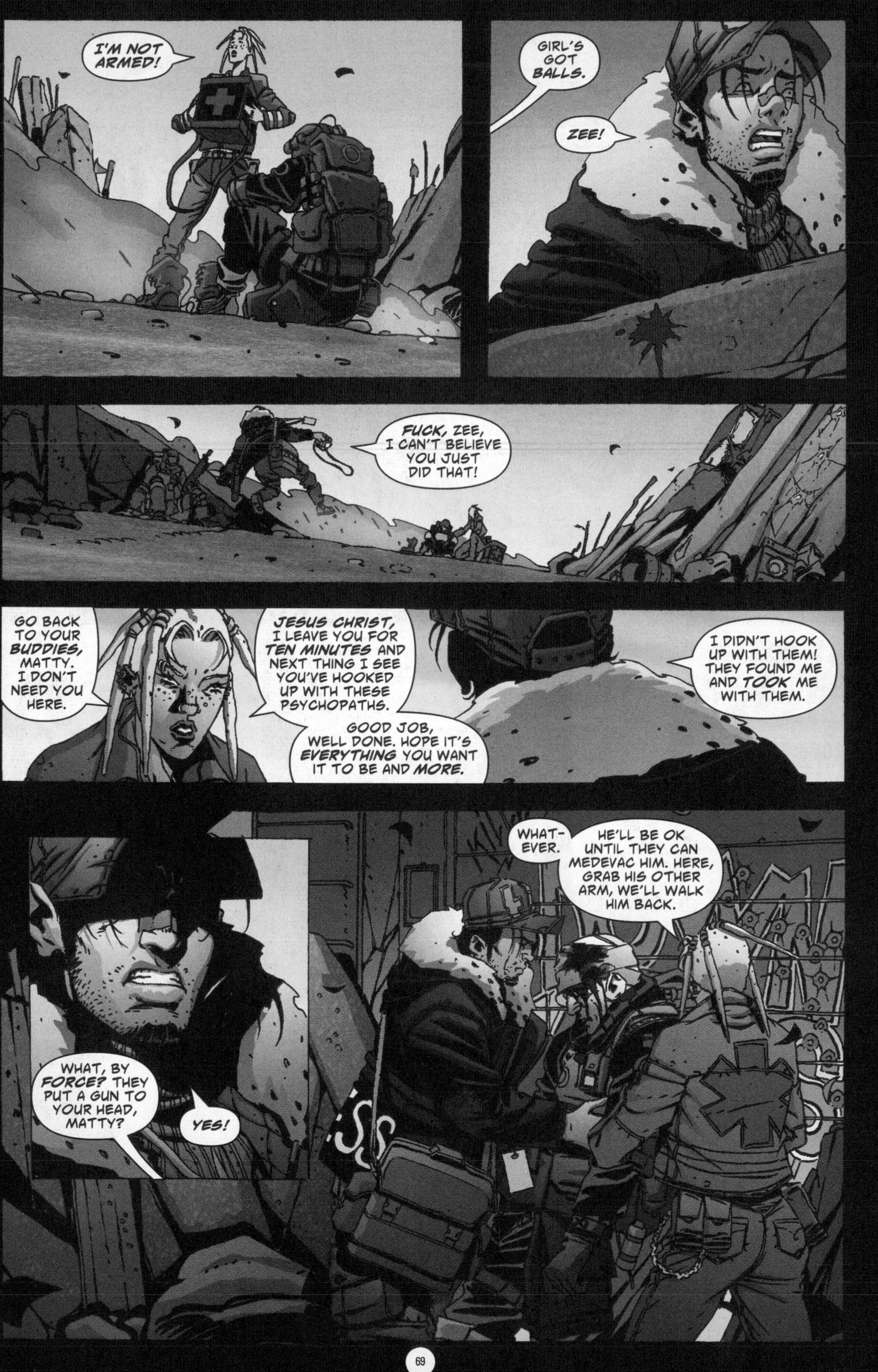
I'M NOT ARMED!
GIRL'S GOT BALLS.
ZEE!
FUCK, ZEE, I CAN'T BELIEVE YOU JUST DID THAT!
GO BACK TO YOUR BUDDIES, MATTY. I DON'T NEED YOU HERE.
JESUS CHRIST, I LEAVE YOU FOR TEN MINUTES AND NEXT THING I SEE YOU'VE HOOKED UP WITH THESE PSYCHOPATHS.
GOOD JOB, WELL DONE. HOPE IT'S EVERYTHING YOU WANT IT TO BE AND MORE.
I DIDN'T HOOK UP WITH THEM! THEY FOUND ME AND TOOK ME WITH THEM.
WHAT, BY FORCE? THEY PUT A GUN TO YOUR HEAD, MATTY?
YES!
WHAT-EVER.
HE'LL BE OK UNTIL THEY CAN MEDEVAC HIM. HERE, GRAB HIS OTHER ARM, WE'LL WALK HIM BACK.

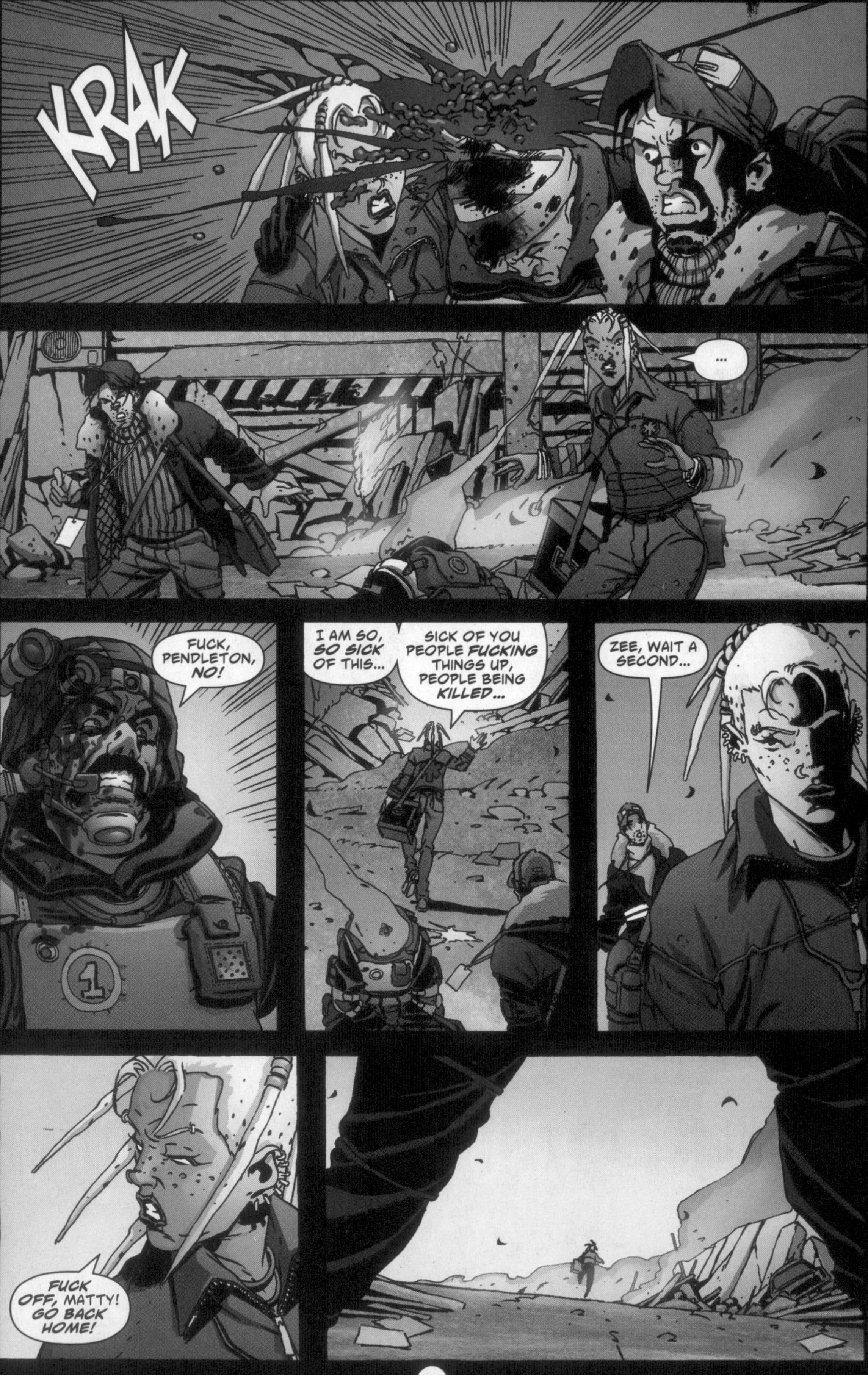

KRAK
...
FUCK, PENDLETON, NO!
I AM SO, SO SICK OF THIS...
SICK OF YOU PEOPLE FUCKING THINGS UP, PEOPLE BEING KILLED...
ZEE, WAIT A SECOND...
FUCK OFF, MATTY! GO BACK HOME!

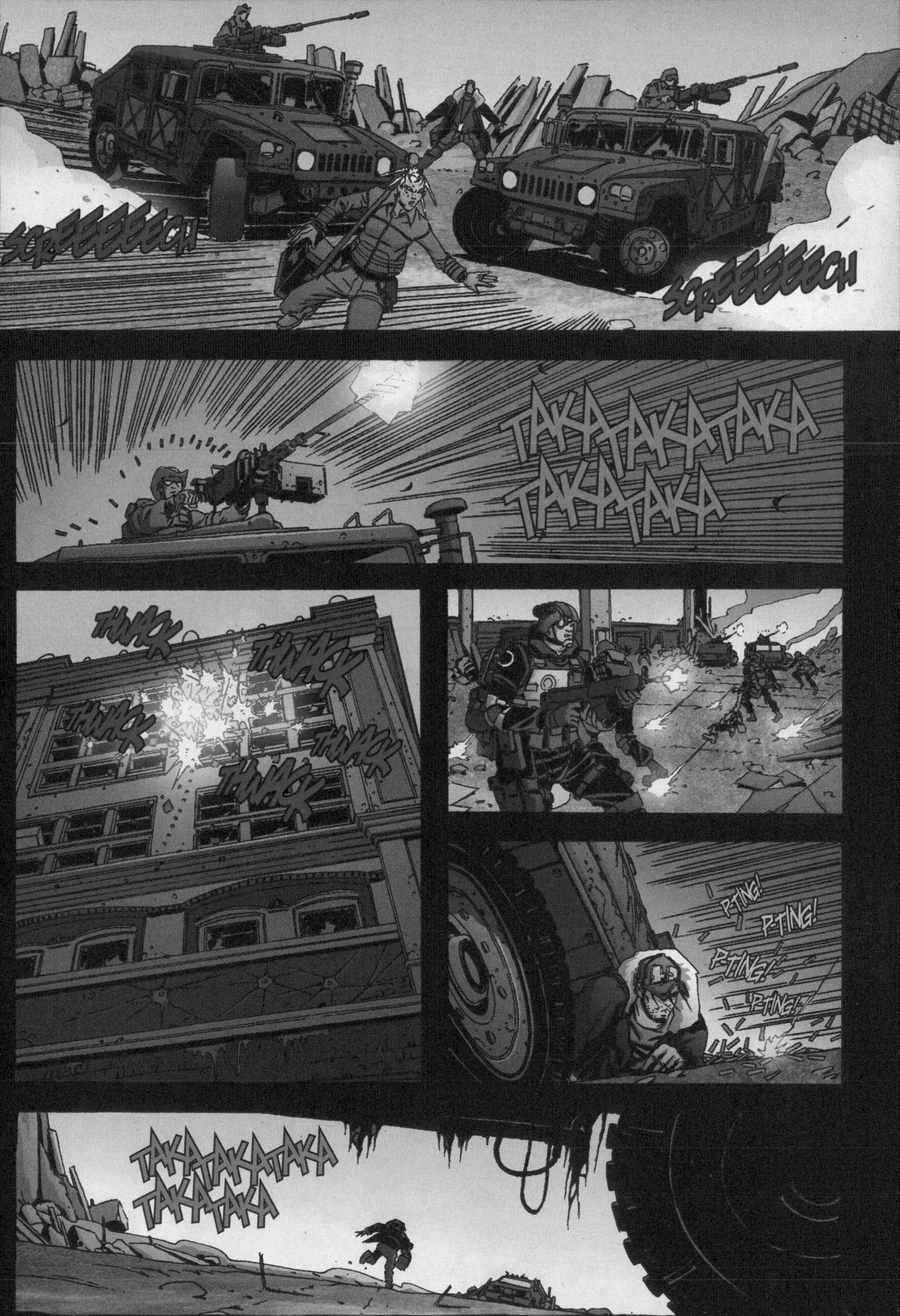
SCREEEEECH
SCREEEEECH
TAKATAKATAKA
TAKATAKA
THWACK
THWACK
THWACK
THWACK
THWACK
P-TING!
P-TING!
P-TING!
P-TING!
TAKATAKATAKA
TAKATAKA

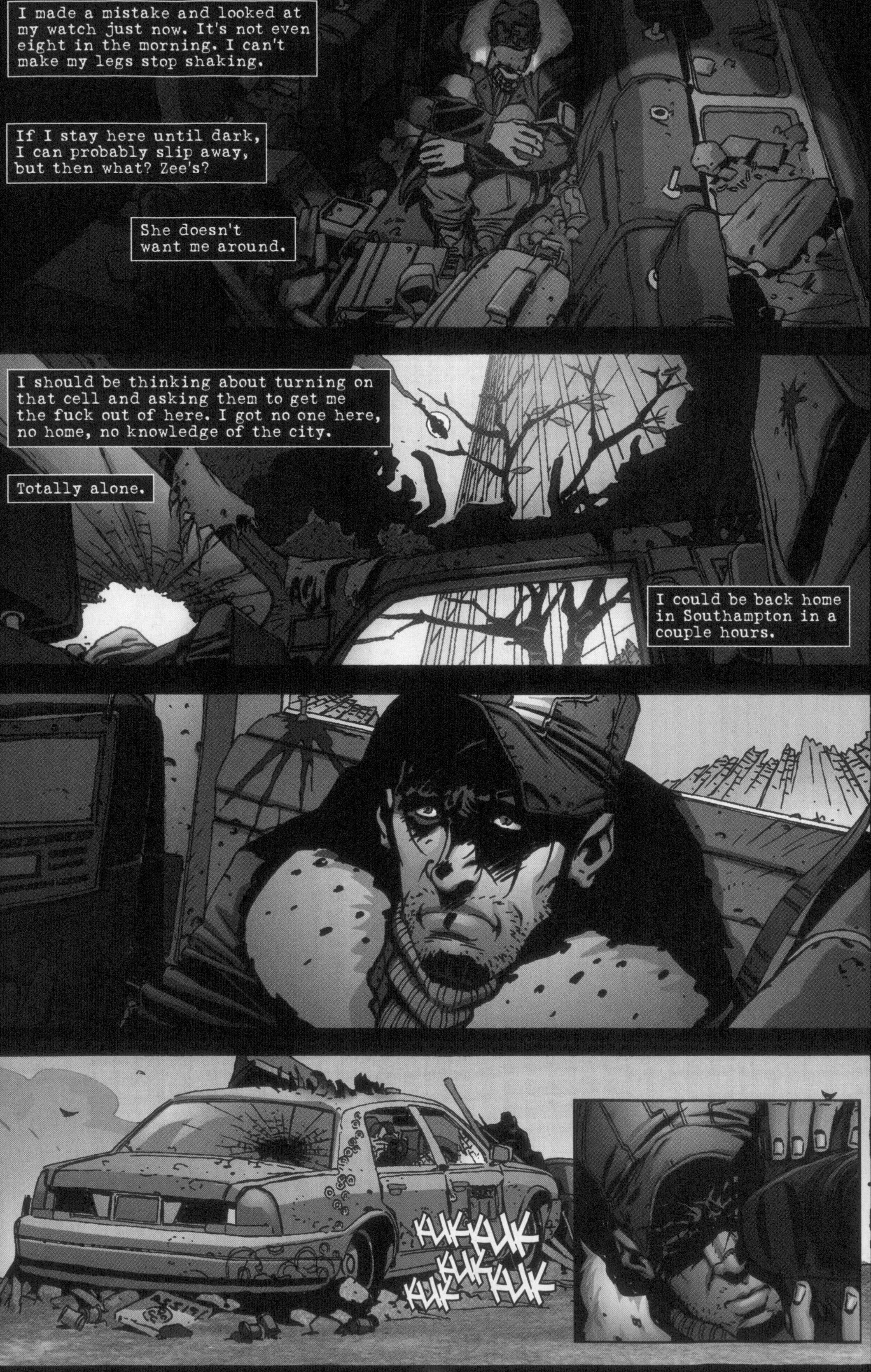

I made a mistake and looked at my watch just now. It's not even eight in the morning. I can't make my legs stop shaking.
If I stay here until dark, I can probably slip away, but then what? Zee's?
She doesn't want me around.
I should be thinking about turning on that cell and asking them to get me the fuck out of here. I got no one here, no home, no knowledge of the city.
Totally alone.
I could be back home in Southampton in a couple hours.
KUK KUK KUK KUK KUK

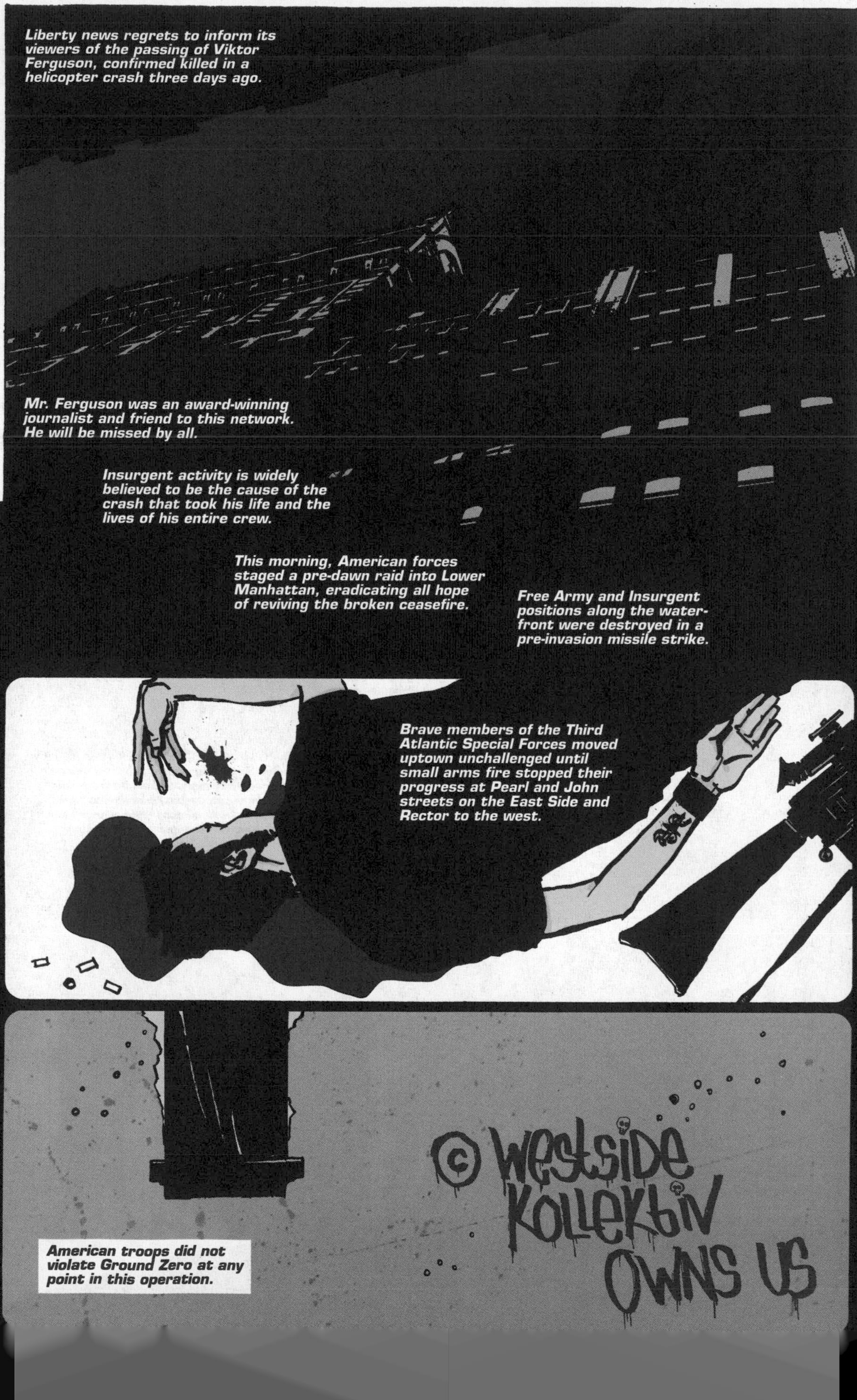

Liberty news regrets to inform its viewers of the passing of Viktor Ferguson, confirmed killed in a helicopter crash three days ago.

Mr. Ferguson was an award-winning journalist and friend to this network. He will be missed by all.

Insurgent activity is widely believed to be the cause of the crash that took his life and the lives of his entire crew.

This morning, American forces staged a pre-dawn raid into Lower Manhattan, eradicating all hope of reviving the broken ceasefire.

Free Army and Insurgent positions along the water-front were destroyed in a pre-invasion missile strike.

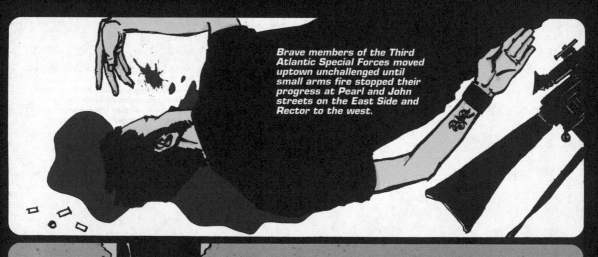

Brave members of the Third Atlantic Special Forces moved uptown unchallenged until small arms fire stopped their progress at Pearl and John streets on the East Side and Rector to the west.

American troops did not violate Ground Zero at any point in this operation.

© WESTSIDE KOLLEKTIV OWNS US

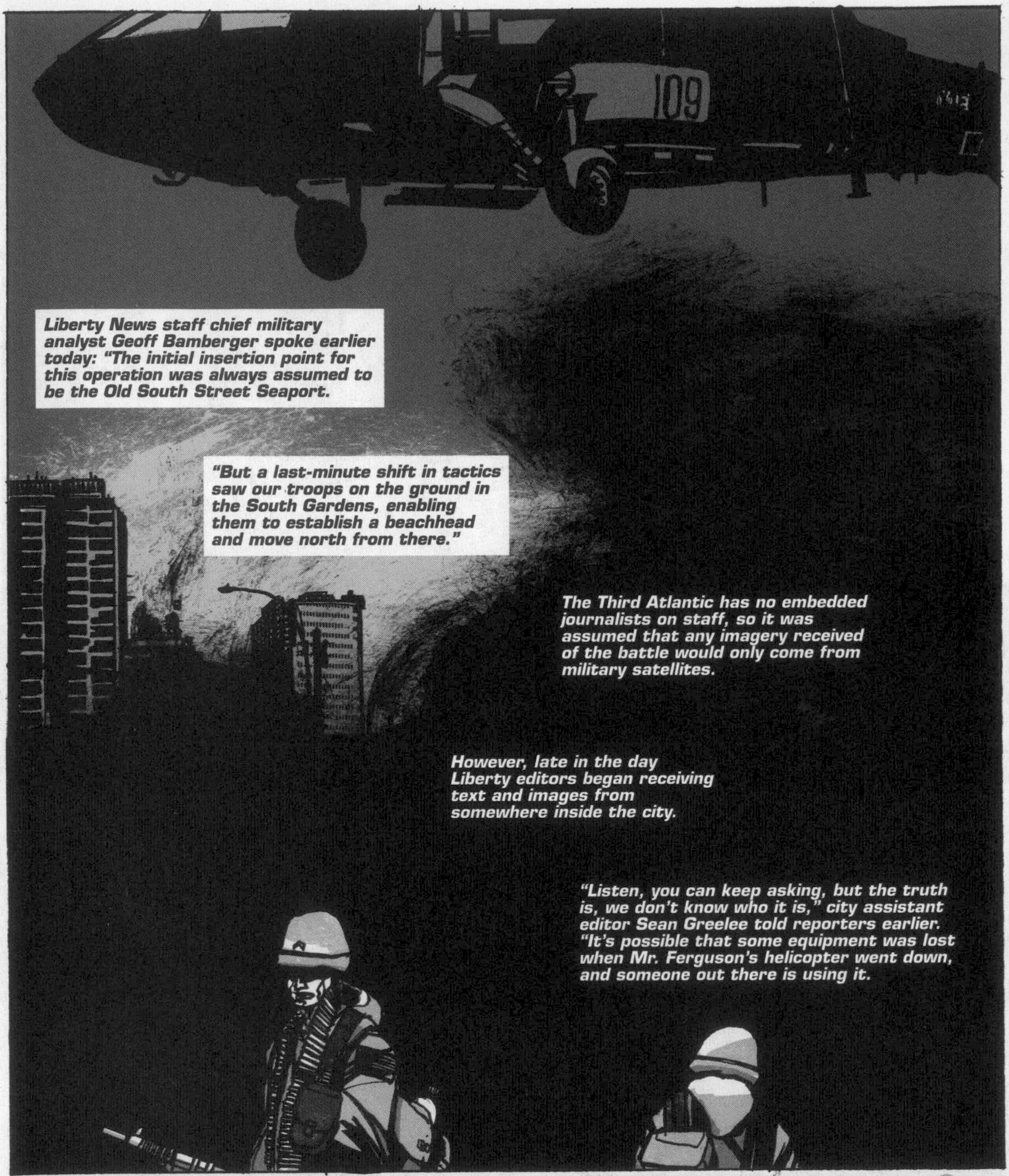
109
Liberty News staff chief military analyst Geoff Bamberger spoke earlier today: "The initial insertion point for this operation was always assumed to be the Old South Street Seaport.
"But a last-minute shift in tactics saw our troops on the ground in the South Gardens, enabling them to establish a beachhead and move north from there."
The Third Atlantic has no embedded journalists on staff, so it was assumed that any imagery received of the battle would only come from military satellites.
However, late in the day Liberty editors began receiving text and images from somewhere inside the city.
"Listen, you can keep asking, but the truth is, we don't know who it is," city assistant editor Sean Greelee told reporters earlier. "It's possible that some equipment was lost when Mr. Ferguson's helicopter went down, and someone out there is using it.

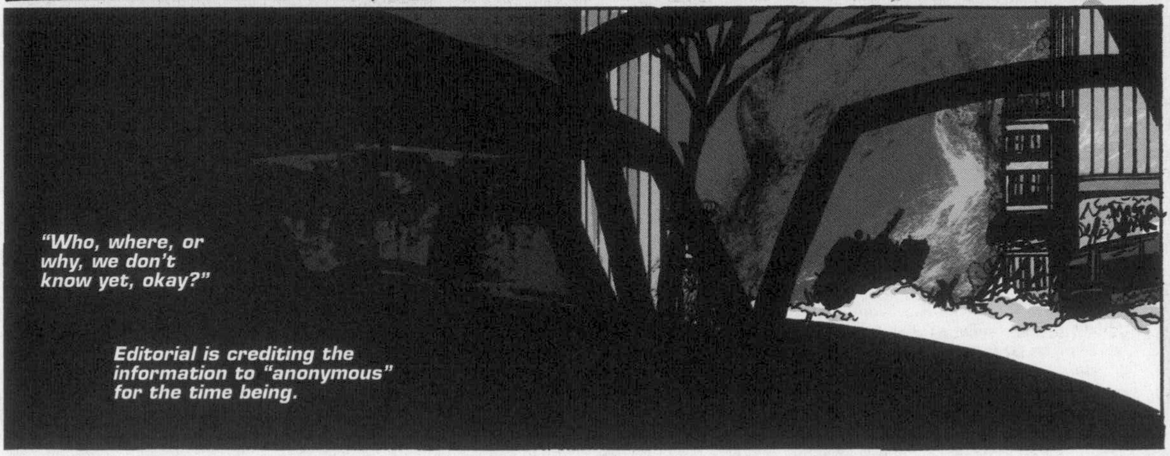
"Who, where, or why, we don't know yet, okay?"
Editorial is crediting the information to "anonymous" for the time being.

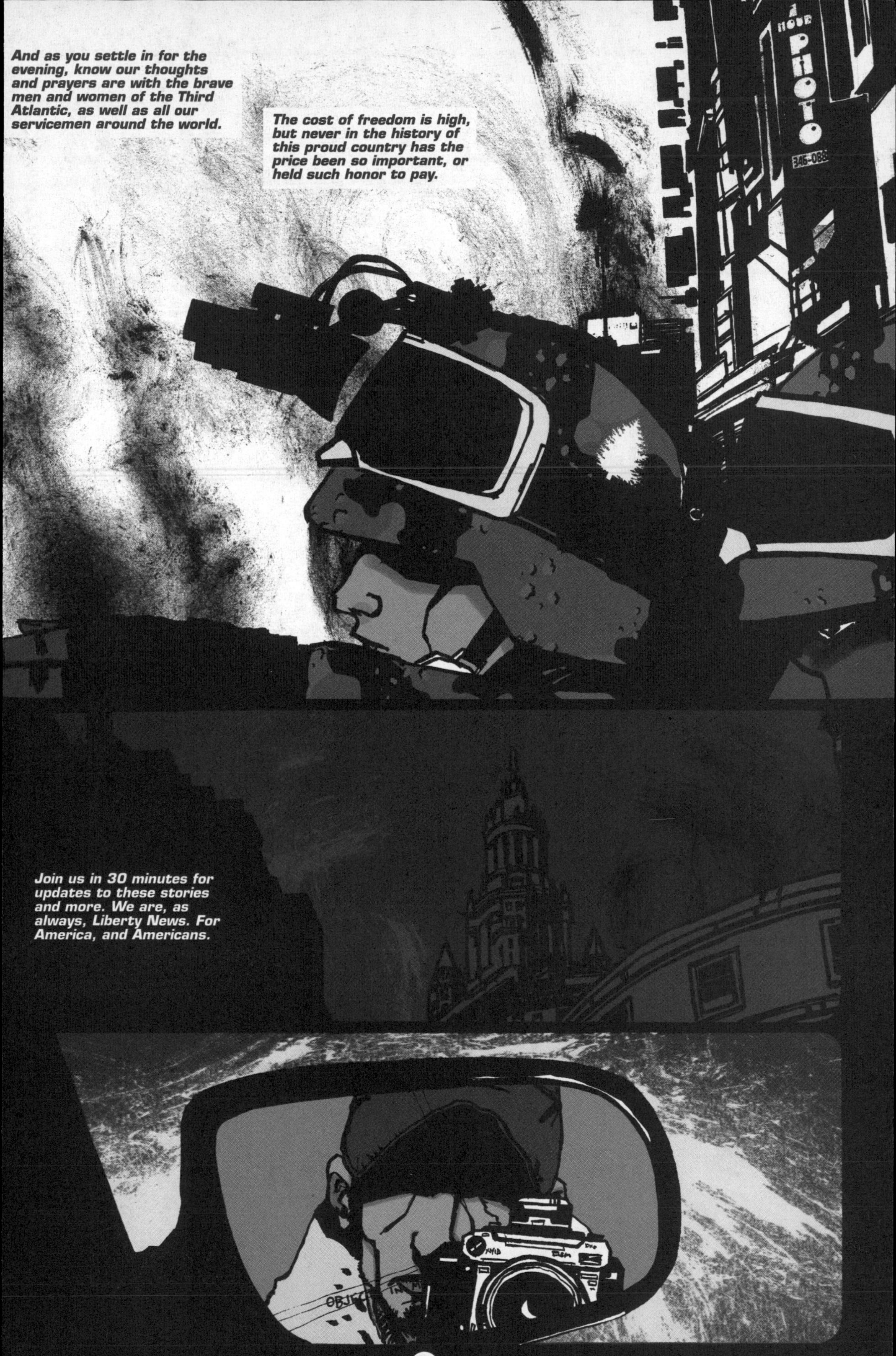
And as you settle in for the evening, know our thoughts and prayers are with the brave men and women of the Third Atlantic, as well as all our servicemen around the world.
The cost of freedom is high, but never in the history of this proud country has the price been so important, or held such honor to pay.
PHOTO
Join us in 30 minutes for updates to these stories and more. We are, as always, Liberty News. For America, and Americans.

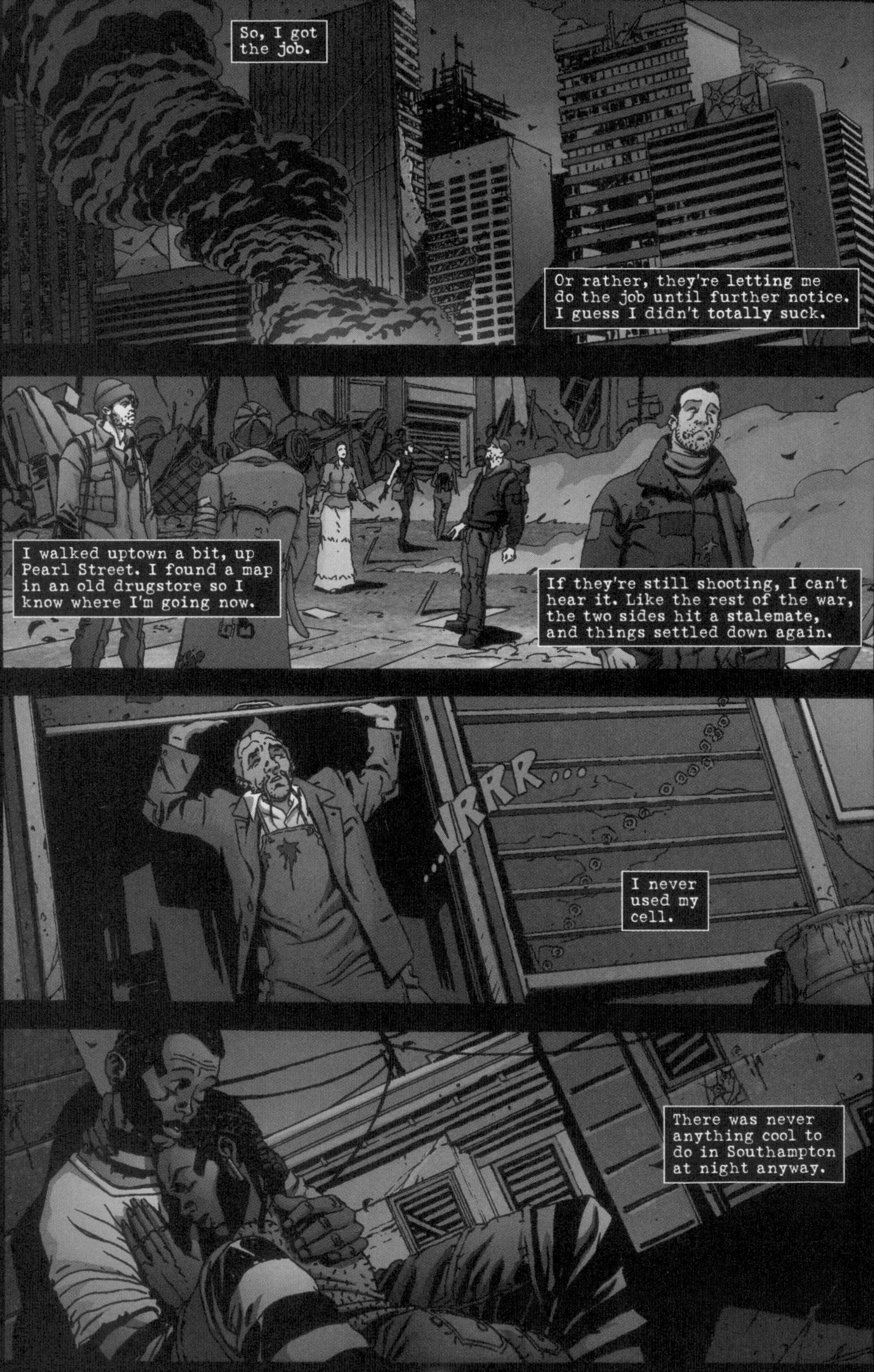
So, I got the job.
Or rather, they're letting me do the job until further notice. I guess I didn't totally suck.
I walked uptown a bit, up Pearl Street. I found a map in an old drugstore so I know where I'm going now.
If they're still shooting, I can't hear it. Like the rest of the war, the two sides hit a stalemate, and things settled down again.
...VRRR...
I never used my cell.
There was never anything cool to do in Southampton at night anyway.

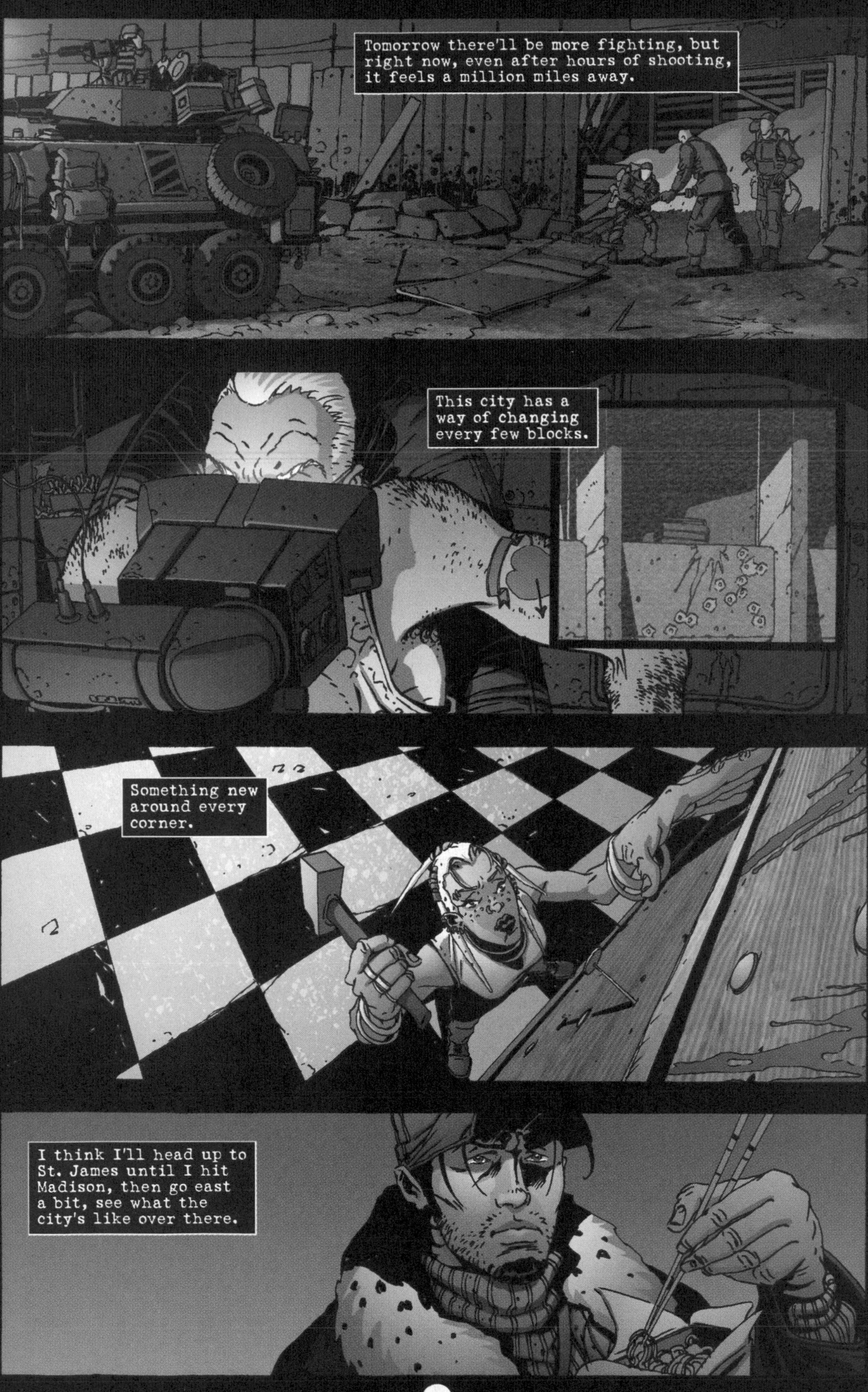
Tomorrow there'll be more fighting, but right now, even after hours of shooting, it feels a million miles away.
This city has a way of changing every few blocks.
Something new around every corner.
I think I'll head up to St. James until I hit Madison, then go east a bit, see what the city's like over there.

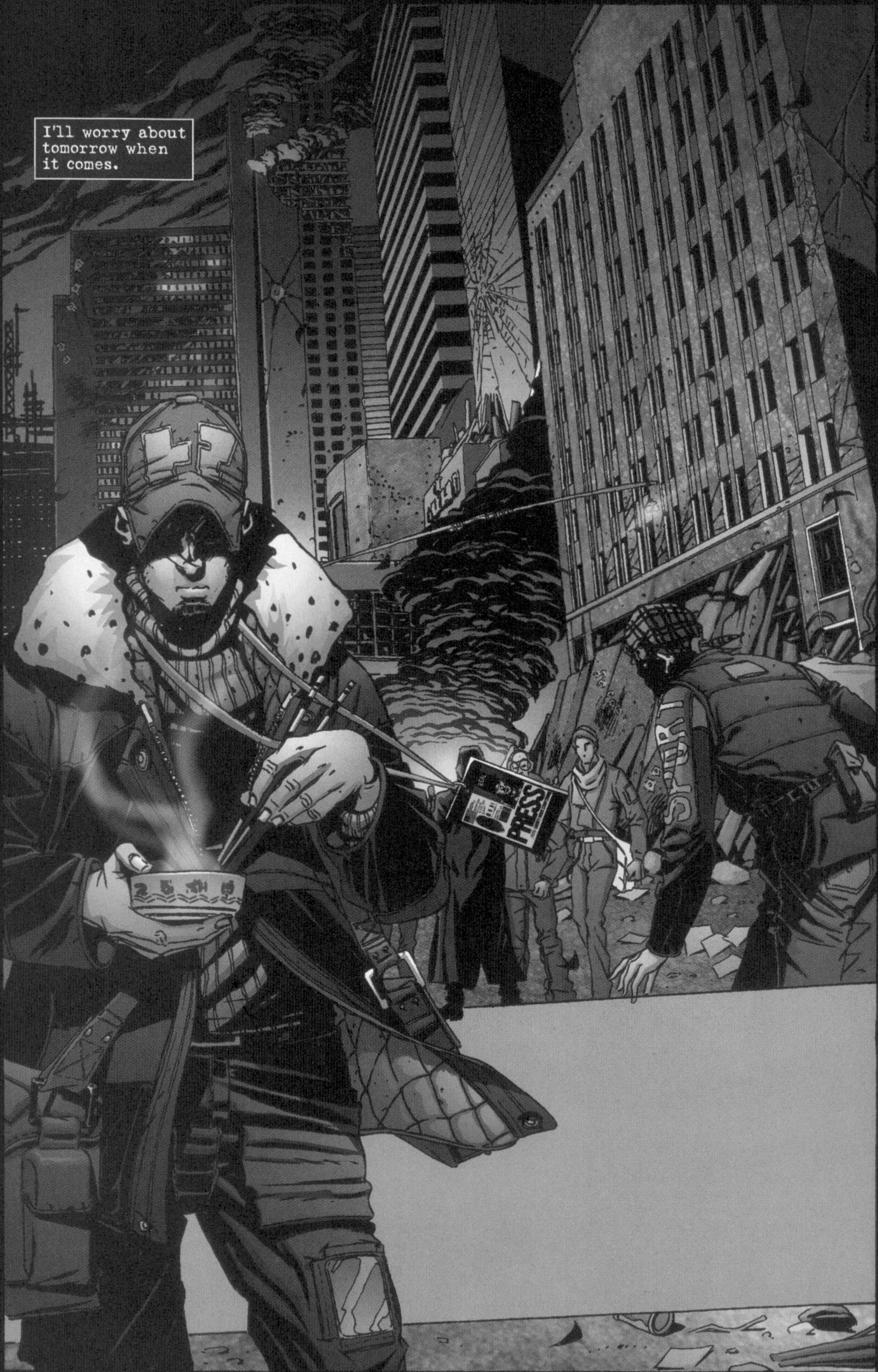
I'll worry about tomorrow when it comes.
PRESS

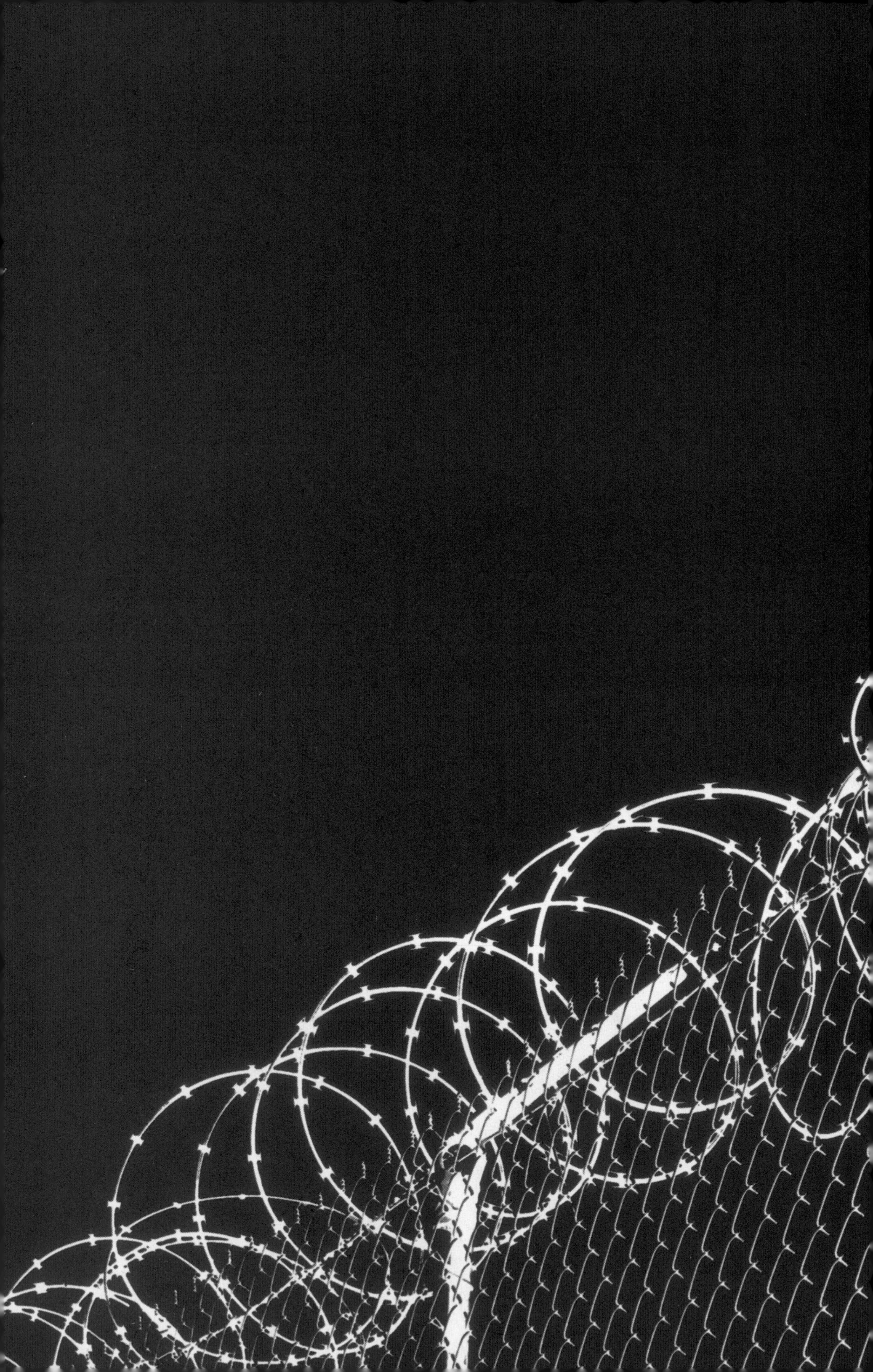

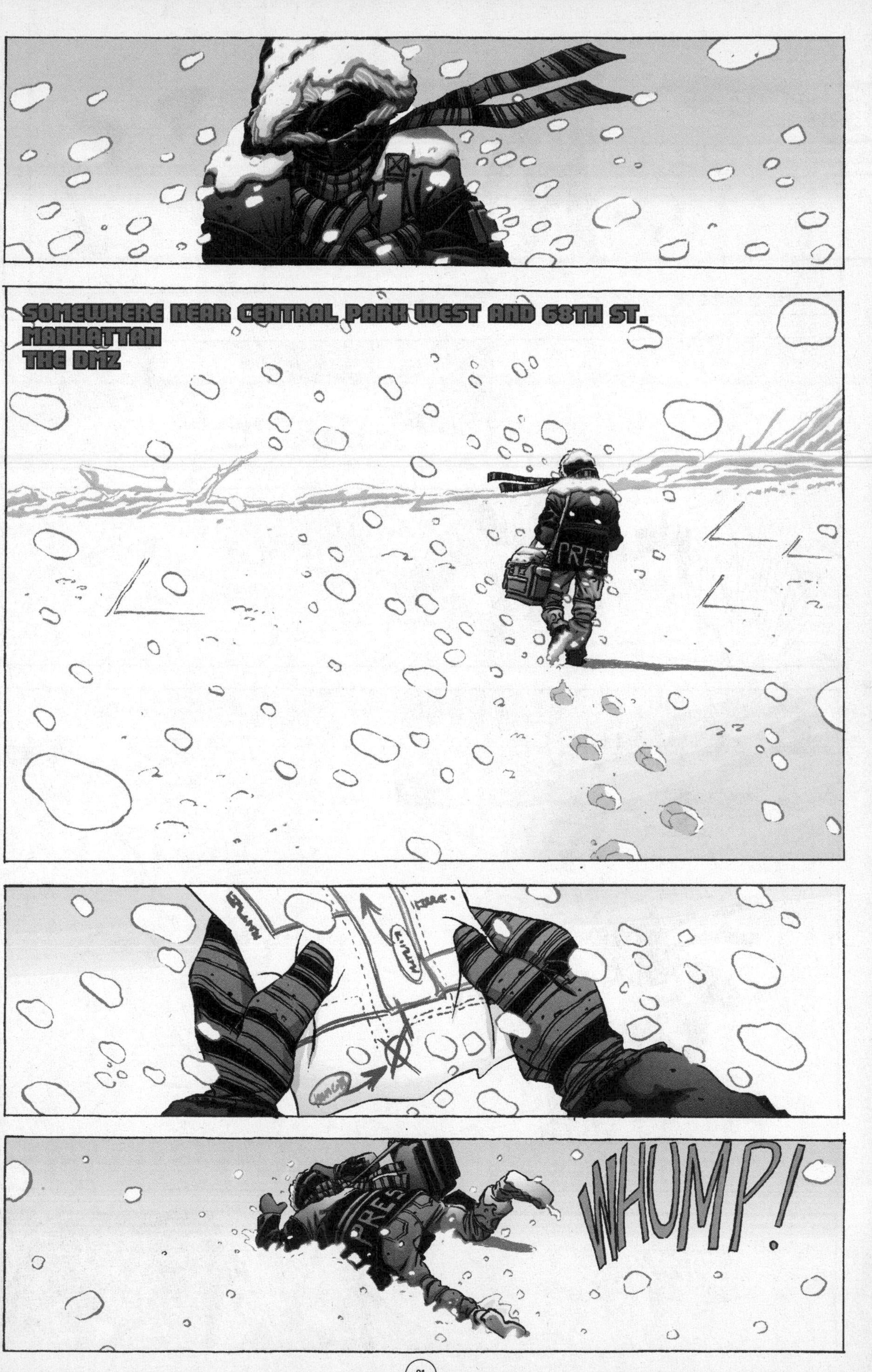
SOMEWHERE NEAR CENTRAL PARK WEST AND 68TH ST.
MANHATTAN
THE DMZ
WHUMP!

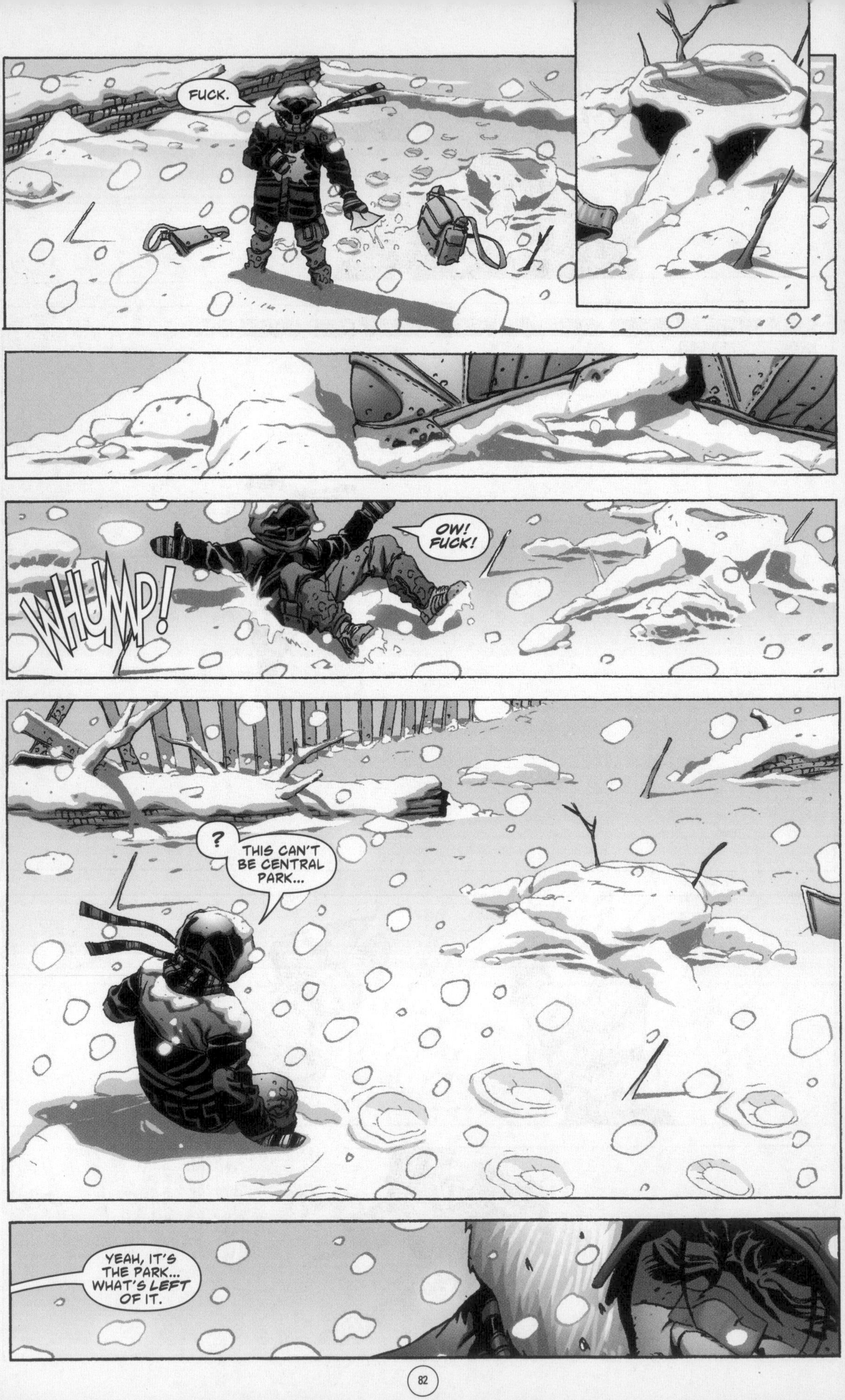
FUCK.
OW! FUCK!
WHUMP!
?
THIS CAN'T BE CENTRAL PARK...
YEAH, IT'S THE PARK... WHAT'S LEFT OF IT.

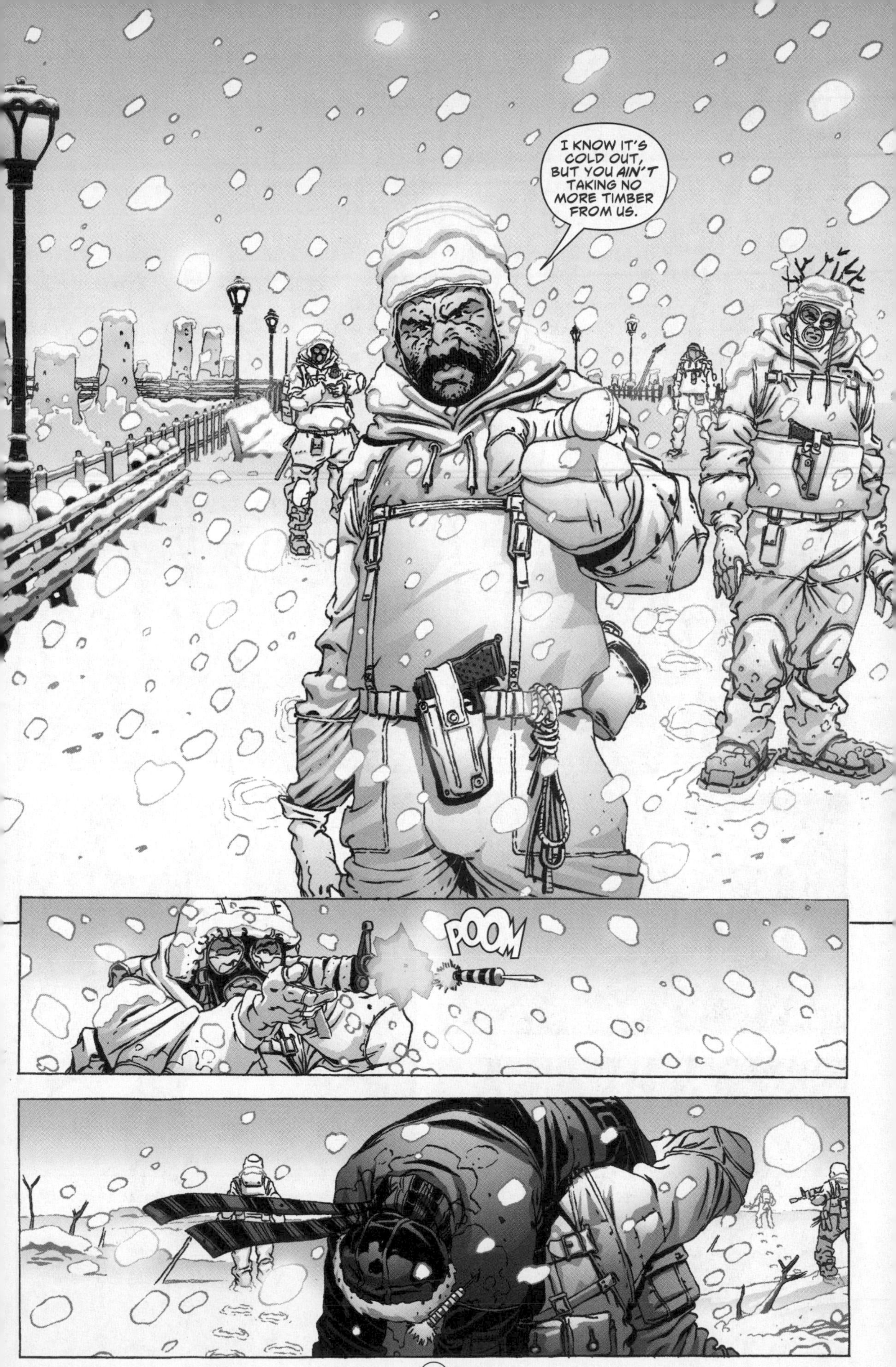
I KNOW IT'S COLD OUT, BUT YOU AIN'T TAKING NO MORE TIMBER FROM US.
POOM

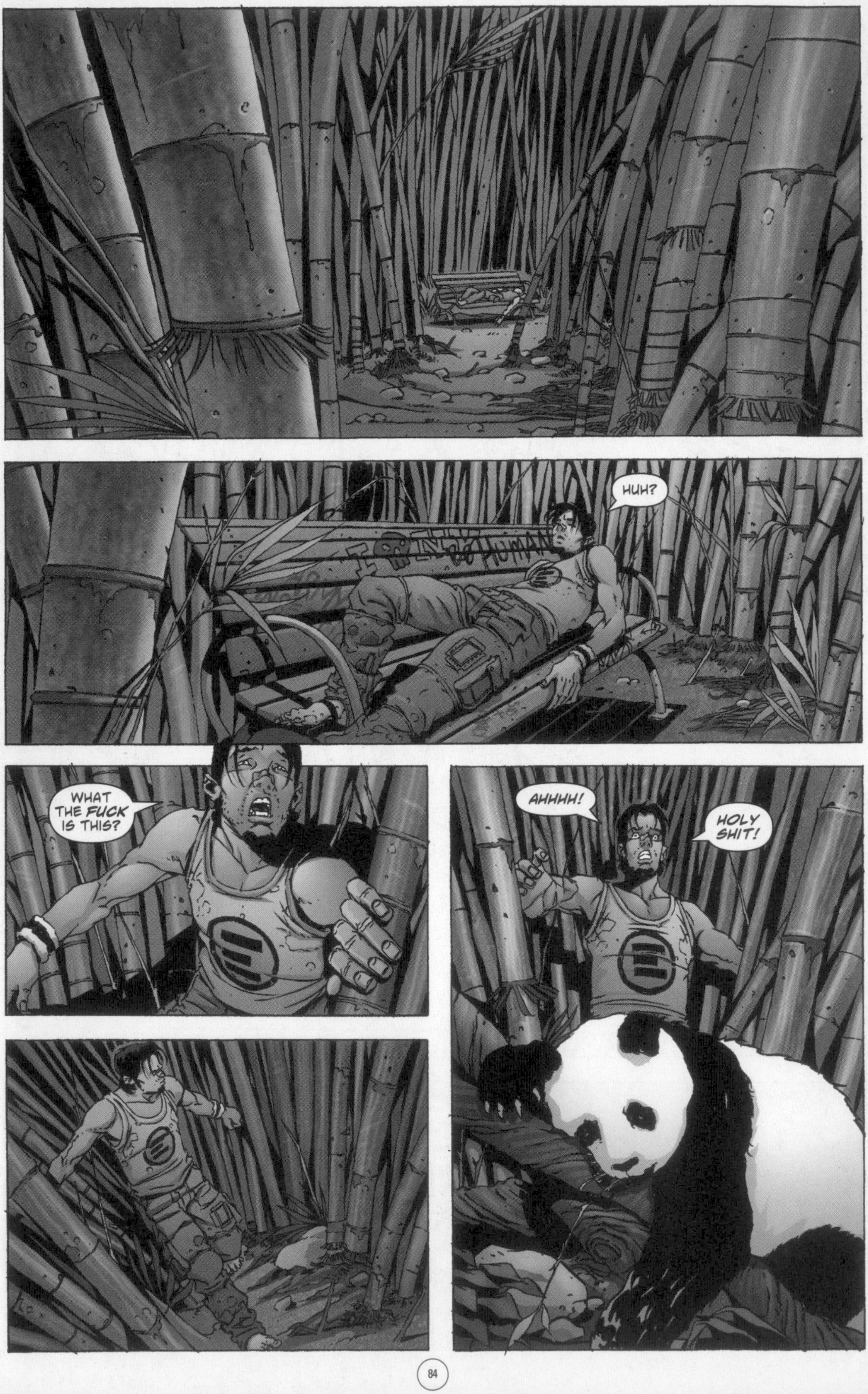
HUH?
WHAT THE *FUCK* IS THIS?
AHHHH!
HOLY SHIT!

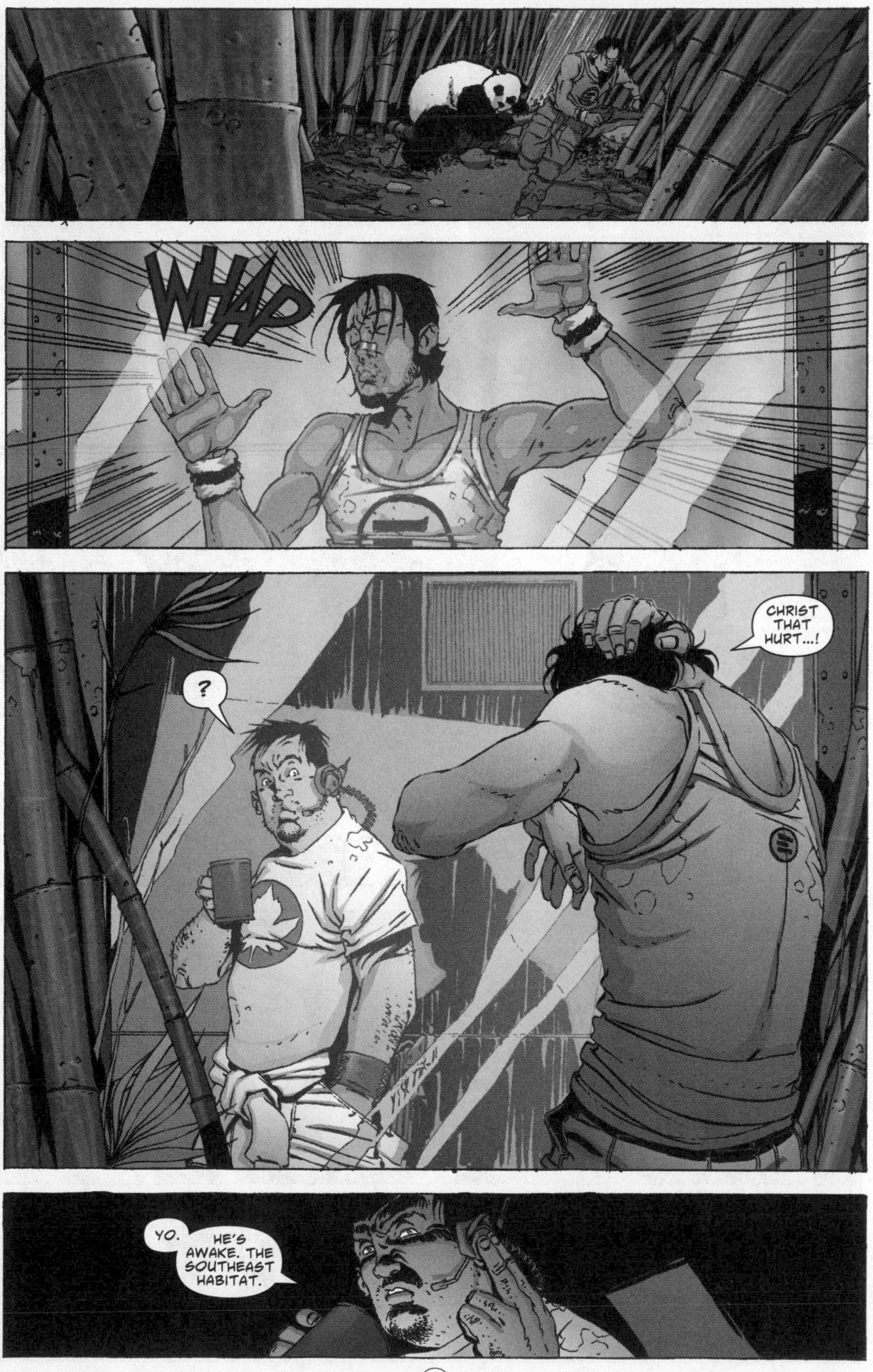
WHAP
?
CHRIST THAT HURT...!
YO.
HE'S AWAKE. THE SOUTHEAST HABITAT.

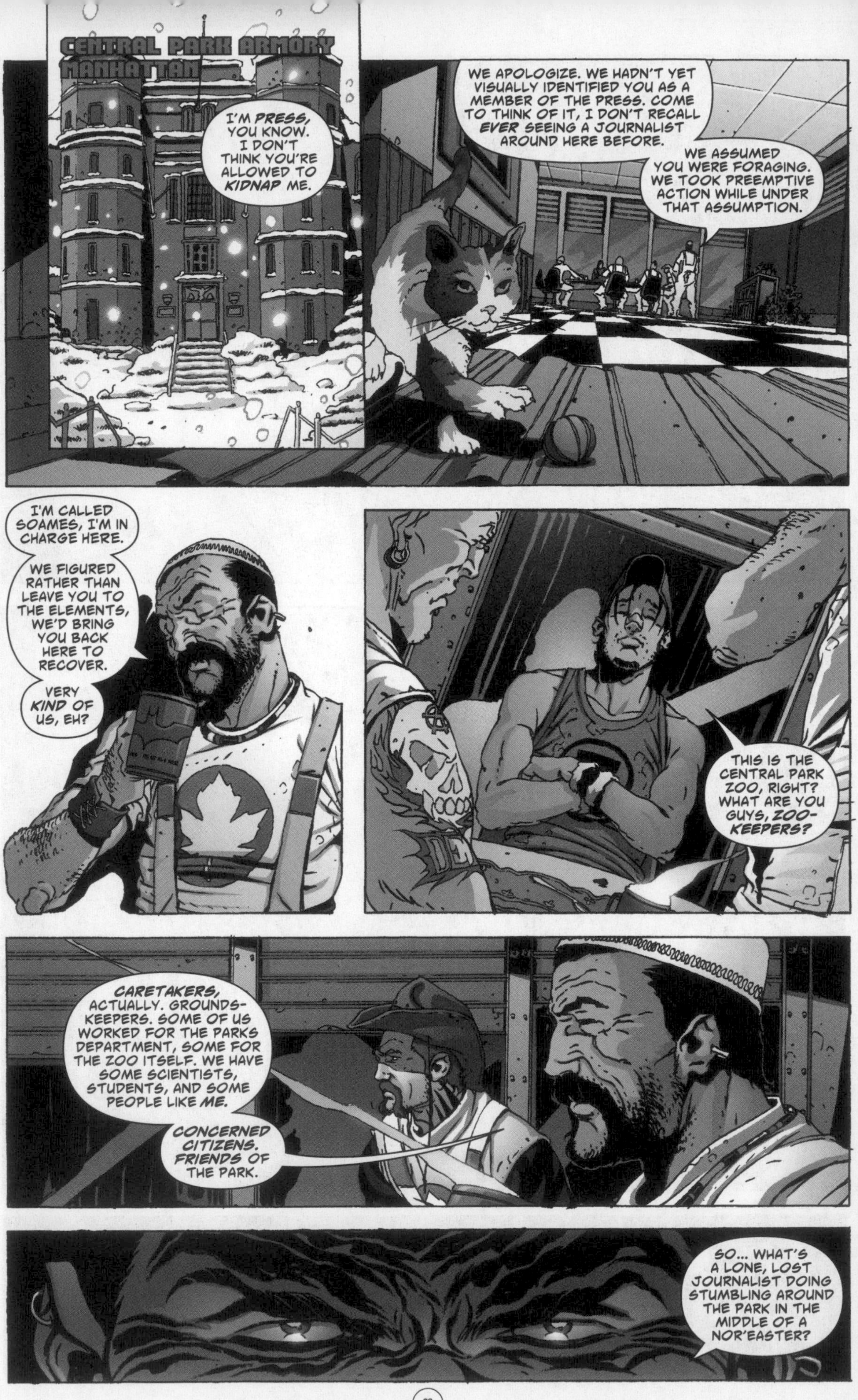
CENTRAL PARK ARMORY
MANHATTAN
I'M PRESS, YOU KNOW. I DON'T THINK YOU'RE ALLOWED TO KIDNAP ME.
WE APOLOGIZE. WE HADN'T YET VISUALLY IDENTIFIED YOU AS A MEMBER OF THE PRESS. COME TO THINK OF IT, I DON'T RECALL EVER SEEING A JOURNALIST AROUND HERE BEFORE.
WE ASSUMED YOU WERE FORAGING. WE TOOK PREEMPTIVE ACTION WHILE UNDER THAT ASSUMPTION.
I'M CALLED SOAMES, I'M IN CHARGE HERE.
WE FIGURED RATHER THAN LEAVE YOU TO THE ELEMENTS, WE'D BRING YOU BACK HERE TO RECOVER.
VERY KIND OF US, EH?
THIS IS THE CENTRAL PARK ZOO, RIGHT? WHAT ARE YOU GUYS, ZOO-KEEPERS?
CARETAKERS, ACTUALLY. GROUNDS-KEEPERS. SOME OF US WORKED FOR THE PARKS DEPARTMENT, SOME FOR THE ZOO ITSELF. WE HAVE SOME SCIENTISTS, STUDENTS, AND SOME PEOPLE LIKE ME.
CONCERNED CITIZENS. FRIENDS OF THE PARK.
SO... WHAT'S A LONE, LOST JOURNALIST DOING STUMBLING AROUND THE PARK IN THE MIDDLE OF A NOR'EASTER?

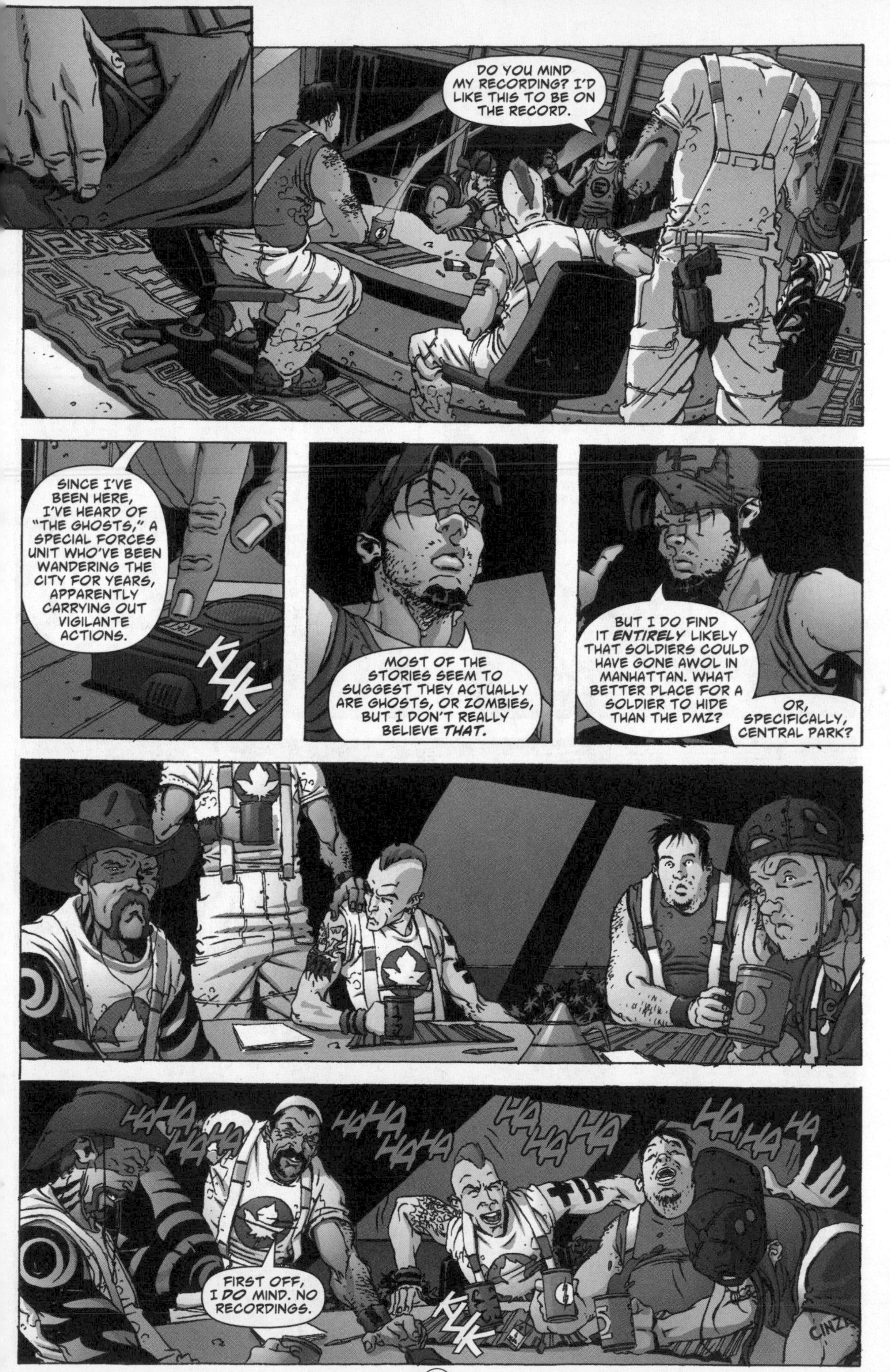
DO YOU MIND MY RECORDING? I'D LIKE THIS TO BE ON THE RECORD.
SINCE I'VE BEEN HERE, I'VE HEARD OF "THE GHOSTS," A SPECIAL FORCES UNIT WHO'VE BEEN WANDERING THE CITY FOR YEARS, APPARENTLY CARRYING OUT VIGILANTE ACTIONS.
KLIK
MOST OF THE STORIES SEEM TO SUGGEST THEY ACTUALLY ARE GHOSTS, OR ZOMBIES, BUT I DON'T REALLY BELIEVE *THAT.*
BUT I DO FIND IT *ENTIRELY* LIKELY THAT SOLDIERS COULD HAVE GONE AWOL IN MANHATTAN. WHAT BETTER PLACE FOR A SOLDIER TO HIDE THAN THE DMZ?
OR, SPECIFICALLY, CENTRAL PARK?
HAHAHAHA
HAHAHA
HAHAHA
HAHAHA
HA HA
FIRST OFF, I *DO* MIND. NO RECORDINGS.
KLIK

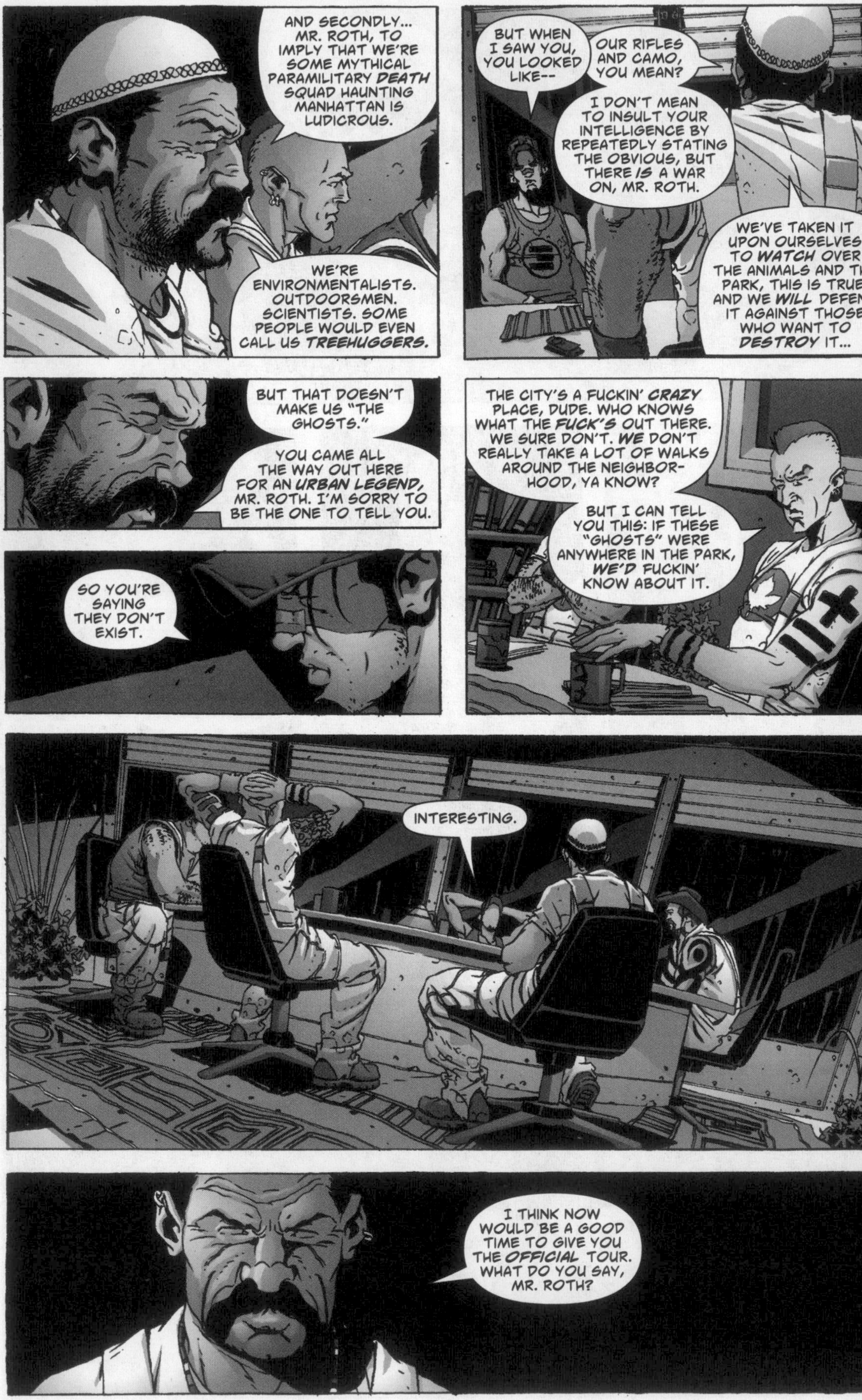
AND SECONDLY... MR. ROTH, TO IMPLY THAT WE'RE SOME MYTHICAL PARAMILITARY *DEATH* SQUAD HAUNTING MANHATTAN IS LUDICROUS.
WE'RE ENVIRONMENTALISTS. OUTDOORSMEN. SCIENTISTS. SOME PEOPLE WOULD EVEN CALL US *TREEHUGGERS.*
BUT WHEN I SAW YOU, YOU LOOKED LIKE--
OUR RIFLES AND CAMO, YOU MEAN?
I DON'T MEAN TO INSULT YOUR INTELLIGENCE BY REPEATEDLY STATING THE OBVIOUS, BUT THERE *IS* A WAR ON, MR. ROTH.
WE'VE TAKEN IT UPON OURSELVES TO *WATCH* OVER THE ANIMALS AND THE PARK, THIS IS TRUE, AND WE *WILL* DEFEND IT AGAINST THOSE WHO WANT TO *DESTROY* IT...
BUT THAT DOESN'T MAKE US "THE GHOSTS."
YOU CAME ALL THE WAY OUT HERE FOR AN *URBAN LEGEND,* MR. ROTH. I'M SORRY TO BE THE ONE TO TELL YOU.
SO YOU'RE SAYING THEY DON'T EXIST.
THE CITY'S A FUCKIN' *CRAZY* PLACE, DUDE. WHO KNOWS WHAT THE *FUCK'S* OUT THERE. WE SURE DON'T. *WE* DON'T REALLY TAKE A LOT OF WALKS AROUND THE NEIGHBORHOOD, YA KNOW?
BUT I CAN TELL YOU THIS: IF THESE "GHOSTS" WERE ANYWHERE IN THE PARK, *WE'D* FUCKIN' KNOW ABOUT IT.
INTERESTING.
I THINK NOW WOULD BE A GOOD TIME TO GIVE YOU THE *OFFICIAL* TOUR. WHAT DO YOU SAY, MR. ROTH?

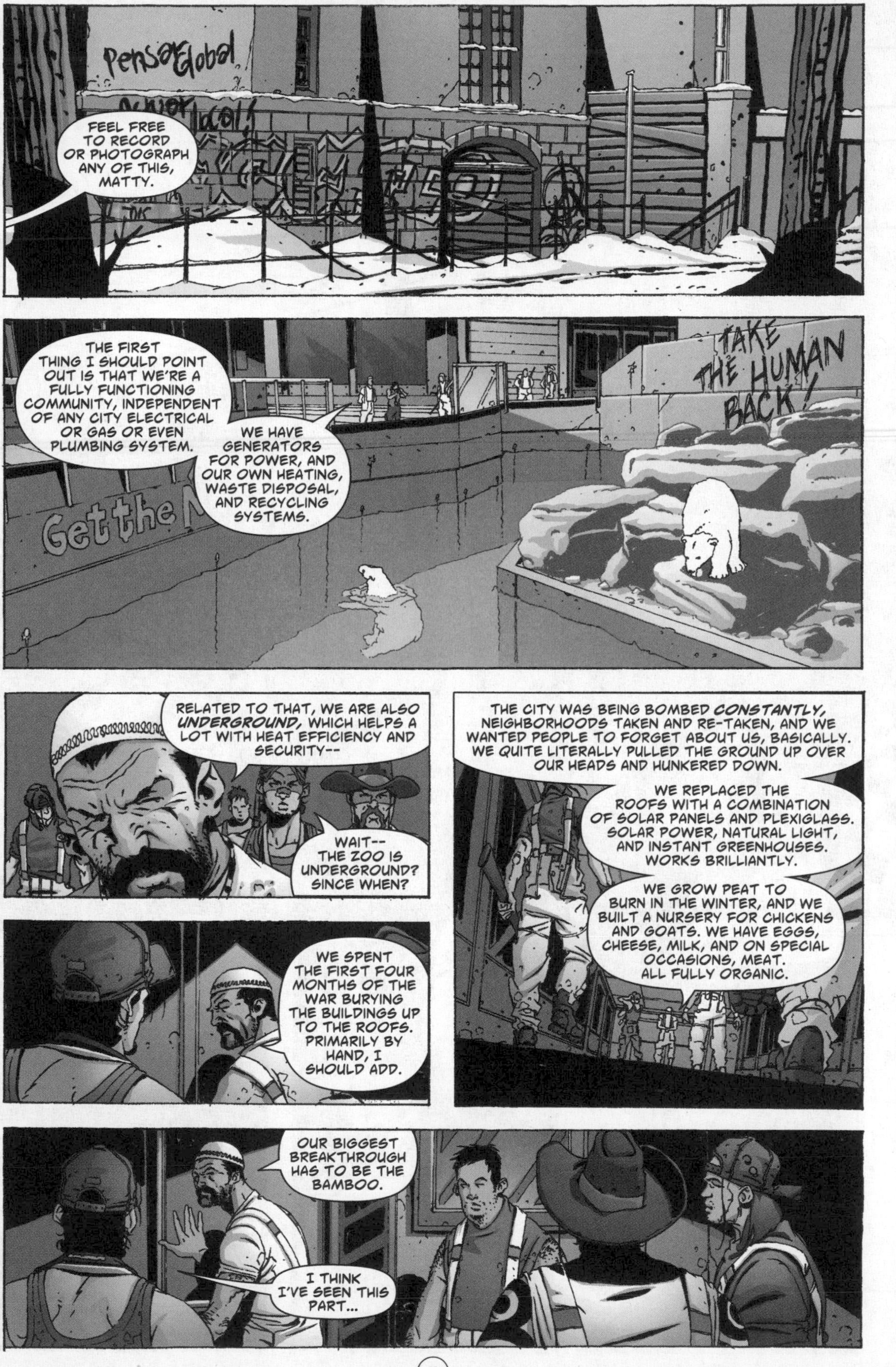

Pensar Global
FEEL FREE TO RECORD OR PHOTOGRAPH ANY OF THIS, MATTY.
TAKE THE HUMAN BACK!
Get the
THE FIRST THING I SHOULD POINT OUT IS THAT WE'RE A FULLY FUNCTIONING COMMUNITY, INDEPENDENT OF ANY CITY ELECTRICAL OR GAS OR EVEN PLUMBING SYSTEM.
WE HAVE GENERATORS FOR POWER, AND OUR OWN HEATING, WASTE DISPOSAL, AND RECYCLING SYSTEMS.
RELATED TO THAT, WE ARE ALSO *UNDERGROUND,* WHICH HELPS A LOT WITH HEAT EFFICIENCY AND SECURITY--
WAIT-- THE ZOO IS UNDERGROUND? SINCE WHEN?
WE SPENT THE FIRST FOUR MONTHS OF THE WAR BURYING THE BUILDINGS UP TO THE ROOFS. PRIMARILY BY HAND, I SHOULD ADD.
THE CITY WAS BEING BOMBED *CONSTANTLY,* NEIGHBORHOODS TAKEN AND RE-TAKEN, AND WE WANTED PEOPLE TO FORGET ABOUT US, BASICALLY. WE QUITE LITERALLY PULLED THE GROUND UP OVER OUR HEADS AND HUNKERED DOWN.
WE REPLACED THE ROOFS WITH A COMBINATION OF SOLAR PANELS AND PLEXIGLASS. SOLAR POWER, NATURAL LIGHT, AND INSTANT GREENHOUSES. WORKS BRILLIANTLY.
WE GROW PEAT TO BURN IN THE WINTER, AND WE BUILT A NURSERY FOR CHICKENS AND GOATS. WE HAVE EGGS, CHEESE, MILK, AND ON SPECIAL OCCASIONS, MEAT. ALL FULLY ORGANIC.
OUR BIGGEST BREAKTHROUGH HAS TO BE THE BAMBOO.
I THINK I'VE SEEN THIS PART...

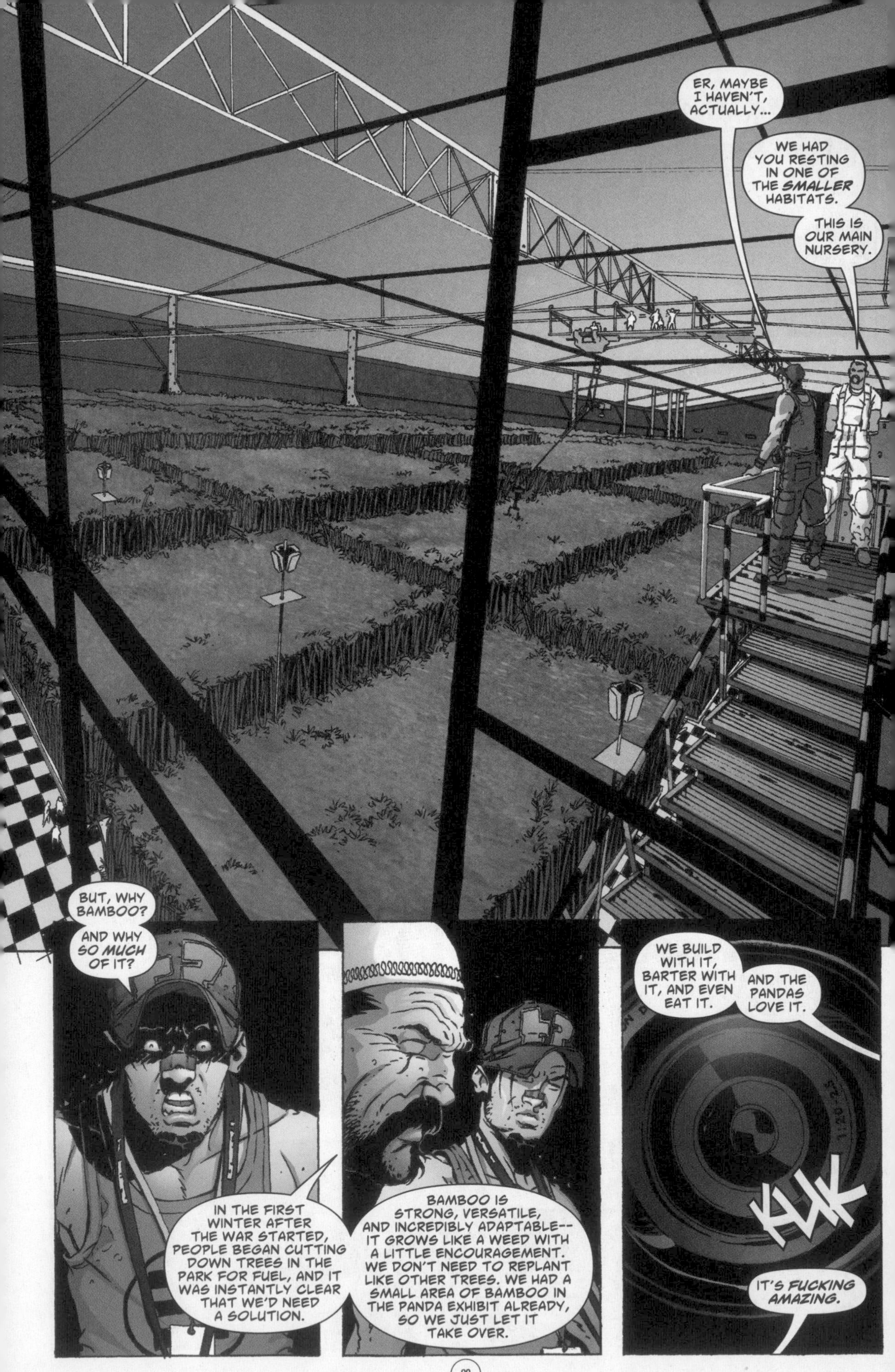
ER, MAYBE I HAVEN'T, ACTUALLY...
WE HAD YOU RESTING IN ONE OF THE SMALLER HABITATS.
THIS IS OUR MAIN NURSERY.
BUT, WHY BAMBOO?
AND WHY SO MUCH OF IT?
IN THE FIRST WINTER AFTER THE WAR STARTED, PEOPLE BEGAN CUTTING DOWN TREES IN THE PARK FOR FUEL, AND IT WAS INSTANTLY CLEAR THAT WE'D NEED A SOLUTION.
BAMBOO IS STRONG, VERSATILE, AND INCREDIBLY ADAPTABLE-- IT GROWS LIKE A WEED WITH A LITTLE ENCOURAGEMENT. WE DON'T NEED TO REPLANT LIKE OTHER TREES. WE HAD A SMALL AREA OF BAMBOO IN THE PANDA EXHIBIT ALREADY, SO WE JUST LET IT TAKE OVER.
WE BUILD WITH IT, BARTER WITH IT, AND EVEN EAT IT.
AND THE PANDAS LOVE IT.
KLIK
IT'S FUCKING AMAZING.

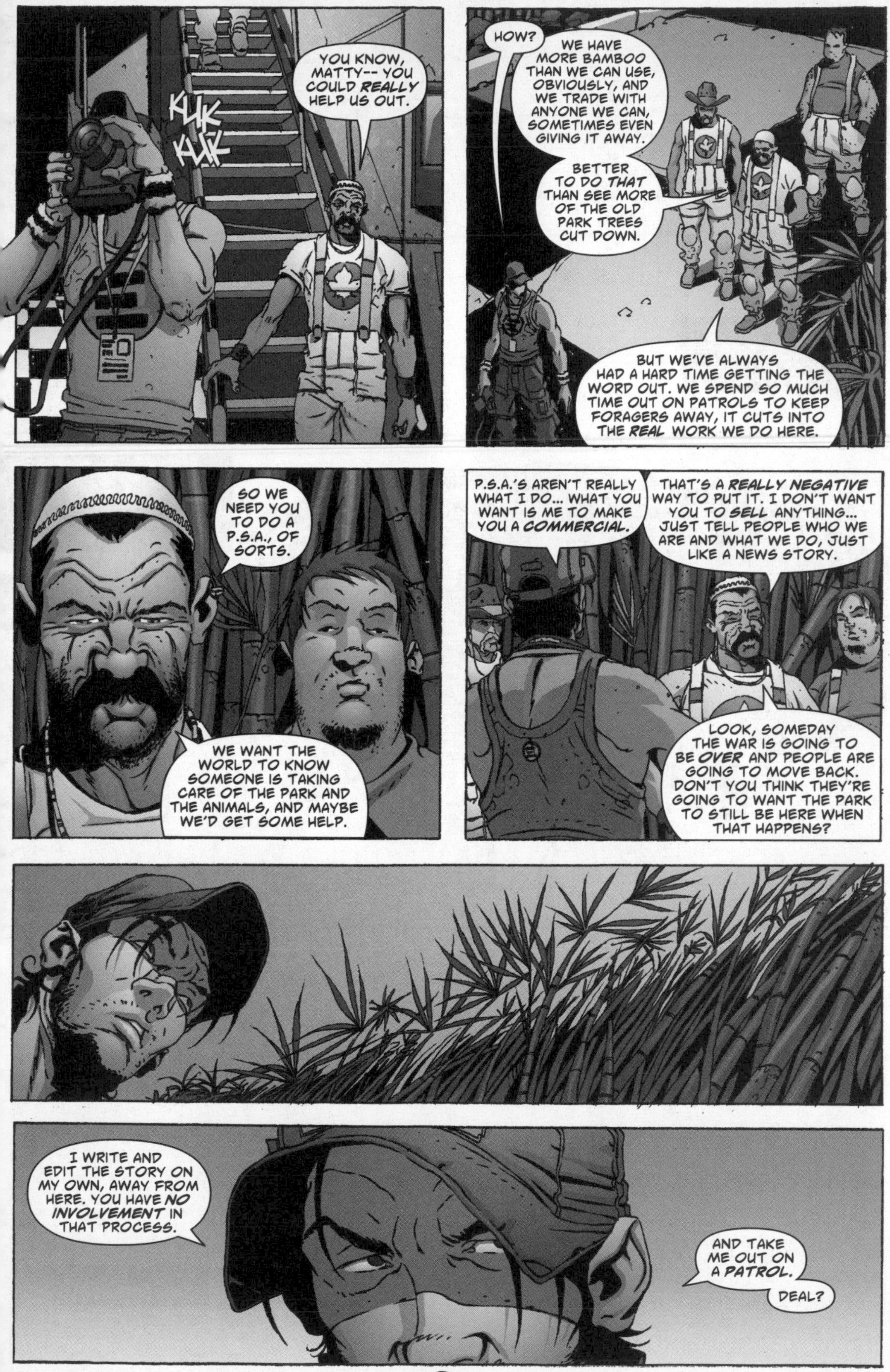

YOU KNOW, MATTY-- YOU COULD REALLY HELP US OUT.
KUK KUK
HOW?
WE HAVE MORE BAMBOO THAN WE CAN USE, OBVIOUSLY, AND WE TRADE WITH ANYONE WE CAN, SOMETIMES EVEN GIVING IT AWAY.
BETTER TO DO THAT THAN SEE MORE OF THE OLD PARK TREES CUT DOWN.
BUT WE'VE ALWAYS HAD A HARD TIME GETTING THE WORD OUT. WE SPEND SO MUCH TIME OUT ON PATROLS TO KEEP FORAGERS AWAY, IT CUTS INTO THE REAL WORK WE DO HERE.
SO WE NEED YOU TO DO A P.S.A., OF SORTS.
WE WANT THE WORLD TO KNOW SOMEONE IS TAKING CARE OF THE PARK AND THE ANIMALS, AND MAYBE WE'D GET SOME HELP.
P.S.A.'S AREN'T REALLY WHAT I DO... WHAT YOU WANT IS ME TO MAKE YOU A COMMERCIAL.
THAT'S A REALLY NEGATIVE WAY TO PUT IT. I DON'T WANT YOU TO SELL ANYTHING... JUST TELL PEOPLE WHO WE ARE AND WHAT WE DO, JUST LIKE A NEWS STORY.
LOOK, SOMEDAY THE WAR IS GOING TO BE OVER AND PEOPLE ARE GOING TO MOVE BACK. DON'T YOU THINK THEY'RE GOING TO WANT THE PARK TO STILL BE HERE WHEN THAT HAPPENS?
I WRITE AND EDIT THE STORY ON MY OWN, AWAY FROM HERE. YOU HAVE NO INVOLVEMENT IN THAT PROCESS.
AND TAKE ME OUT ON A PATROL.
DEAL?

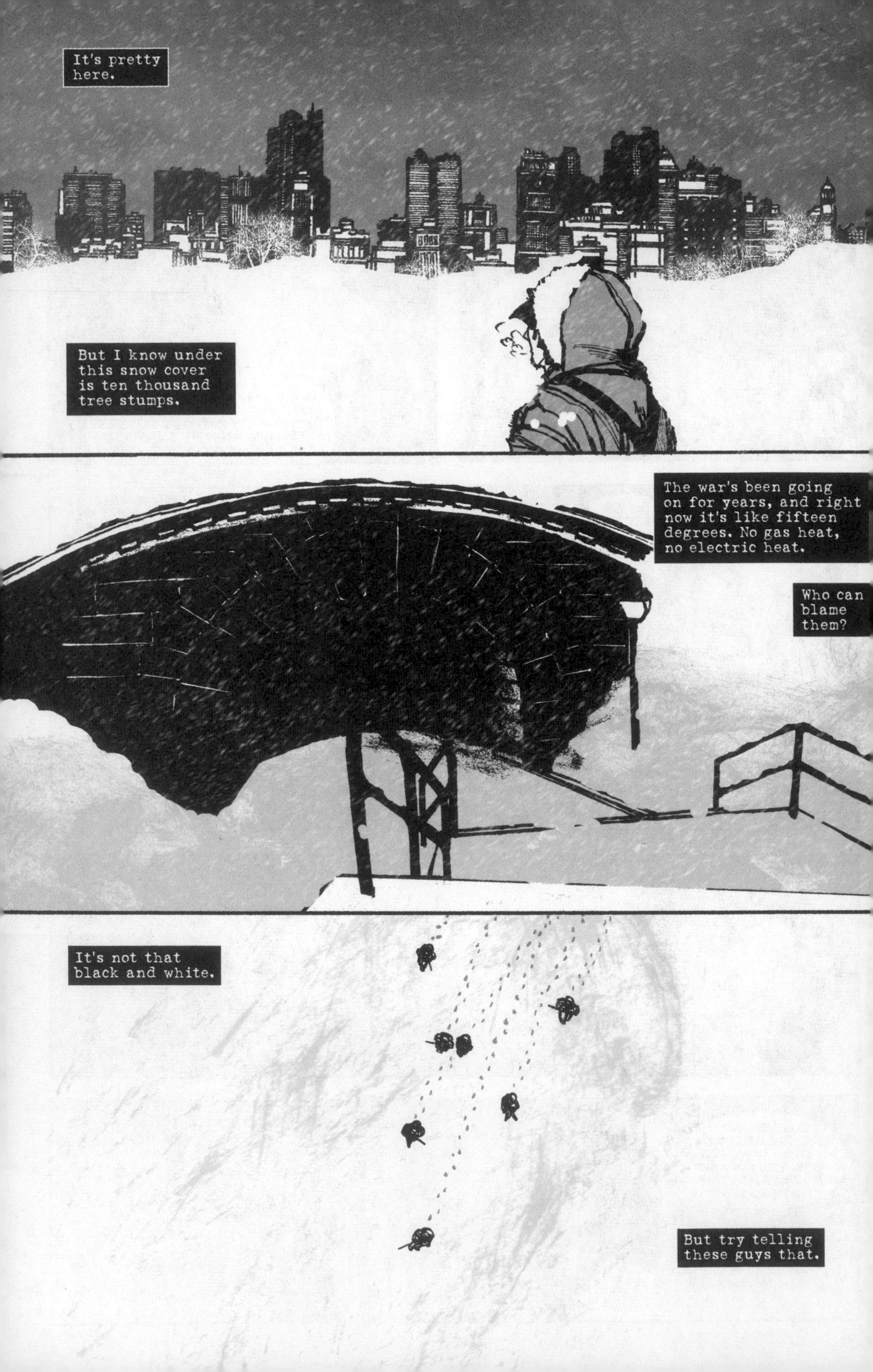
It's pretty here.
But I know under this snow cover is ten thousand tree stumps.
The war's been going on for years, and right now it's like fifteen degrees. No gas heat, no electric heat.
Who can blame them?
It's not that black and white.
But try telling these guys that.

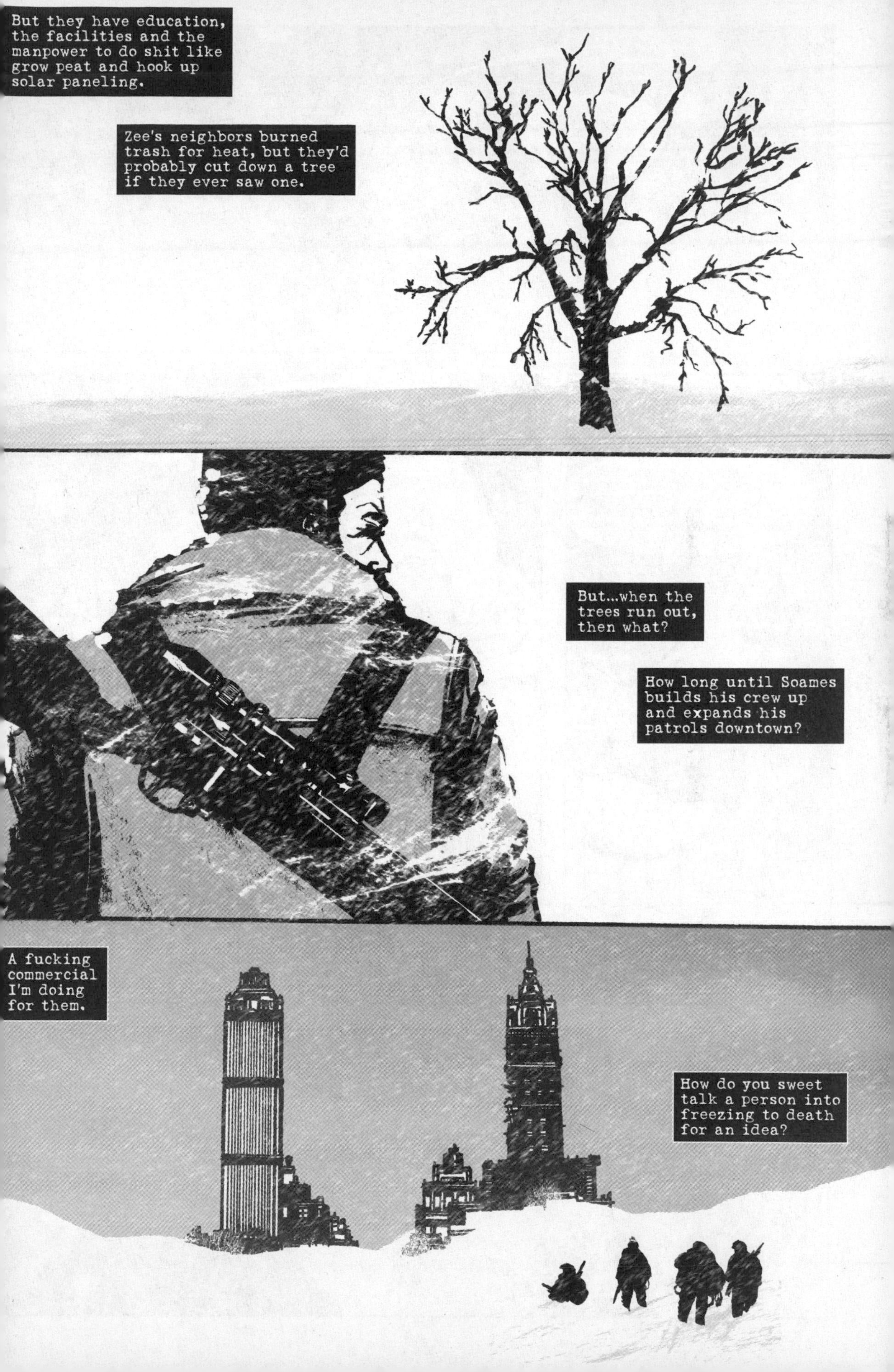
But they have education, the facilities and the manpower to do shit like grow peat and hook up solar paneling.
Zee's neighbors burned trash for heat, but they'd probably cut down a tree if they ever saw one.
But...when the trees run out, then what?
How long until Soames builds his crew up and expands his patrols downtown?
A fucking commercial I'm doing for them.
How do you sweet talk a person into freezing to death for an idea?

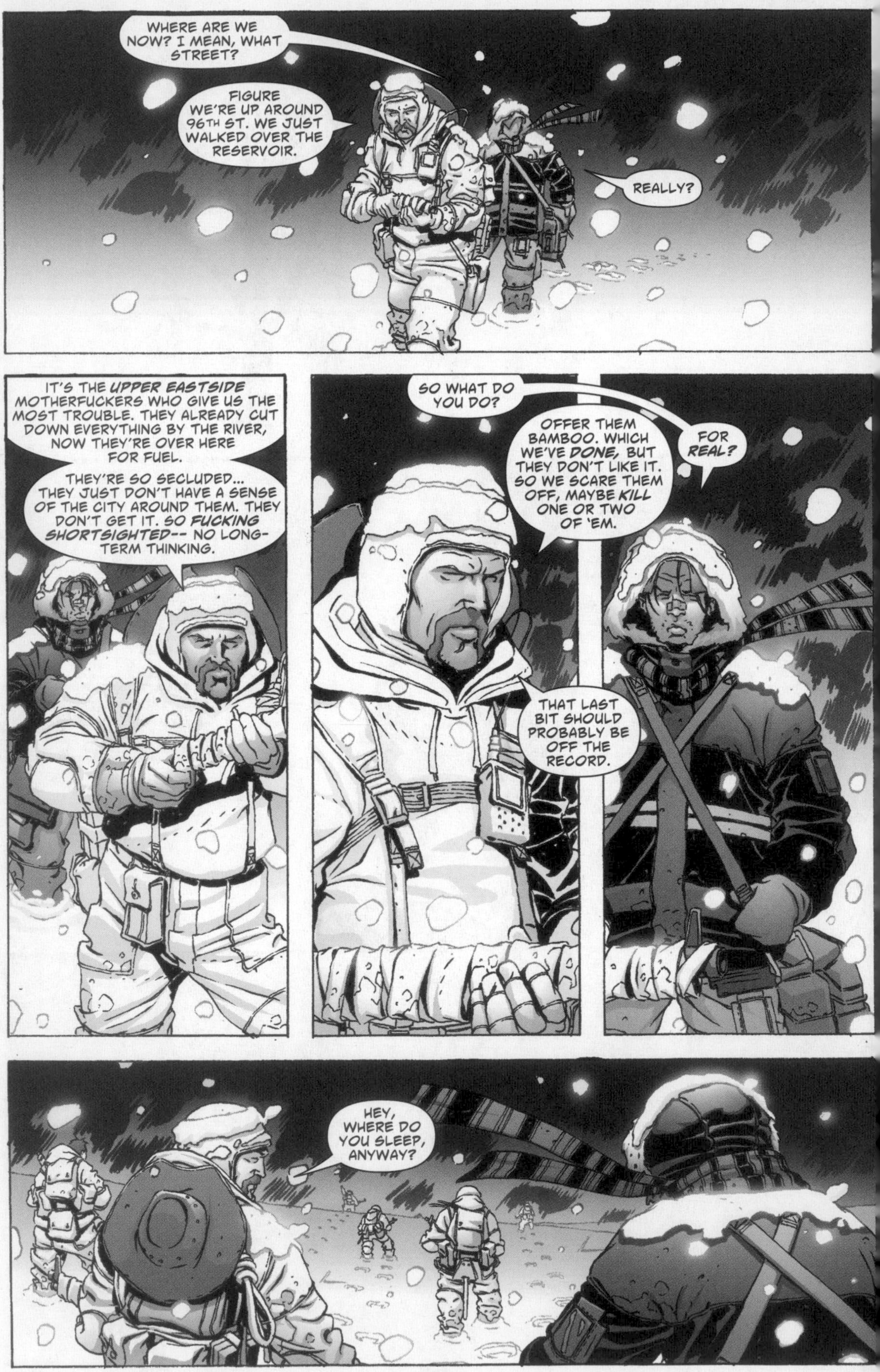
WHERE ARE WE NOW? I MEAN, WHAT STREET?
FIGURE WE'RE UP AROUND 96TH ST. WE JUST WALKED OVER THE RESERVOIR.
REALLY?
IT'S THE UPPER EASTSIDE MOTHERFUCKERS WHO GIVE US THE MOST TROUBLE. THEY ALREADY CUT DOWN EVERYTHING BY THE RIVER, NOW THEY'RE OVER HERE FOR FUEL.
THEY'RE SO SECLUDED... THEY JUST DON'T HAVE A SENSE OF THE CITY AROUND THEM. THEY DON'T GET IT. SO FUCKING SHORTSIGHTED-- NO LONG-TERM THINKING.
SO WHAT DO YOU DO?
OFFER THEM BAMBOO. WHICH WE'VE DONE, BUT THEY DON'T LIKE IT. SO WE SCARE THEM OFF, MAYBE KILL ONE OR TWO OF 'EM.
FOR REAL?
THAT LAST BIT SHOULD PROBABLY BE OFF THE RECORD.
HEY, WHERE DO YOU SLEEP, ANYWAY?

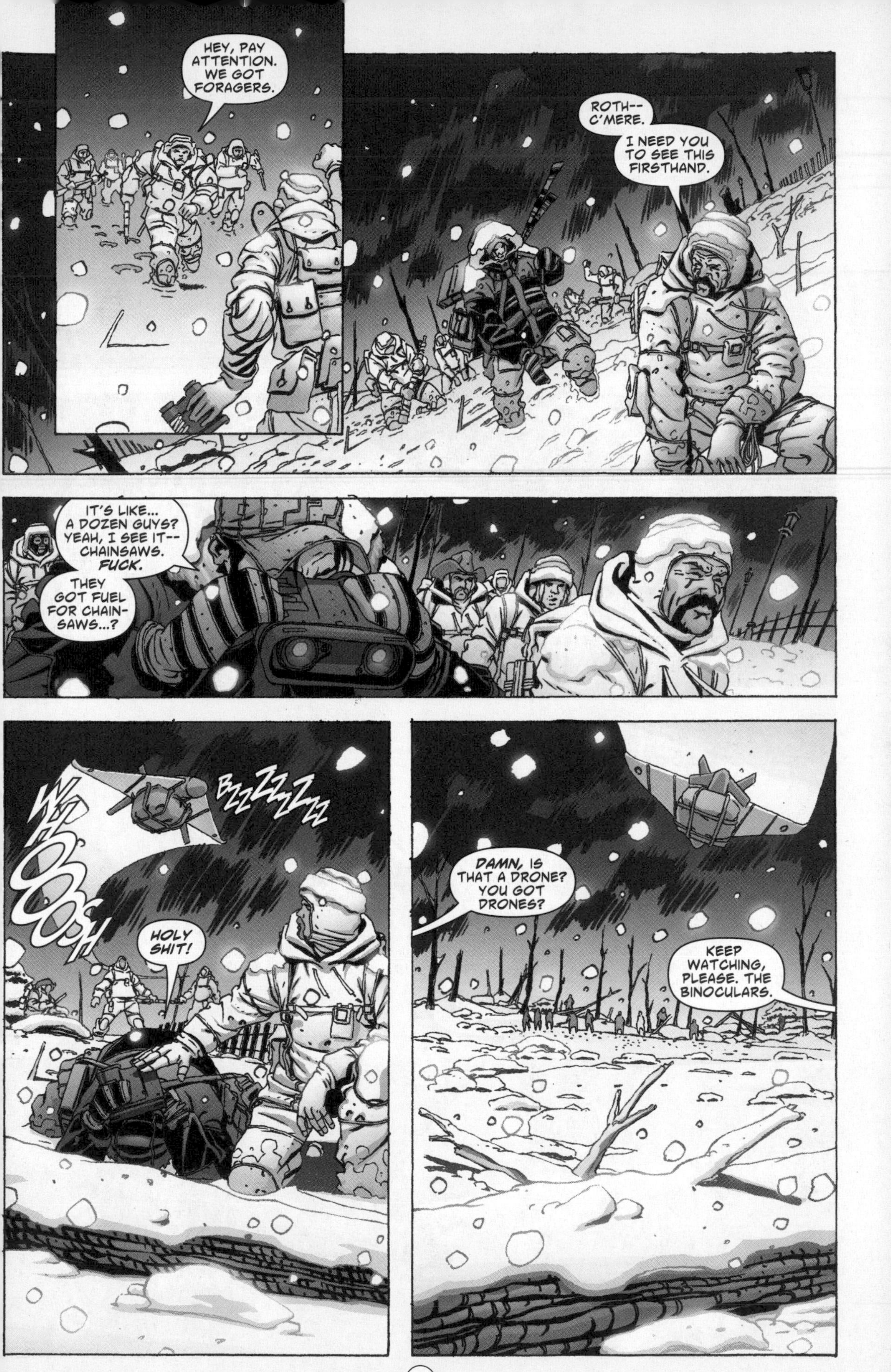
HEY, PAY ATTENTION. WE GOT FORAGERS.
ROTH-- C'MERE.
I NEED YOU TO SEE THIS FIRSTHAND.
IT'S LIKE... A DOZEN GUYS? YEAH, I SEE IT-- CHAINSAWS. *FUCK.*
THEY GOT FUEL FOR CHAIN-SAWS...?
WHOOOOSH
BZZZZZZZ
HOLY SHIT!
DAMN, IS THAT A DRONE? YOU GOT DRONES?
KEEP WATCHING, PLEASE. THE BINOCULARS.

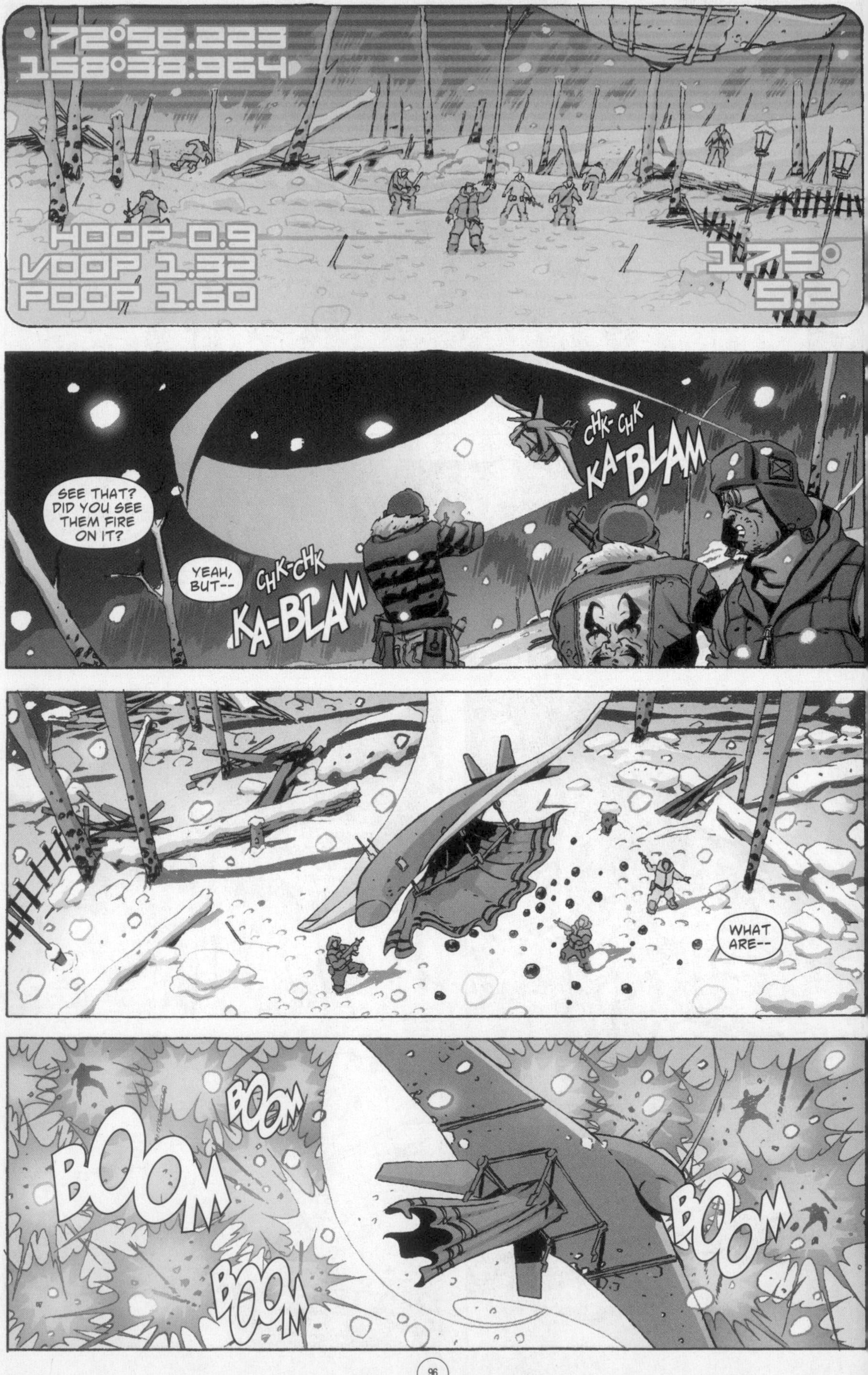
72°56.223
158°38.964
HOOP 0.9
VOOP 1.32
POOP 1.60
175°
5.2
CHK-CHK
KA-BLAM
SEE THAT? DID YOU SEE THEM FIRE ON IT?
YEAH, BUT--
CHK-CHK
KA-BLAM
WHAT ARE--
BOOM
BOOM
BOOM
BOOM

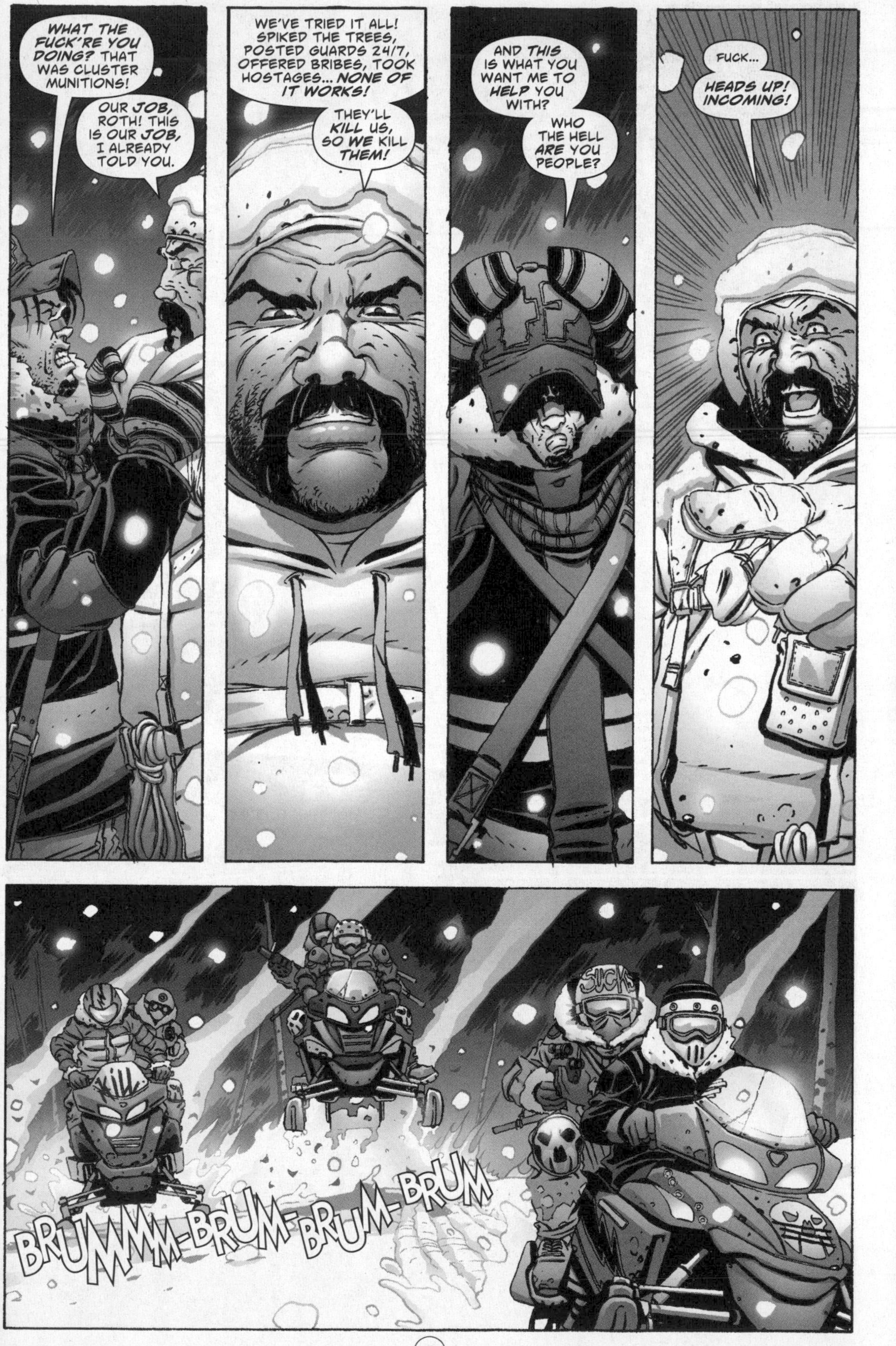

WHAT THE FUCK'RE YOU DOING? THAT WAS CLUSTER MUNITIONS!
OUR JOB, ROTH! THIS IS OUR JOB, I ALREADY TOLD YOU.
WE'VE TRIED IT ALL! SPIKED THE TREES, POSTED GUARDS 24/7, OFFERED BRIBES, TOOK HOSTAGES... NONE OF IT WORKS!
THEY'LL KILL US, SO WE KILL THEM!
AND THIS IS WHAT YOU WANT ME TO HELP YOU WITH?
WHO THE HELL ARE YOU PEOPLE?
FUCK...
HEADS UP! INCOMING!
BRUMMM-BRUM-BRUM-BRUM

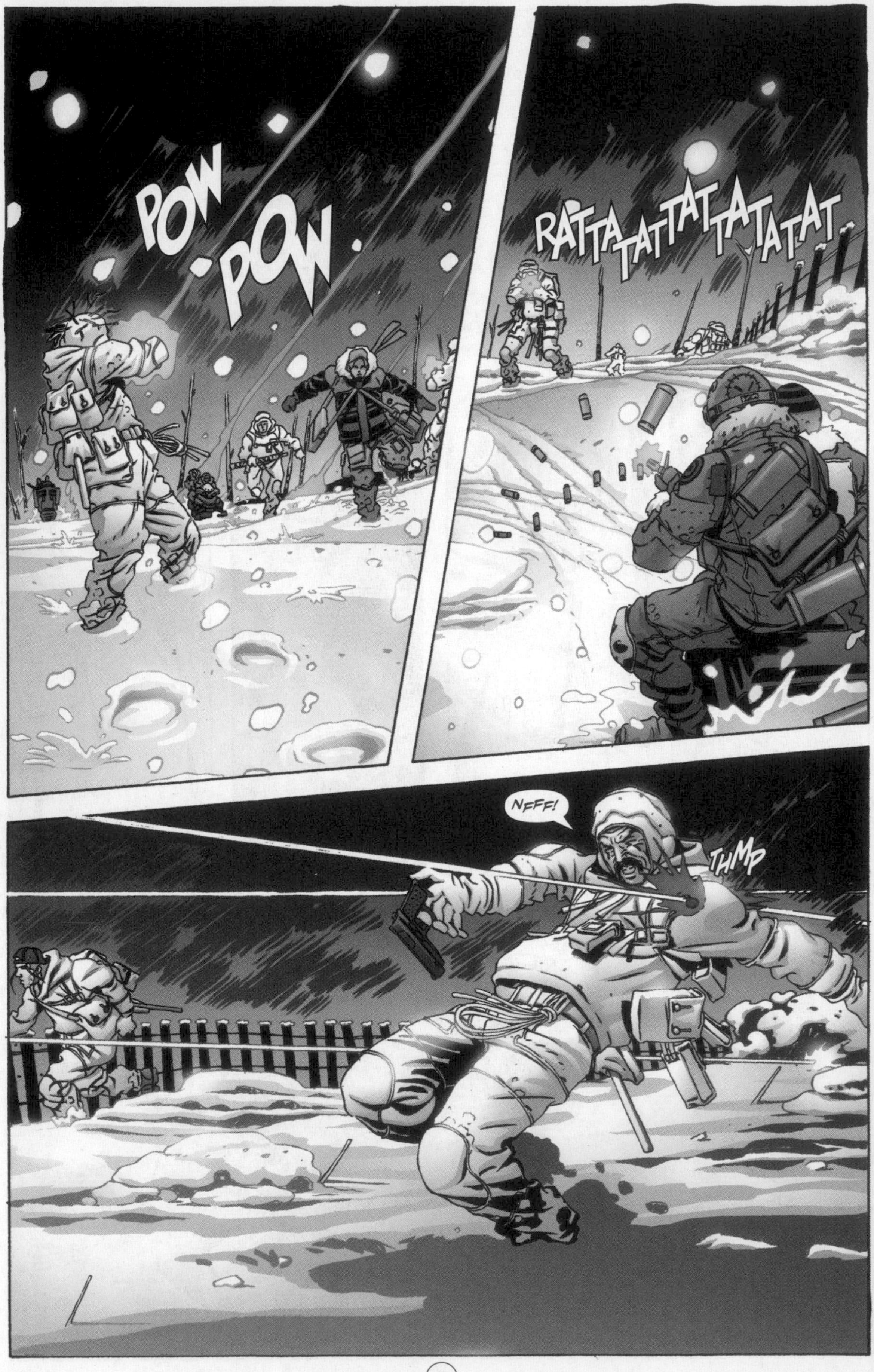
POW
POW
RATTATATTATTATATAT
NFFF!
THMP

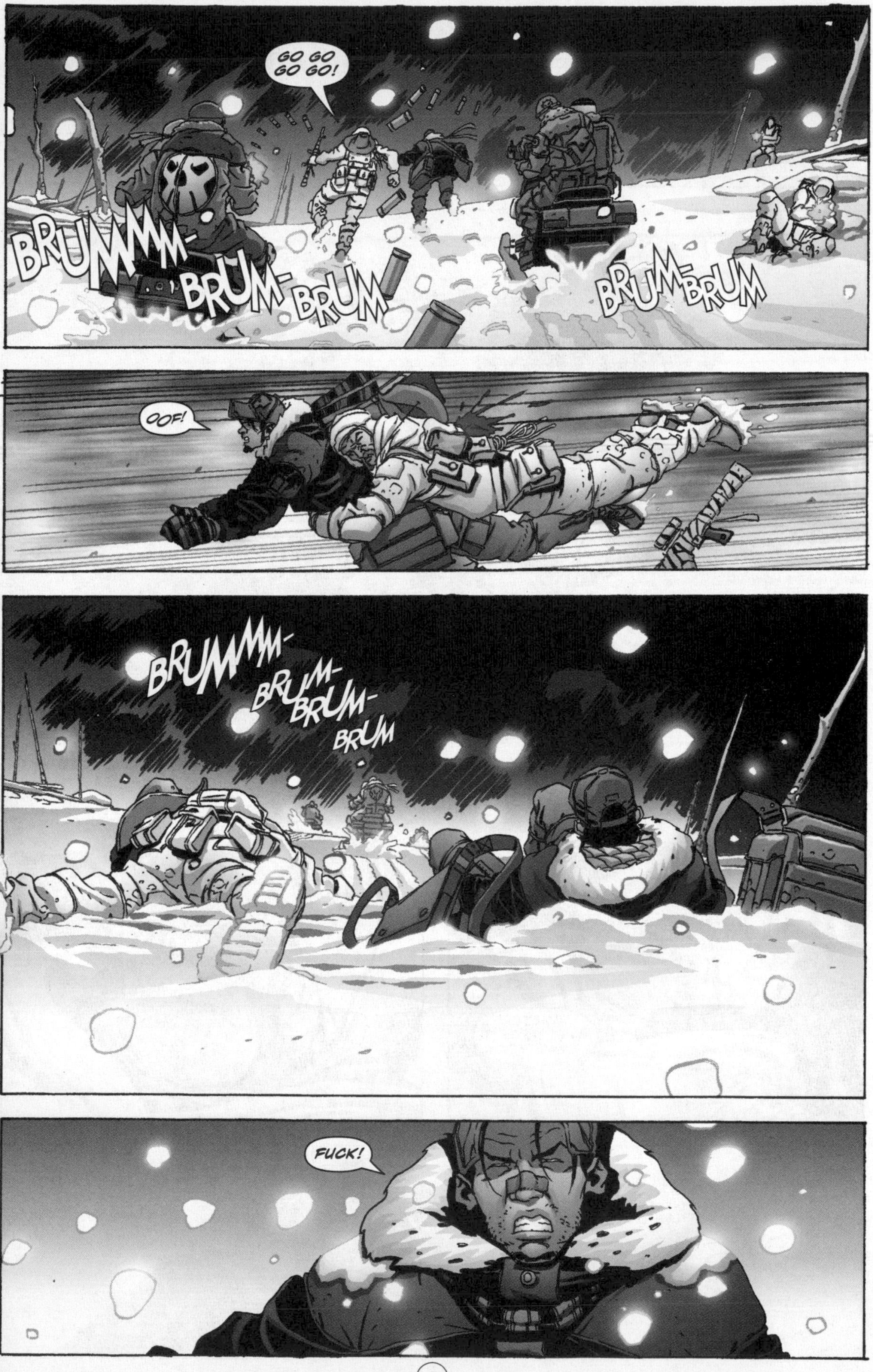
GO GO
GO GO!
BRUMMMM-
BRUM-
BRUM
BRUM-BRUM
OOF!
BRUMMMM-
BRUM-
BRUM-
BRUM
FUCK!

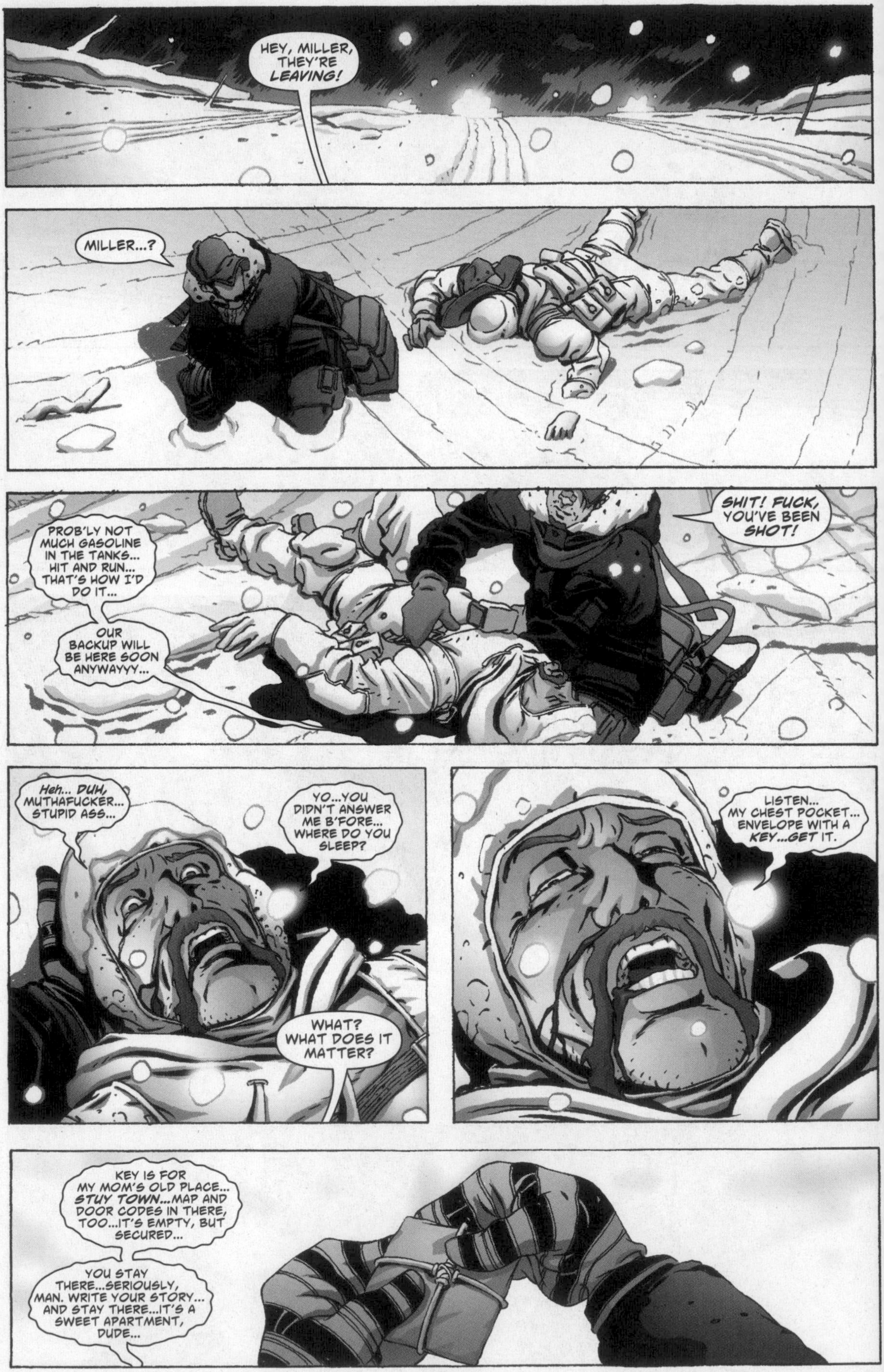
HEY, MILLER, THEY'RE *LEAVING!*
MILLER...?
PROB'LY NOT MUCH GASOLINE IN THE TANKS... HIT AND RUN... THAT'S HOW I'D DO IT...
OUR BACKUP WILL BE HERE SOON ANYWAYYY...
SHIT! FUCK, YOU'VE BEEN *SHOT!*
Heh... DUH, MUTHAFUCKER... STUPID ASS...
YO...YOU DIDN'T ANSWER ME B'FORE... WHERE DO YOU SLEEP?
WHAT? WHAT DOES IT MATTER?
LISTEN... MY CHEST POCKET... ENVELOPE WITH A *KEY...GET* IT.
KEY IS FOR MY MOM'S OLD PLACE... *STUY TOWN...*MAP AND DOOR CODES IN THERE, TOO...IT'S EMPTY, BUT SECURED...
YOU STAY THERE...SERIOUSLY, MAN. WRITE YOUR STORY... AND STAY THERE...IT'S A SWEET APARTMENT, DUDE...

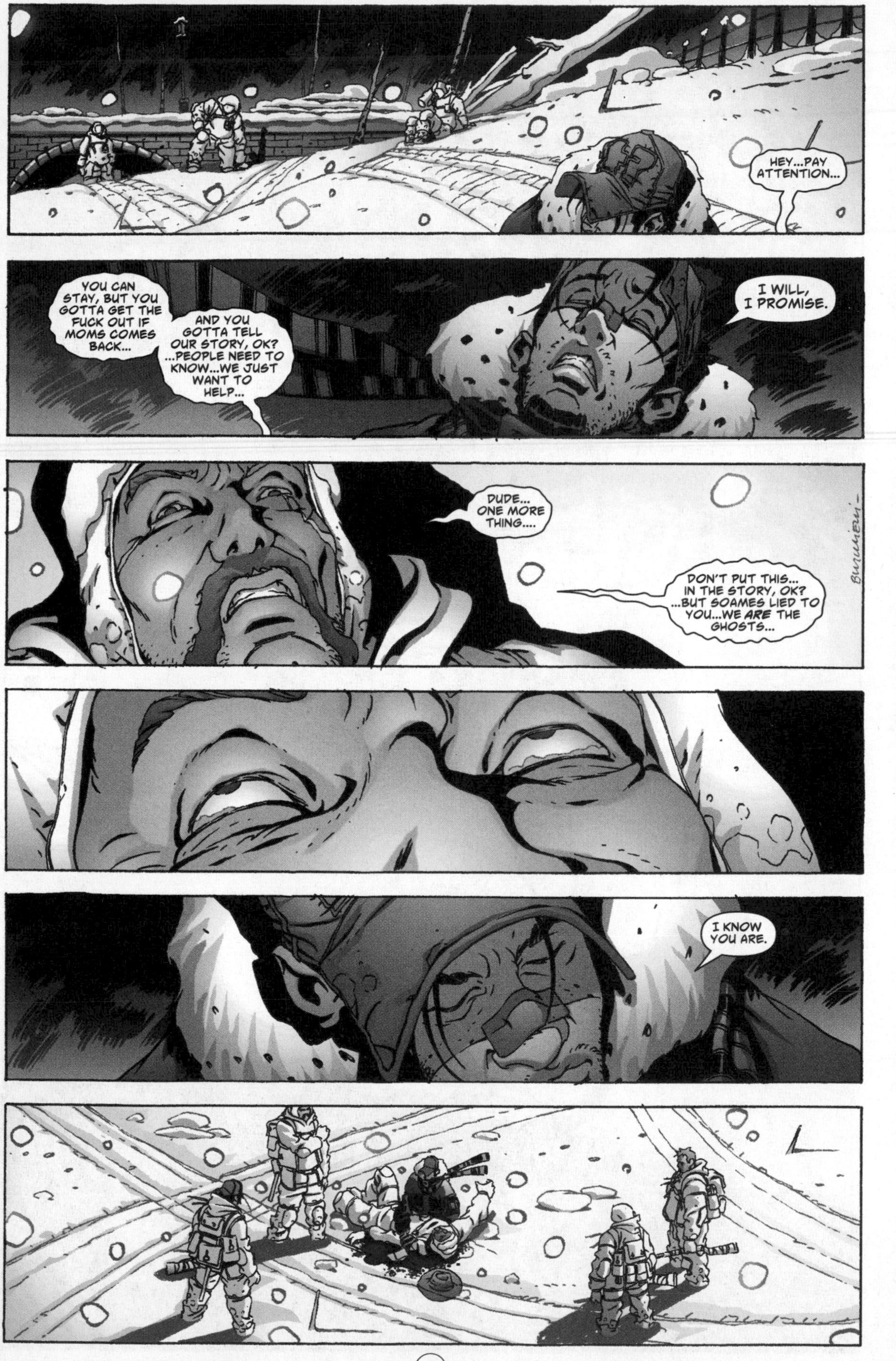
HEY...PAY ATTENTION...
YOU CAN STAY, BUT YOU GOTTA GET THE FUCK OUT IF MOMS COMES BACK...
AND YOU GOTTA TELL OUR STORY, OK? ...PEOPLE NEED TO KNOW...WE JUST WANT TO HELP...
I WILL, I PROMISE.
DUDE... ONE MORE THING....
DON'T PUT THIS... IN THE STORY, OK? ...BUT SOAMES LIED TO YOU...WE *ARE* THE GHOSTS...
I KNOW YOU ARE.

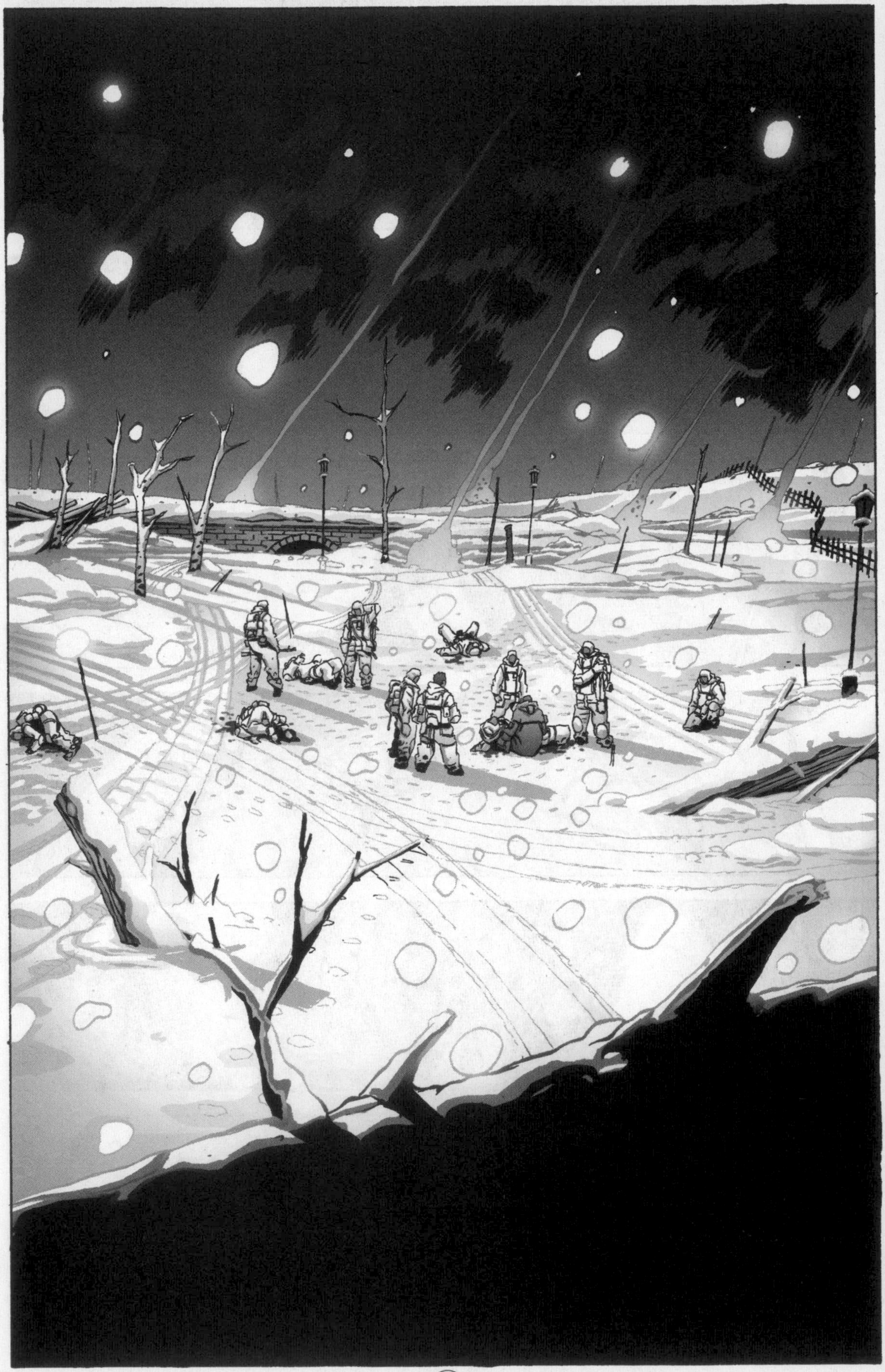

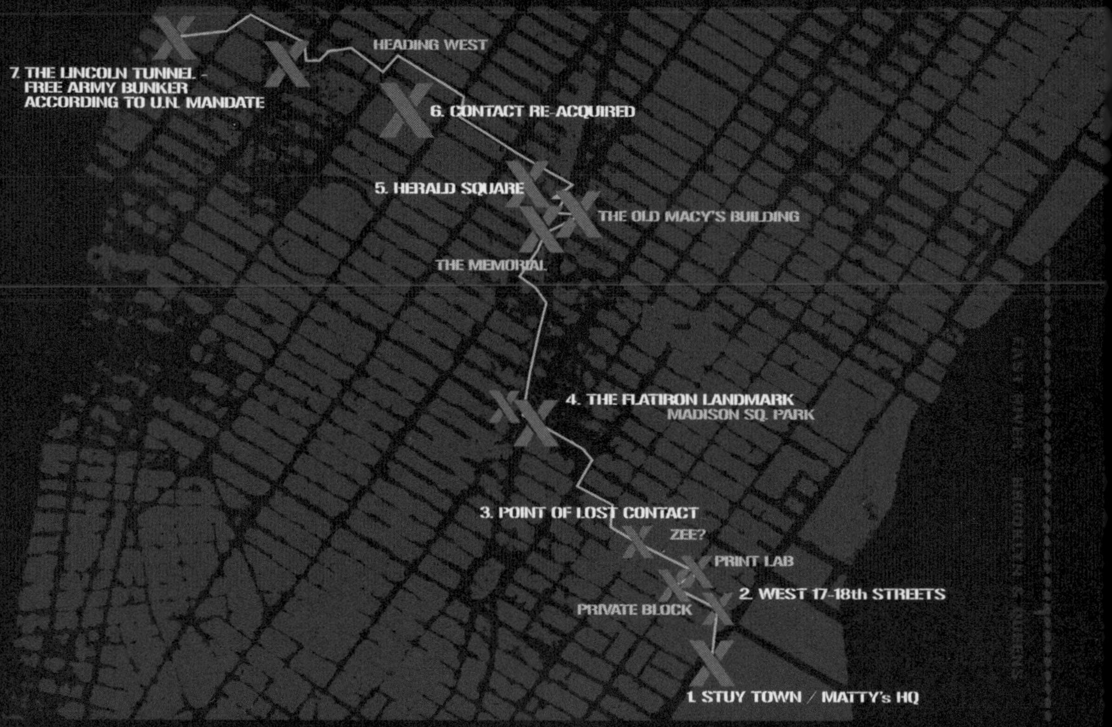

7. THE LINCOLN TUNNEL -
FREE ARMY BUNKER
ACCORDING TO U.N. MANDATE
HEADING WEST
6. CONTACT RE-ACQUIRED
5. HERALD SQUARE
THE OLD MACY'S BUILDING
THE MEMORIAL
4. THE FLATIRON LANDMARK
MADISON SQ. PARK
3. POINT OF LOST CONTACT
ZEE?
PRINT LAB
2. WEST 17-18th STREETS
PRIVATE BLOCK
1. STUY TOWN / MATTY's HQ

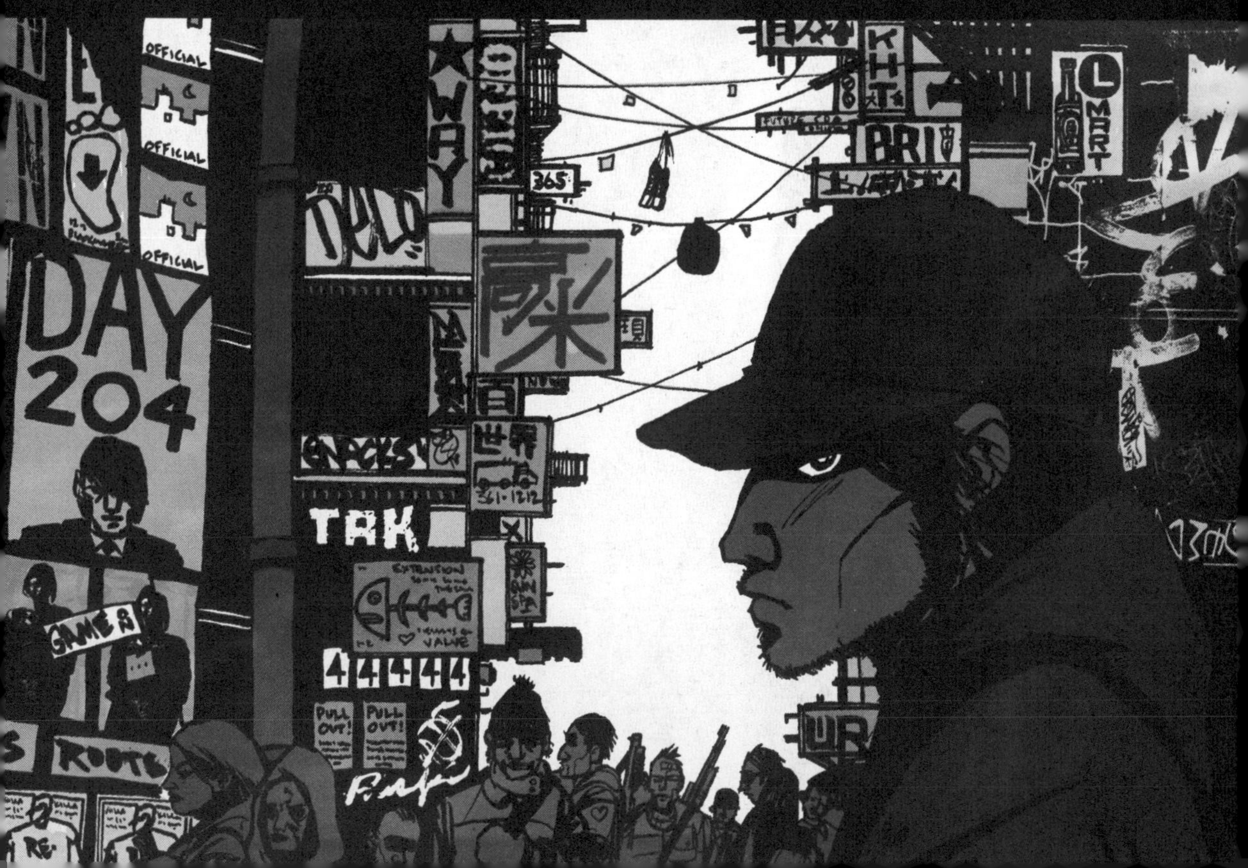

OFFICIAL
OFFICIAL
OFFICIAL
DAY
204
WAY
365
BRI
世界
361-1212
TRK
44444
PULL OUT!
PULL OUT!
GAMES
ROOTS

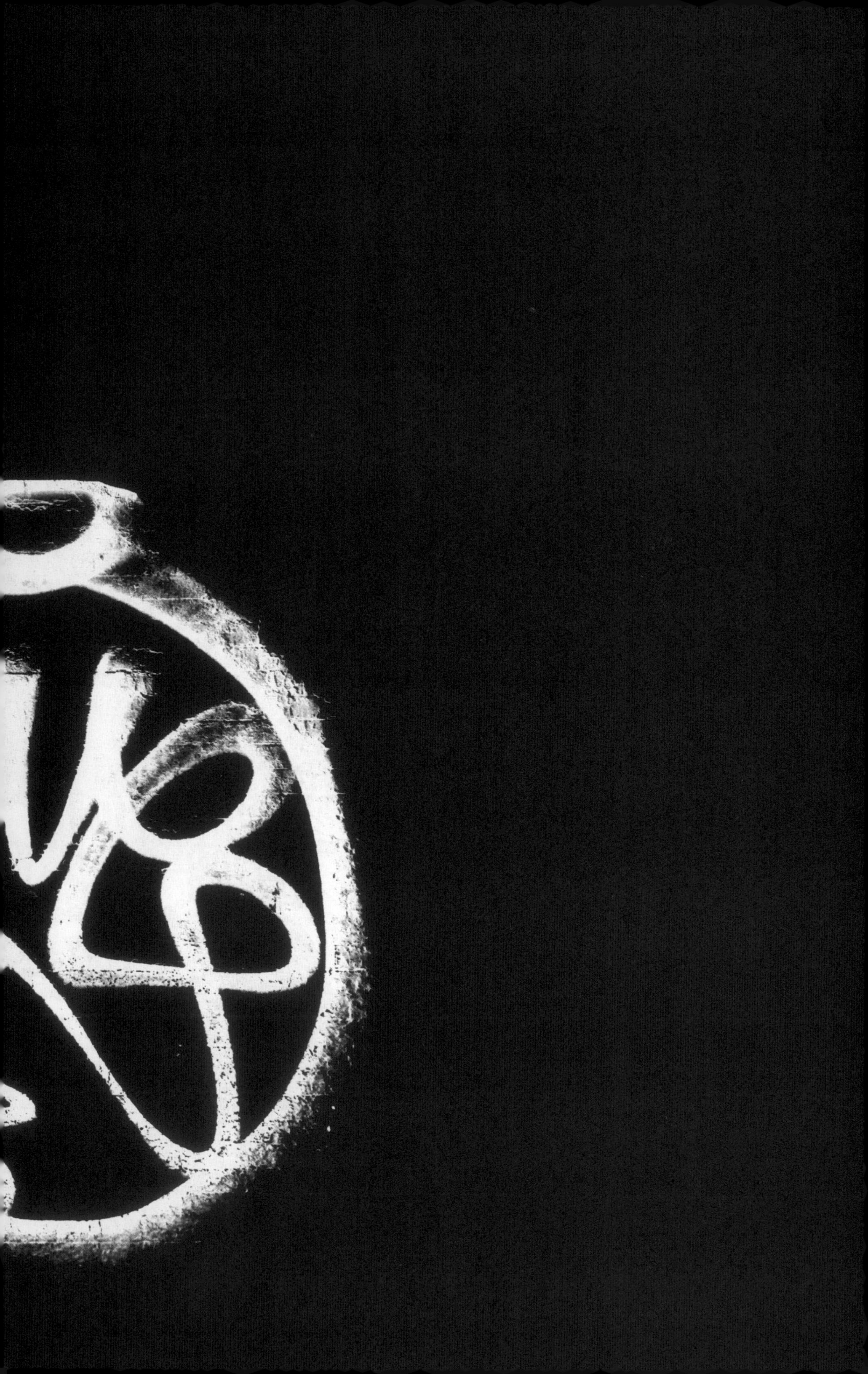

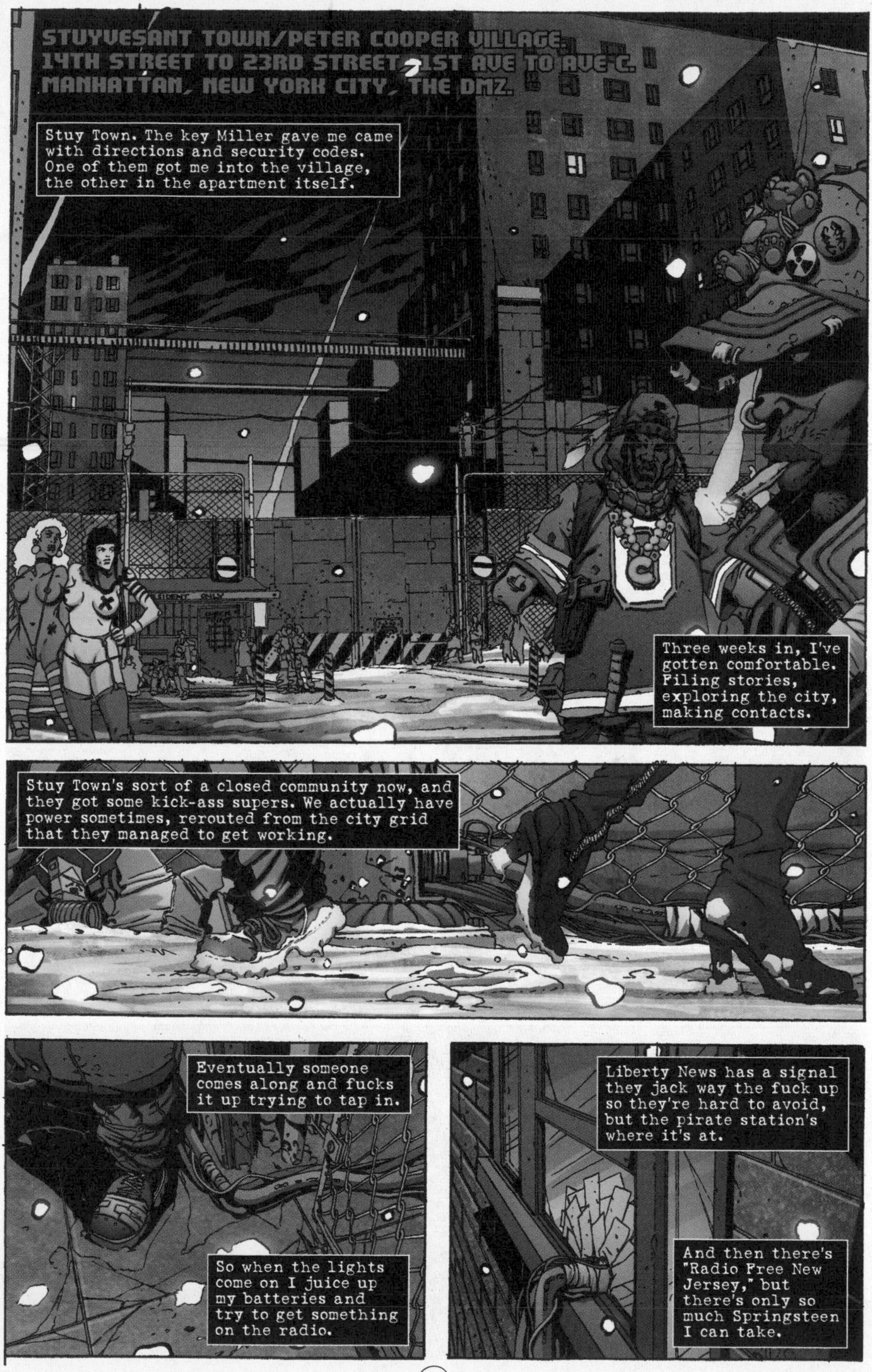
STUYVESANT TOWN/PETER COOPER VILLAGE.
14TH STREET TO 23RD STREET, 1ST AVE TO AVE C.
MANHATTAN, NEW YORK CITY, THE DMZ.
Stuy Town. The key Miller gave me came with directions and security codes. One of them got me into the village, the other in the apartment itself.
Three weeks in, I've gotten comfortable. Filing stories, exploring the city, making contacts.
Stuy Town's sort of a closed community now, and they got some kick-ass supers. We actually have power sometimes, rerouted from the city grid that they managed to get working.
Eventually someone comes along and fucks it up trying to tap in.
So when the lights come on I juice up my batteries and try to get something on the radio.
Liberty News has a signal they jack way the fuck up so they're hard to avoid, but the pirate station's where it's at.
And then there's "Radio Free New Jersey," but there's only so much Springsteen I can take.

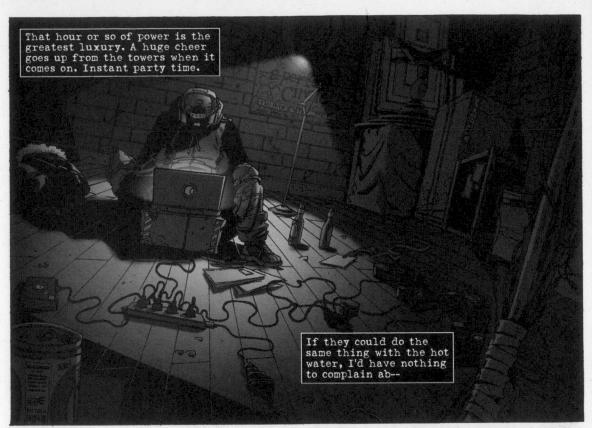

That hour or so of power is the greatest luxury. A huge cheer goes up from the towers when it comes on. Instant party time.

If they could do the same thing with the hot water, I'd have nothing to complain ab--

WHO'S THERE?

HELLO?

CRASH

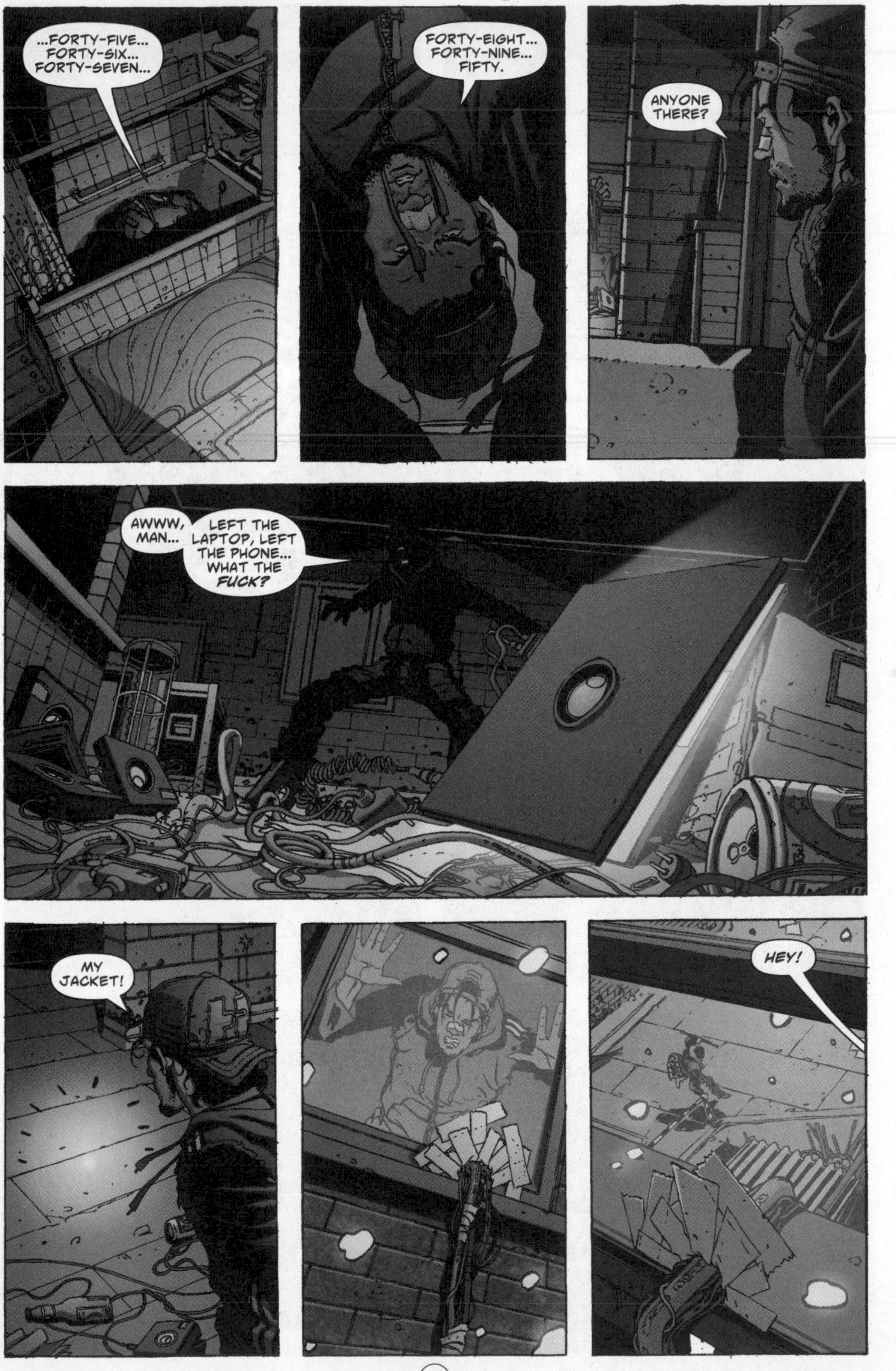
...FORTY-FIVE... FORTY-SIX... FORTY-SEVEN...
FORTY-EIGHT... FORTY-NINE... FIFTY.
ANYONE THERE?
AWWW, MAN...
LEFT THE LAPTOP, LEFT THE PHONE... WHAT THE *FUCK?*
MY JACKET!
HEY!

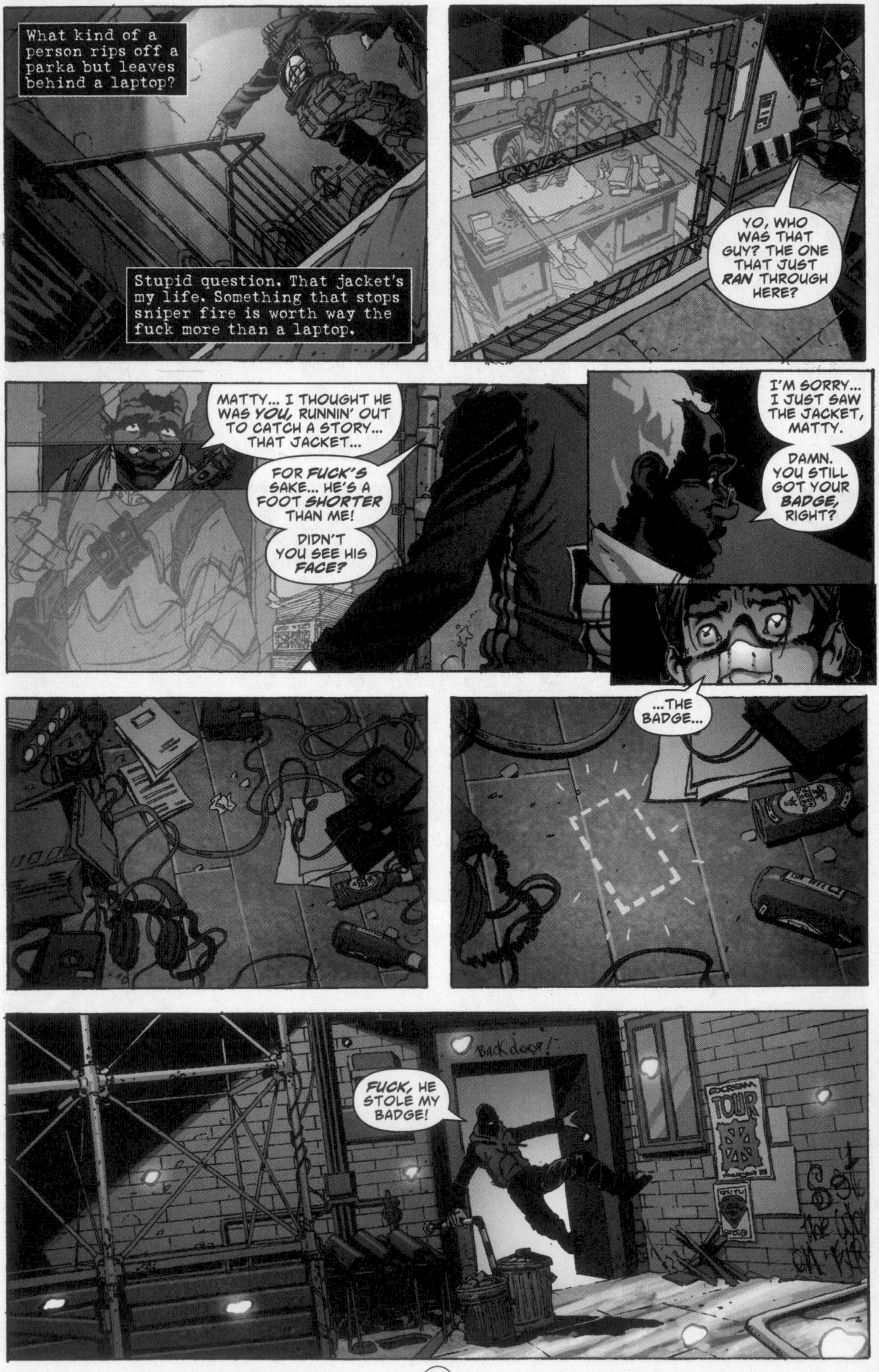

What kind of a person rips off a parka but leaves behind a laptop?
Stupid question. That jacket's my life. Something that stops sniper fire is worth way the fuck more than a laptop.
YO, WHO WAS THAT GUY? THE ONE THAT JUST RAN THROUGH HERE?
MATTY... I THOUGHT HE WAS YOU, RUNNIN' OUT TO CATCH A STORY... THAT JACKET...
FOR FUCK'S SAKE... HE'S A FOOT SHORTER THAN ME!
DIDN'T YOU SEE HIS FACE?
I'M SORRY... I JUST SAW THE JACKET, MATTY.
DAMN. YOU STILL GOT YOUR BADGE, RIGHT?
...THE BADGE...
FUCK, HE STOLE MY BADGE!
Back door!
TOUR

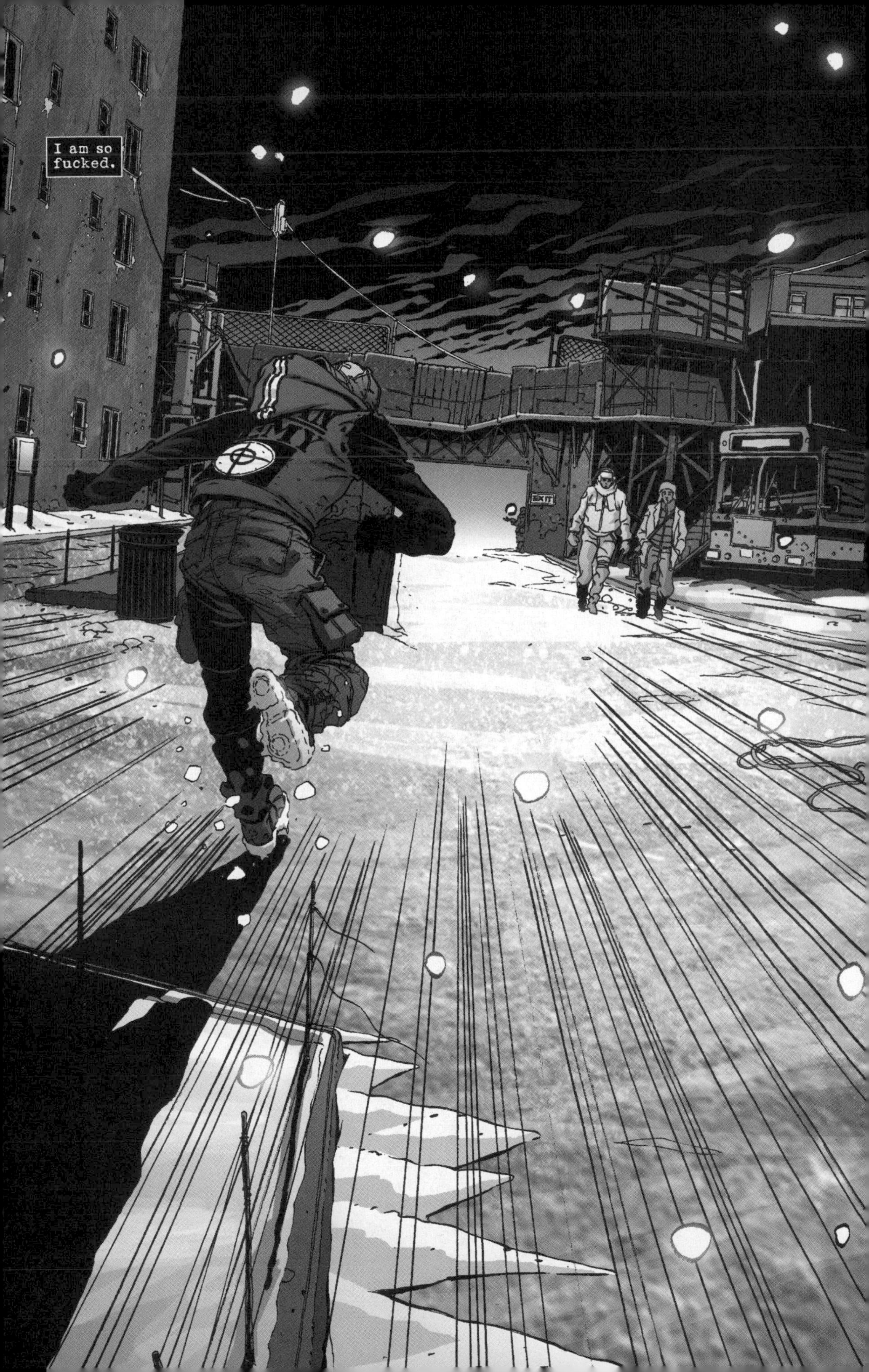
I am so fucked.
EXIT

WHICH WAY?

...MATTY?

THE GUY WITH MY JACKET-- WHICH WAY DID HE GO?

I am so fucked.

UPTOWN! TURNED WEST ON 17TH!

The jacket... the jacket might make a shooter pause.

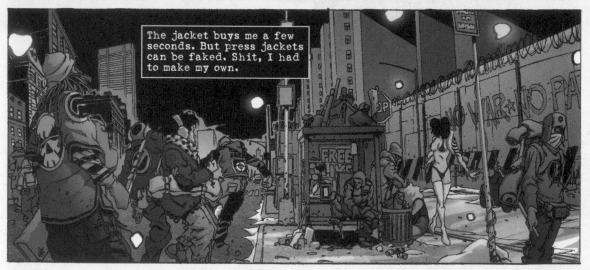

The jacket buys me a few seconds. But press jackets can be faked. Shit, I had to make my own.

The badge is what keeps me alive. Gets me access, gives me my cred.

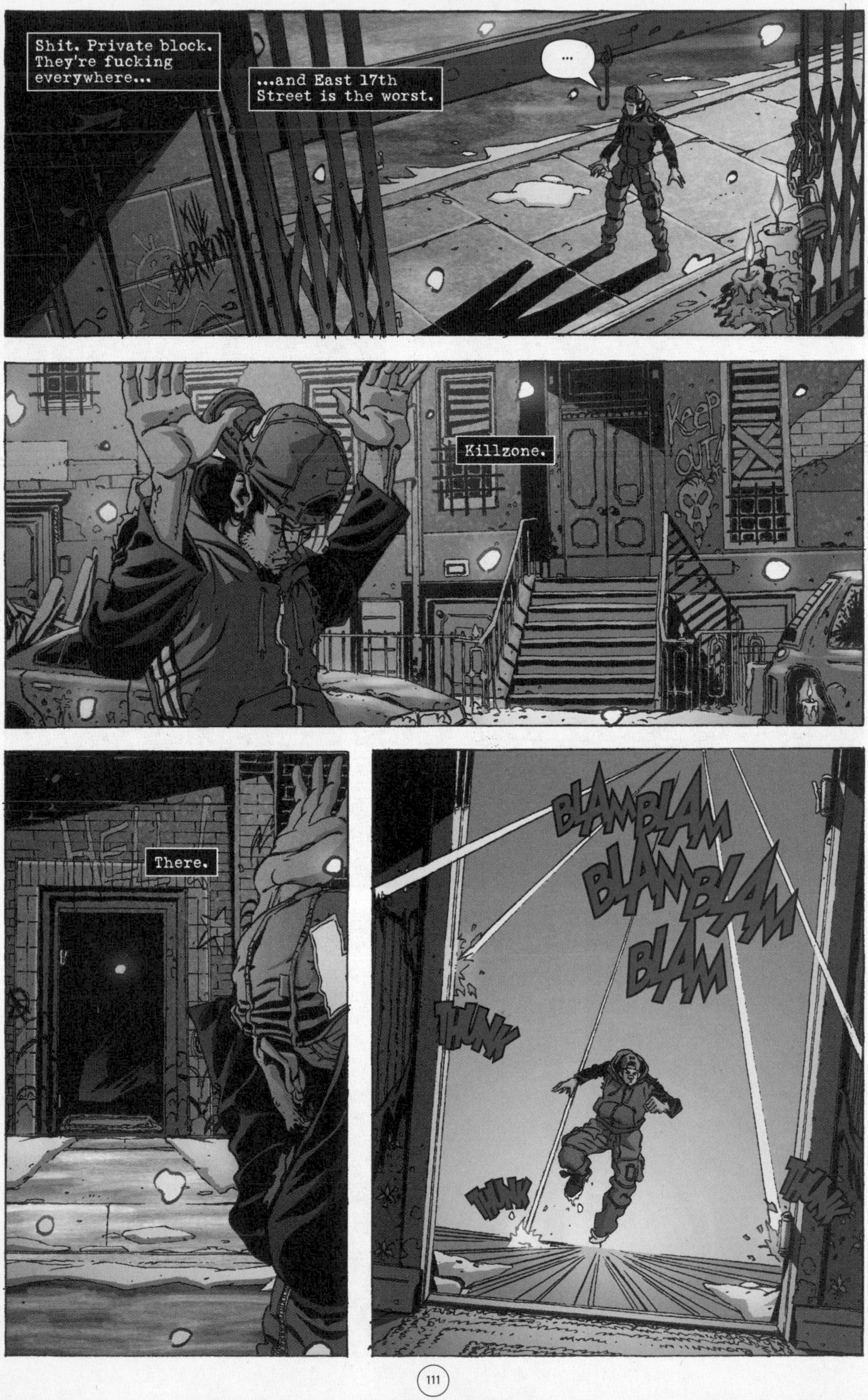
Shit. Private block. They're fucking everywhere...
...and East 17th Street is the worst.
...
Killzone.
There.
BLAMBLAM
BLAMBLAMBLAM
BLAM
THUNK
THUNK
THUNK

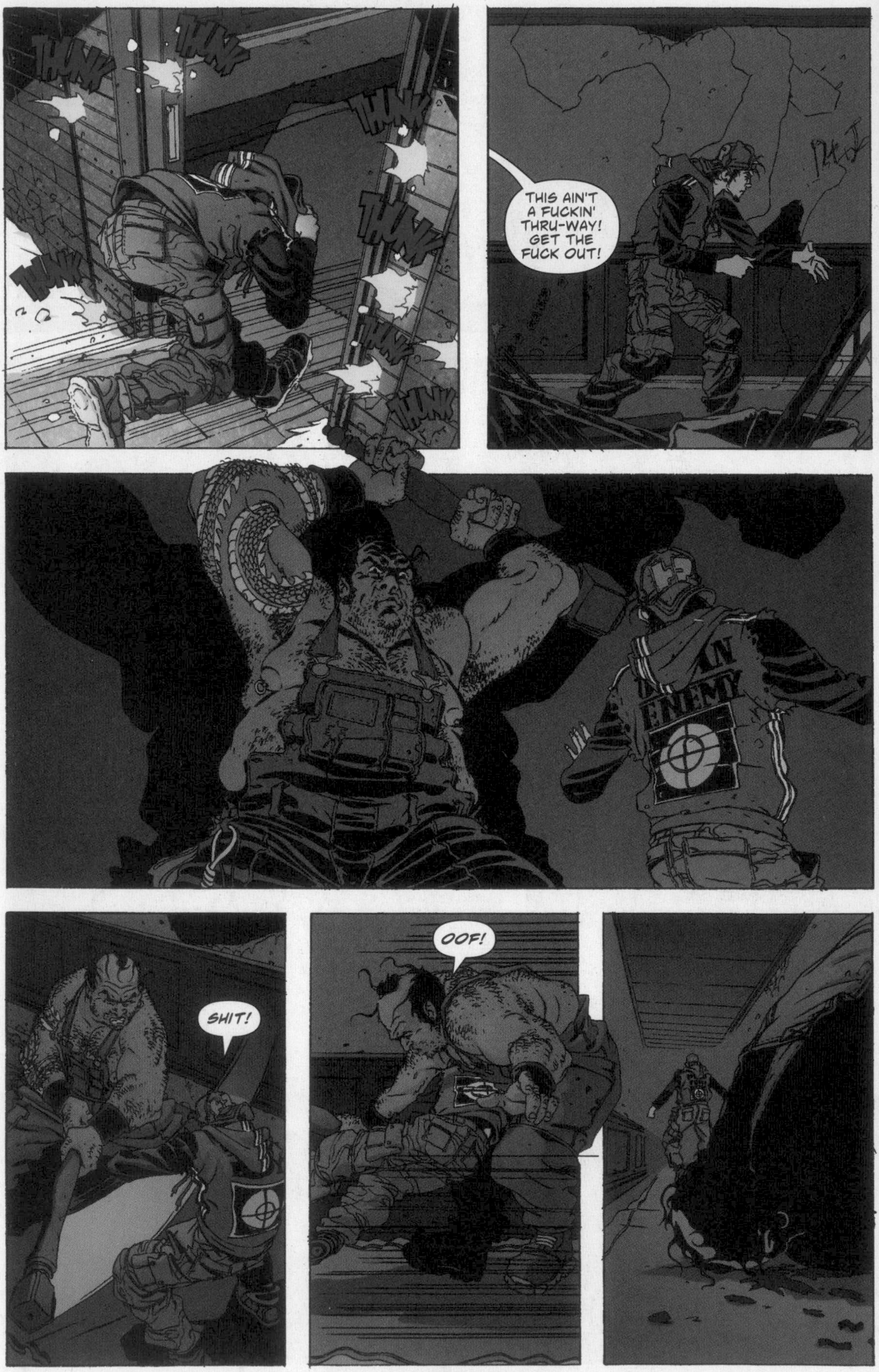
THUNK
THUNK
THUNK
THUNK
THUNK
THUNK
THUNK
THIS AIN'T A FUCKIN' THRU-WAY! GET THE FUCK OUT!
SHIT!
OOF!

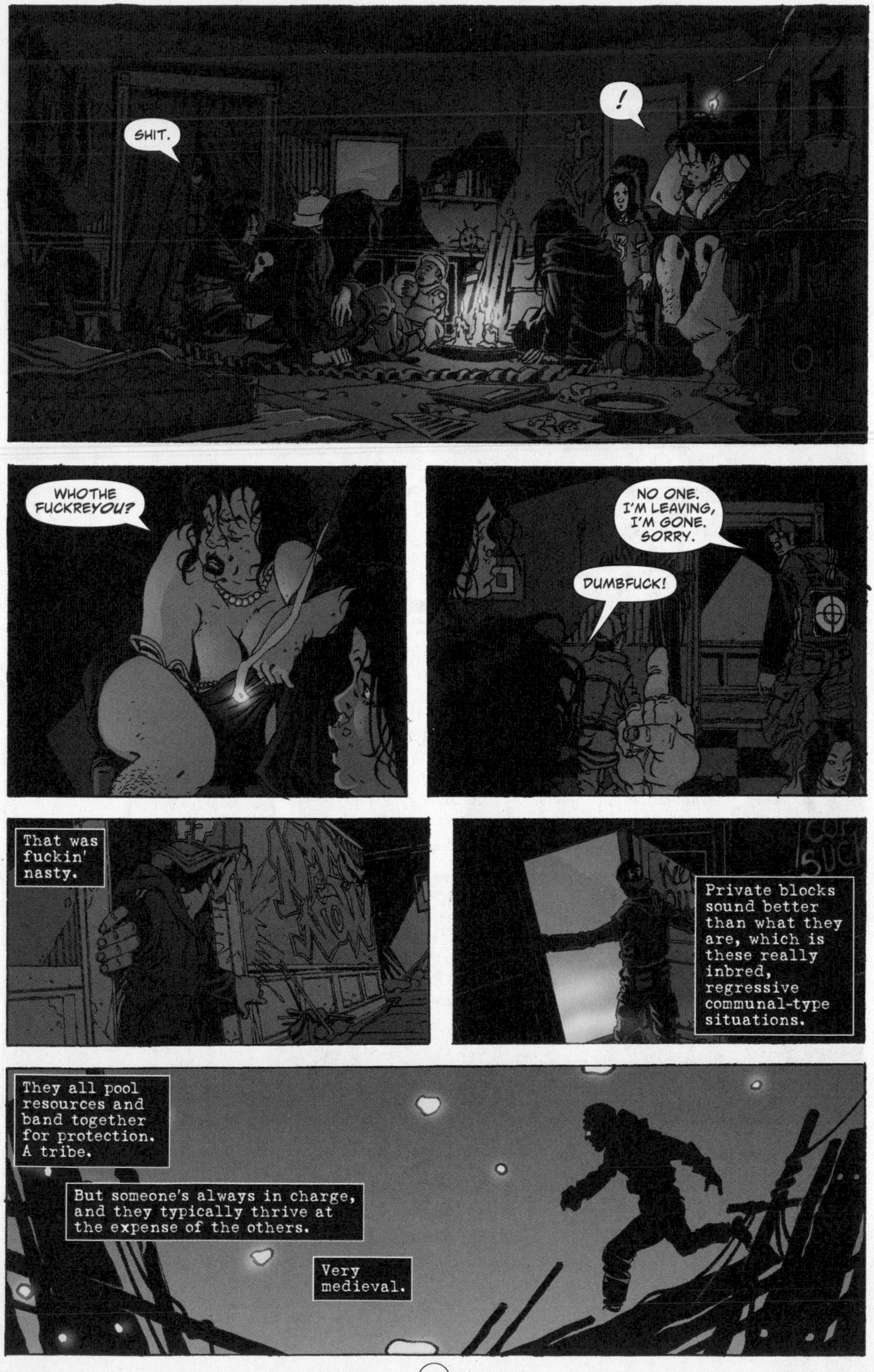
SHIT.
!
WHOTHE FUCKREYOU?
NO ONE. I'M LEAVING, I'M GONE. SORRY.
DUMBFUCK!
That was fuckin' nasty.
Private blocks sound better than what they are, which is these really inbred, regressive communal-type situations.
They all pool resources and band together for protection. A tribe.
But someone's always in charge, and they typically thrive at the expense of the others.
Very medieval.

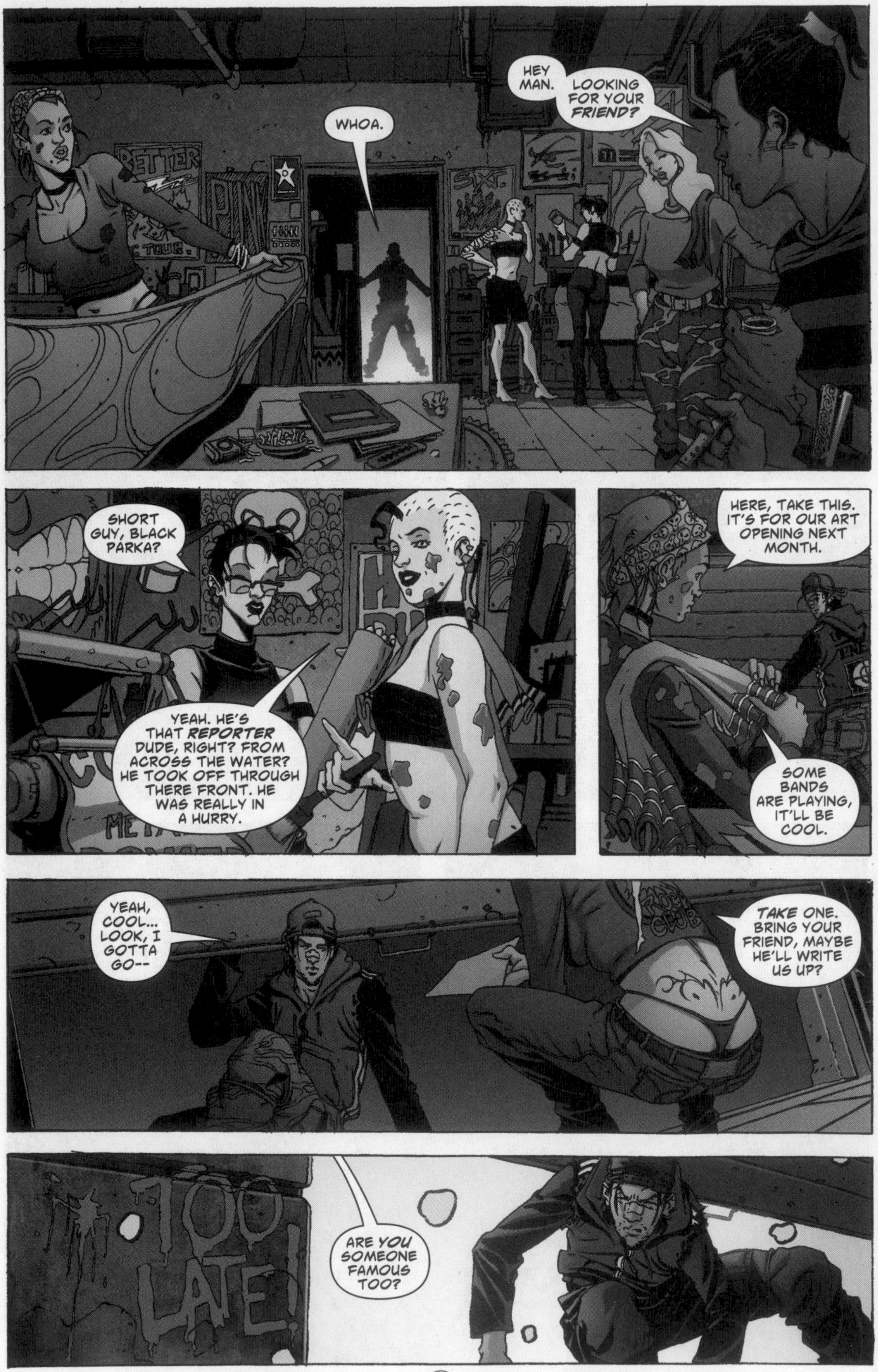
WHOA.
HEY MAN.
LOOKING FOR YOUR *FRIEND?*
SHORT GUY, BLACK PARKA?
YEAH. HE'S THAT *REPORTER* DUDE, RIGHT? FROM ACROSS THE WATER? HE TOOK OFF THROUGH THERE FRONT. HE WAS REALLY IN A HURRY.
HERE, TAKE THIS. IT'S FOR OUR ART OPENING NEXT MONTH.
SOME BANDS ARE PLAYING, IT'LL BE COOL.
YEAH, COOL... LOOK, I GOTTA GO--
TAKE ONE. BRING YOUR FRIEND, MAYBE HE'LL WRITE US UP?
TOO LATE!
ARE *YOU* SOMEONE FAMOUS TOO?

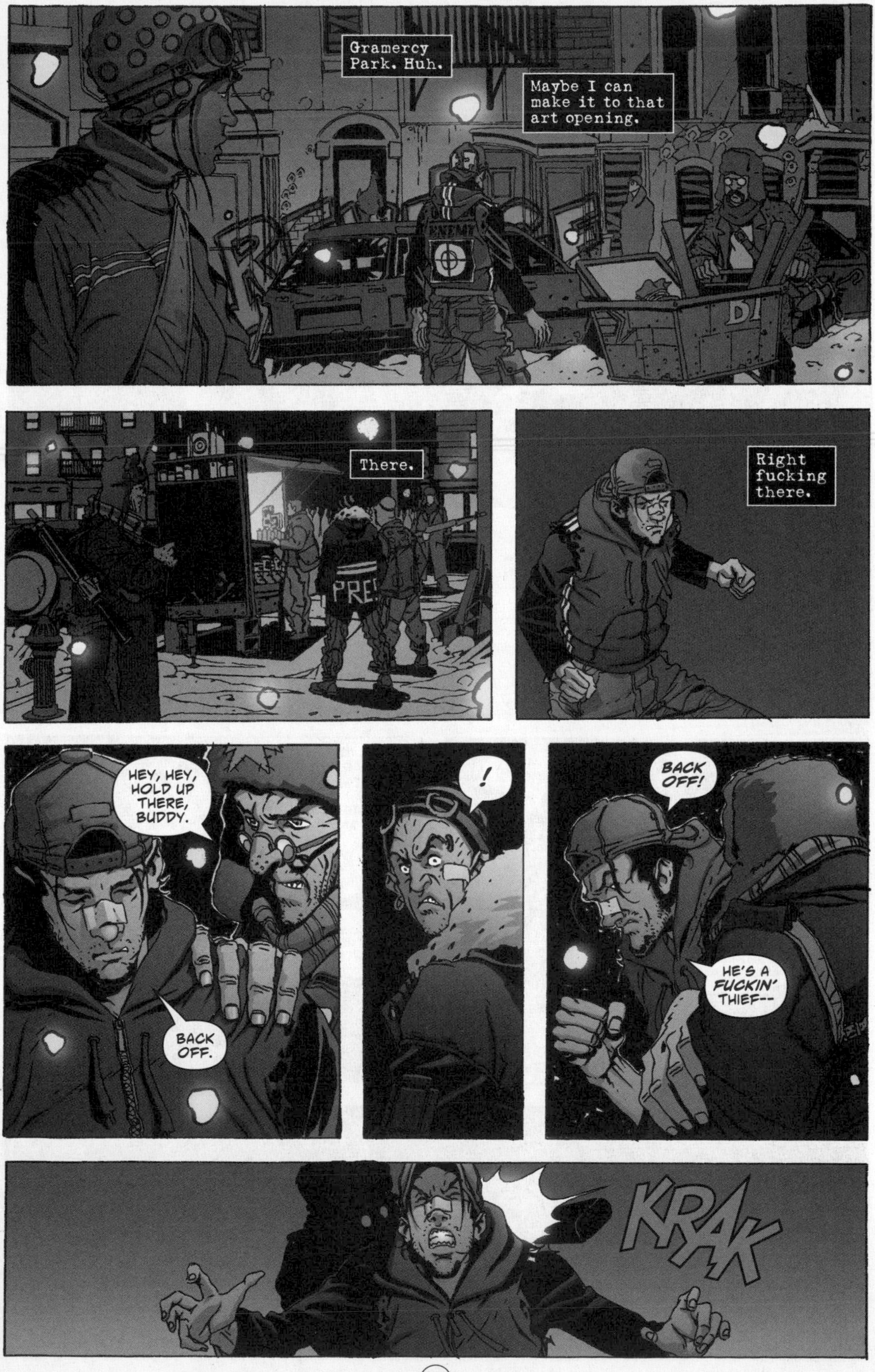

Gramercy Park. Huh.
Maybe I can make it to that art opening.
ENEMY
There.
PRES
Right fucking there.
HEY, HEY, HOLD UP THERE, BUDDY.
BACK OFF.
!
BACK OFF!
HE'S A FUCKIN' THIEF--
KRAK

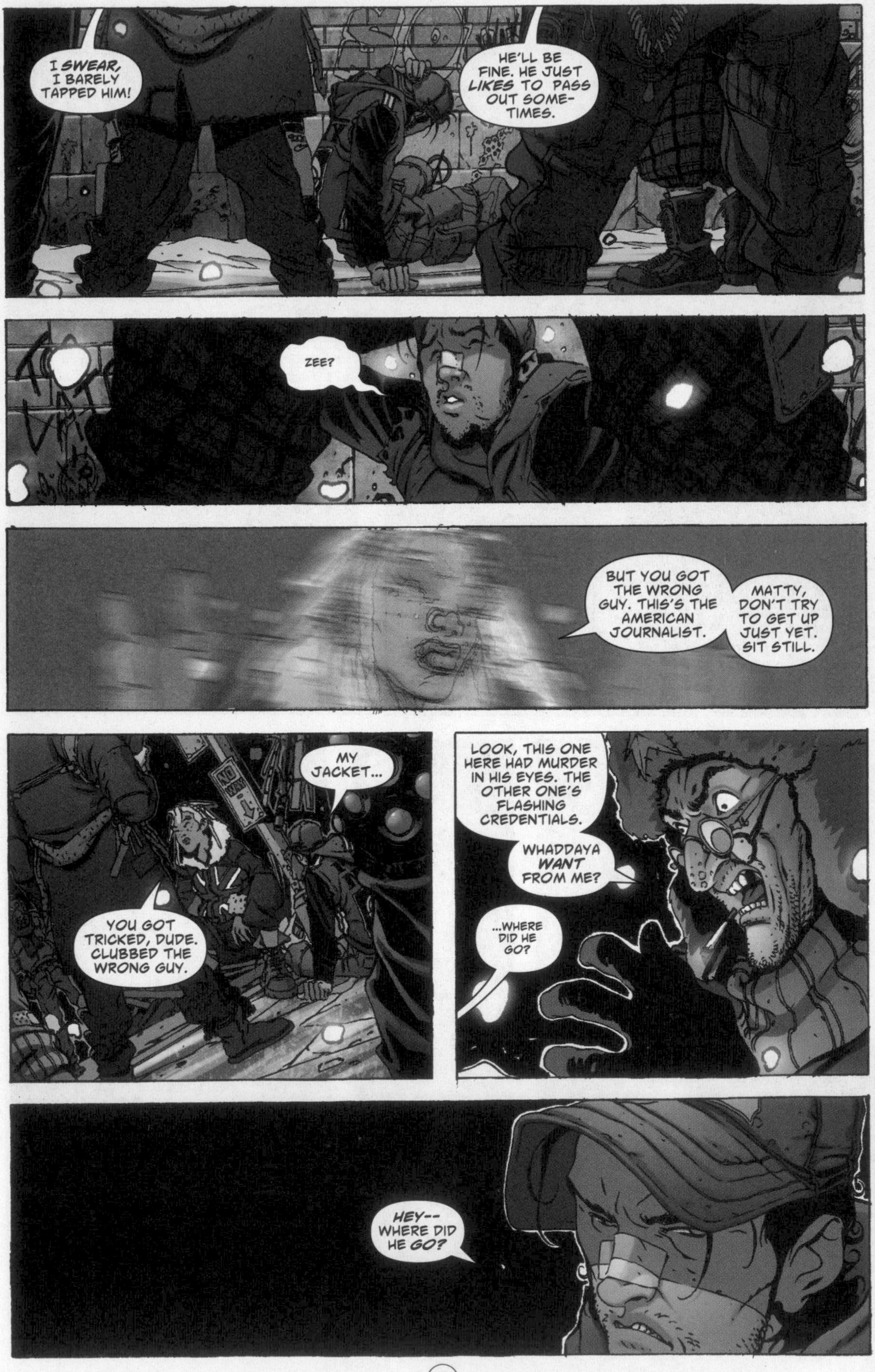

I SWEAR, I BARELY TAPPED HIM!
HE'LL BE FINE. HE JUST LIKES TO PASS OUT SOMETIMES.
ZEE?
BUT YOU GOT THE WRONG GUY. THIS'S THE AMERICAN JOURNALIST.
MATTY, DON'T TRY TO GET UP JUST YET. SIT STILL.
MY JACKET...
YOU GOT TRICKED, DUDE. CLUBBED THE WRONG GUY.
NO WAY
LOOK, THIS ONE HERE HAD MURDER IN HIS EYES. THE OTHER ONE'S FLASHING CREDENTIALS.
WHADDAYA WANT FROM ME?
...WHERE DID HE GO?
HEY--WHERE DID HE GO?

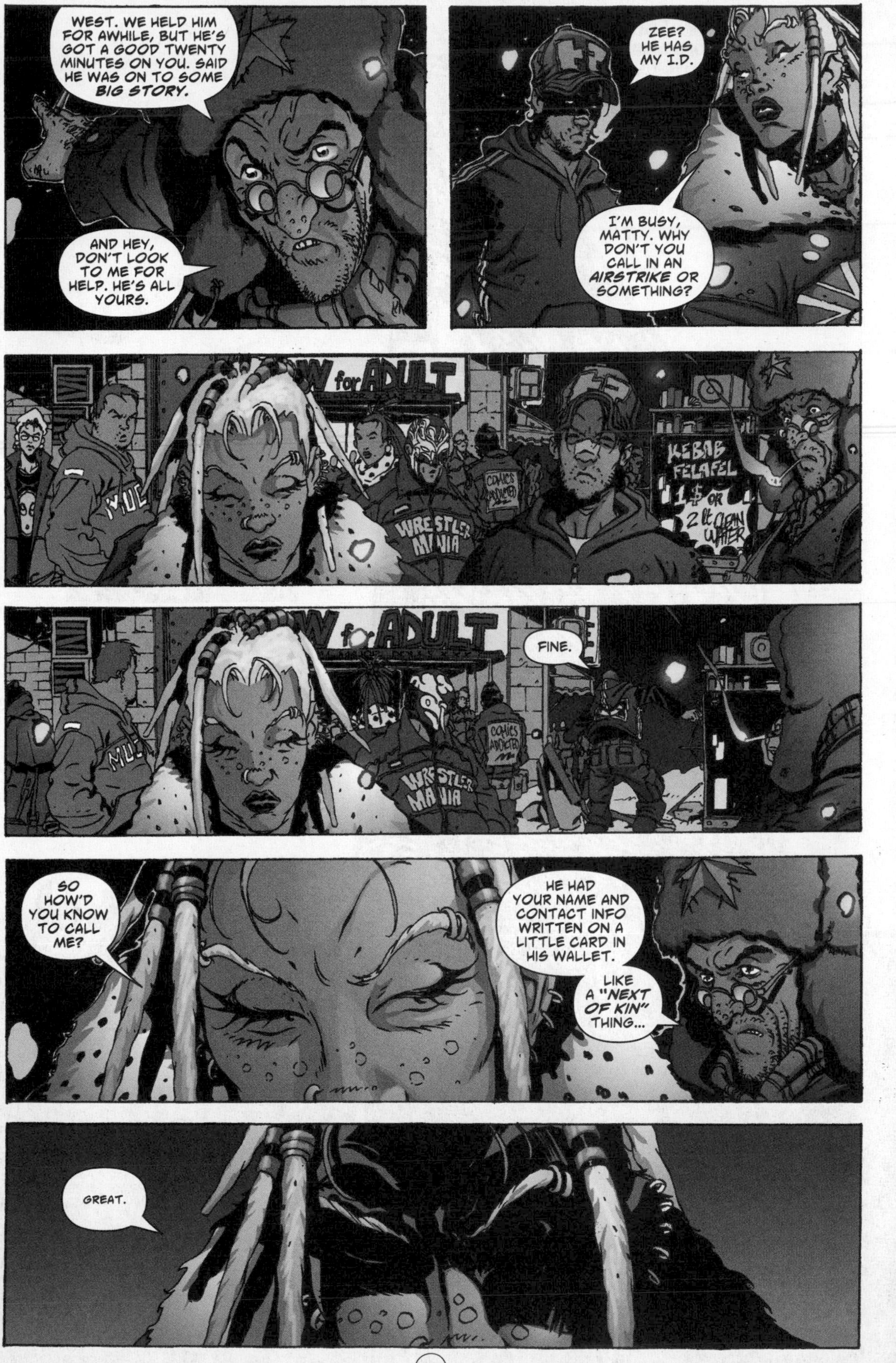
WEST. WE HELD HIM FOR AWHILE, BUT HE'S GOT A GOOD TWENTY MINUTES ON YOU. SAID HE WAS ON TO SOME BIG STORY.
AND HEY, DON'T LOOK TO ME FOR HELP. HE'S ALL YOURS.
ZEE? HE HAS MY I.D.
I'M BUSY, MATTY. WHY DON'T YOU CALL IN AN AIRSTRIKE OR SOMETHING?
W for ADULT
KEBAB FELAFEL 1$ OR 2 lt CLEAN WATER
WRESTLER MANIA
FINE.
SO HOW'D YOU KNOW TO CALL ME?
HE HAD YOUR NAME AND CONTACT INFO WRITTEN ON A LITTLE CARD IN HIS WALLET.
LIKE A "NEXT OF KIN" THING...
GREAT.

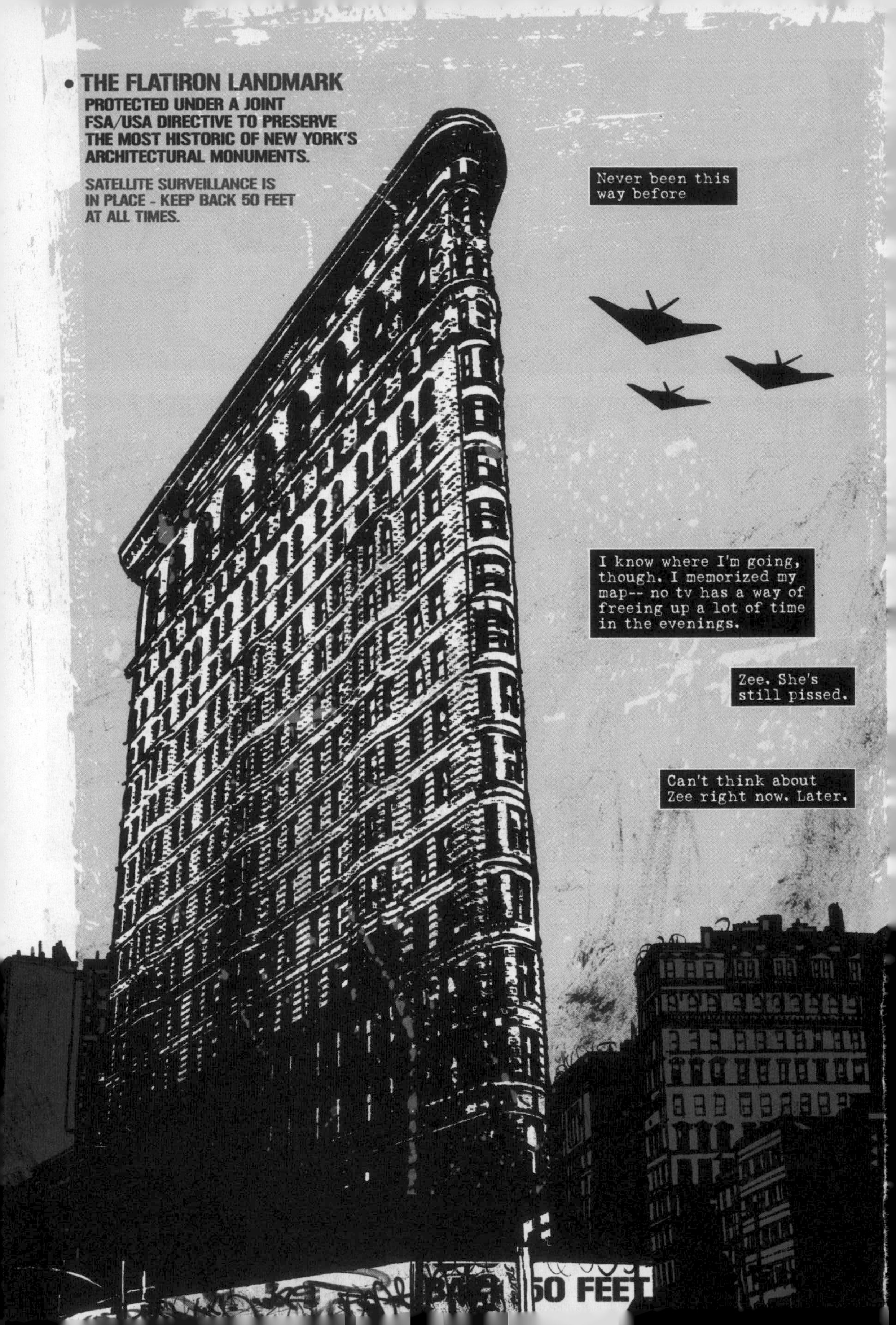
• THE FLATIRON LANDMARK
PROTECTED UNDER A JOINT FSA/USA DIRECTIVE TO PRESERVE THE MOST HISTORIC OF NEW YORK'S ARCHITECTURAL MONUMENTS.
SATELLITE SURVEILLANCE IS IN PLACE - KEEP BACK 50 FEET AT ALL TIMES.
Never been this way before
I know where I'm going, though. I memorized my map-- no tv has a way of freeing up a lot of time in the evenings.
Zee. She's still pissed.
Can't think about Zee right now. Later.
50 FEET

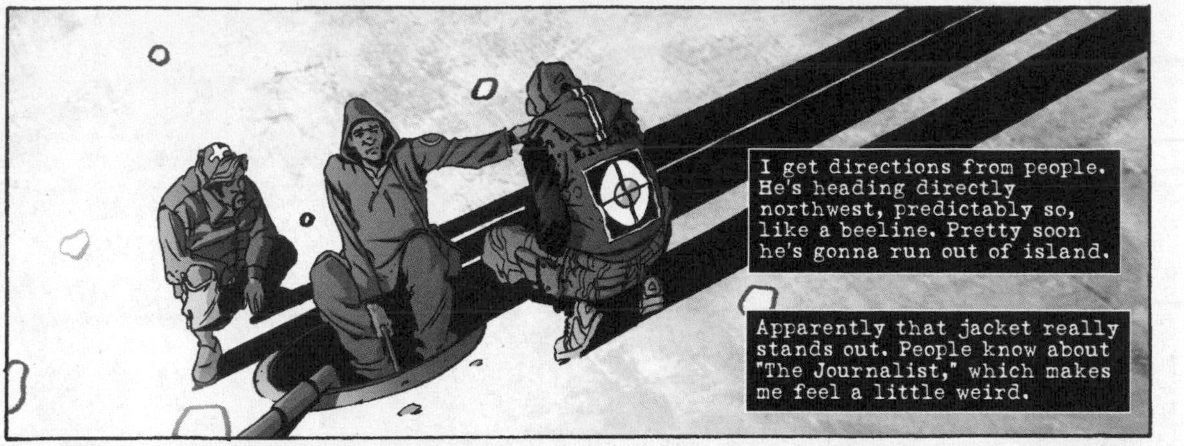
I get directions from people. He's heading directly northwest, predictably so, like a beeline. Pretty soon he's gonna run out of island.
Apparently that jacket really stands out. People know about "The Journalist," which makes me feel a little weird.

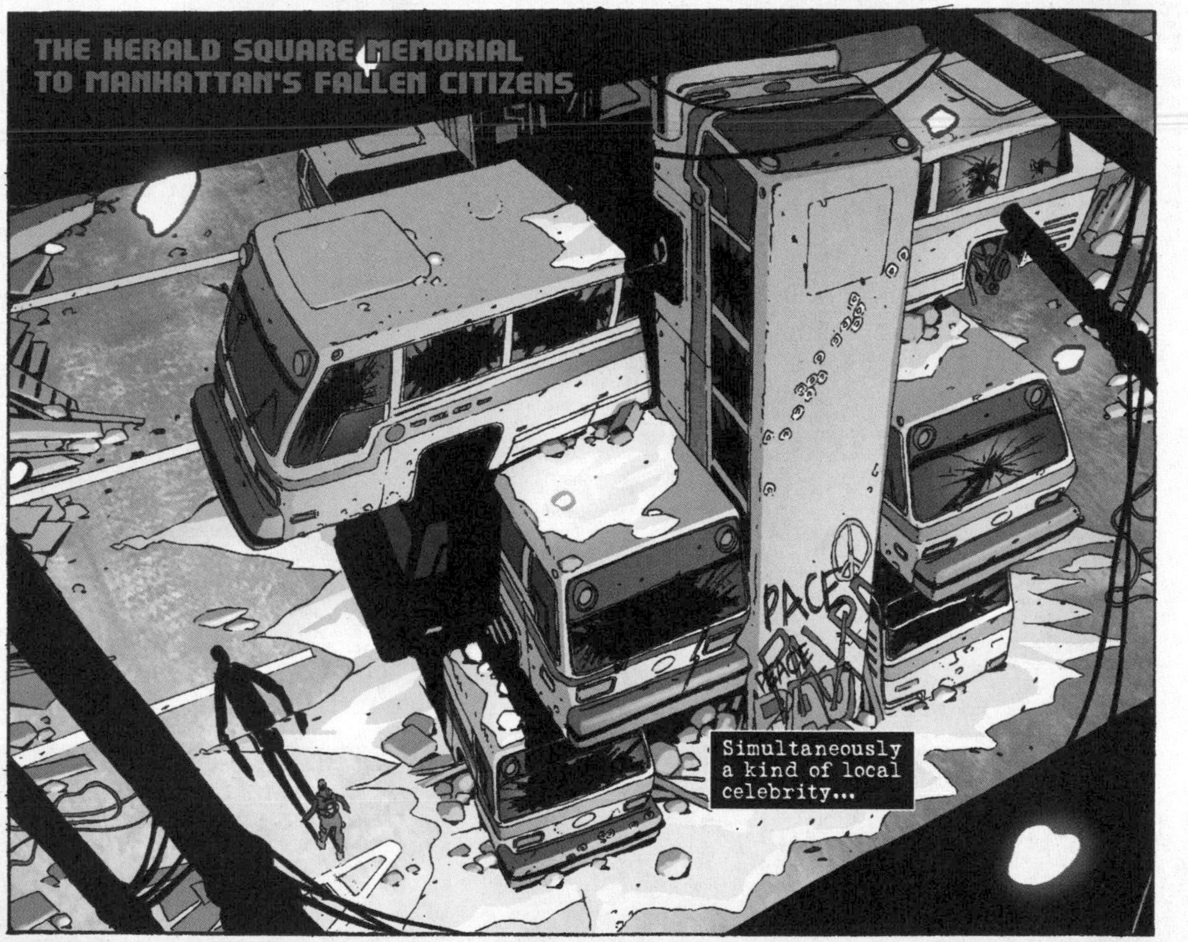
THE HERALD SQUARE MEMORIAL TO MANHATTAN'S FALLEN CITIZENS
PACE
Simultaneously a kind of local celebrity...

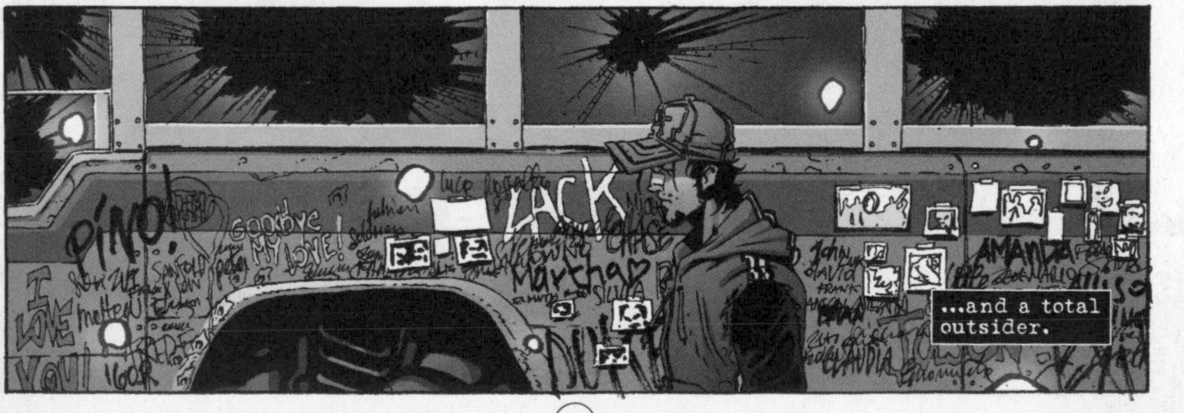
PINO!
GOODBYE MY LOVE!
JACK
CHASE
Martha
AMANDA
CLAUDIA
...and a total outsider.

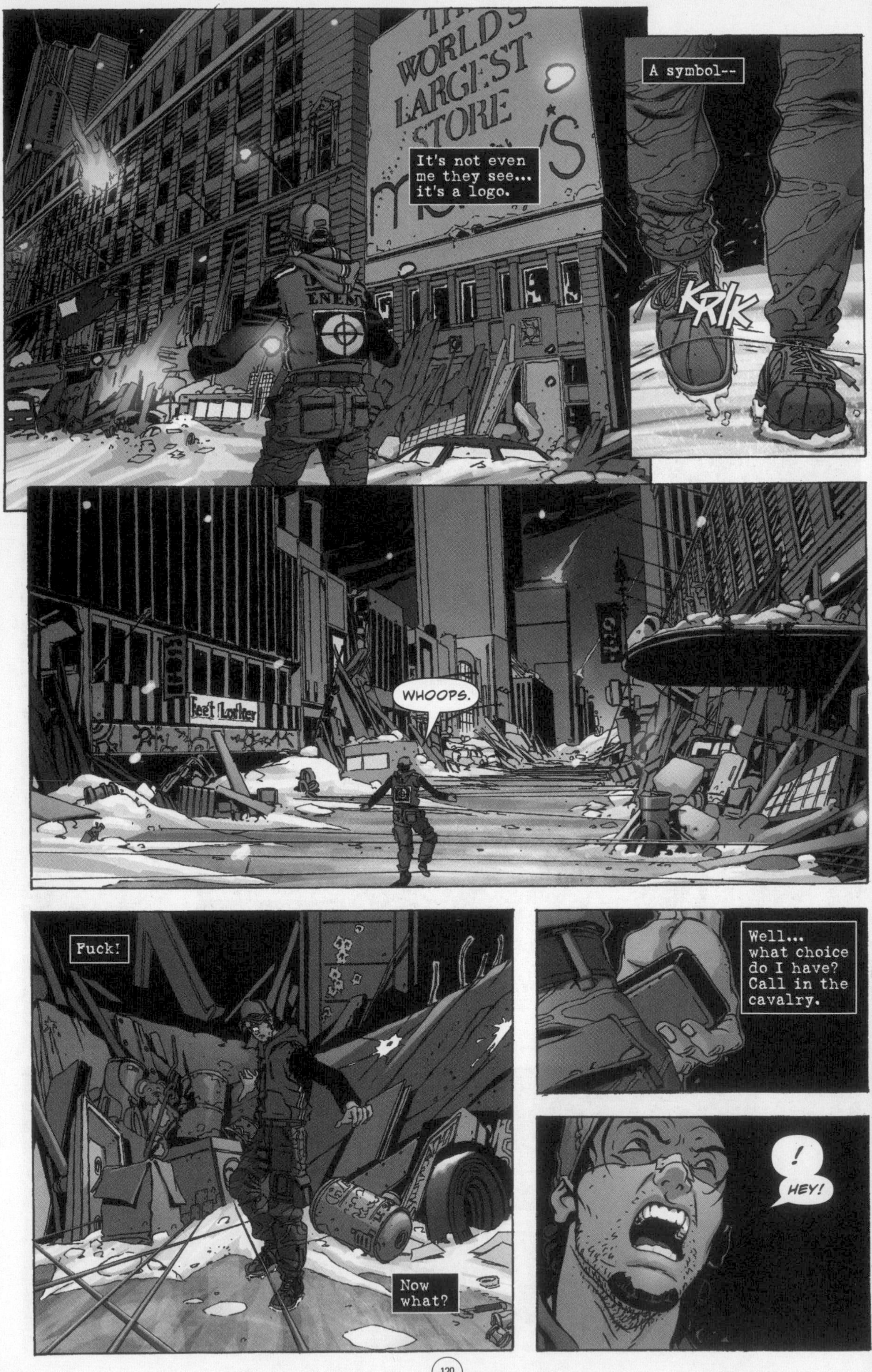
THE WORLD'S LARGEST STORE
It's not even me they see... it's a logo.
A symbol--
KRIK
Foot Locker
WHOOPS.
Fuck!
Now what?
Well... what choice do I have? Call in the cavalry.
!
HEY!

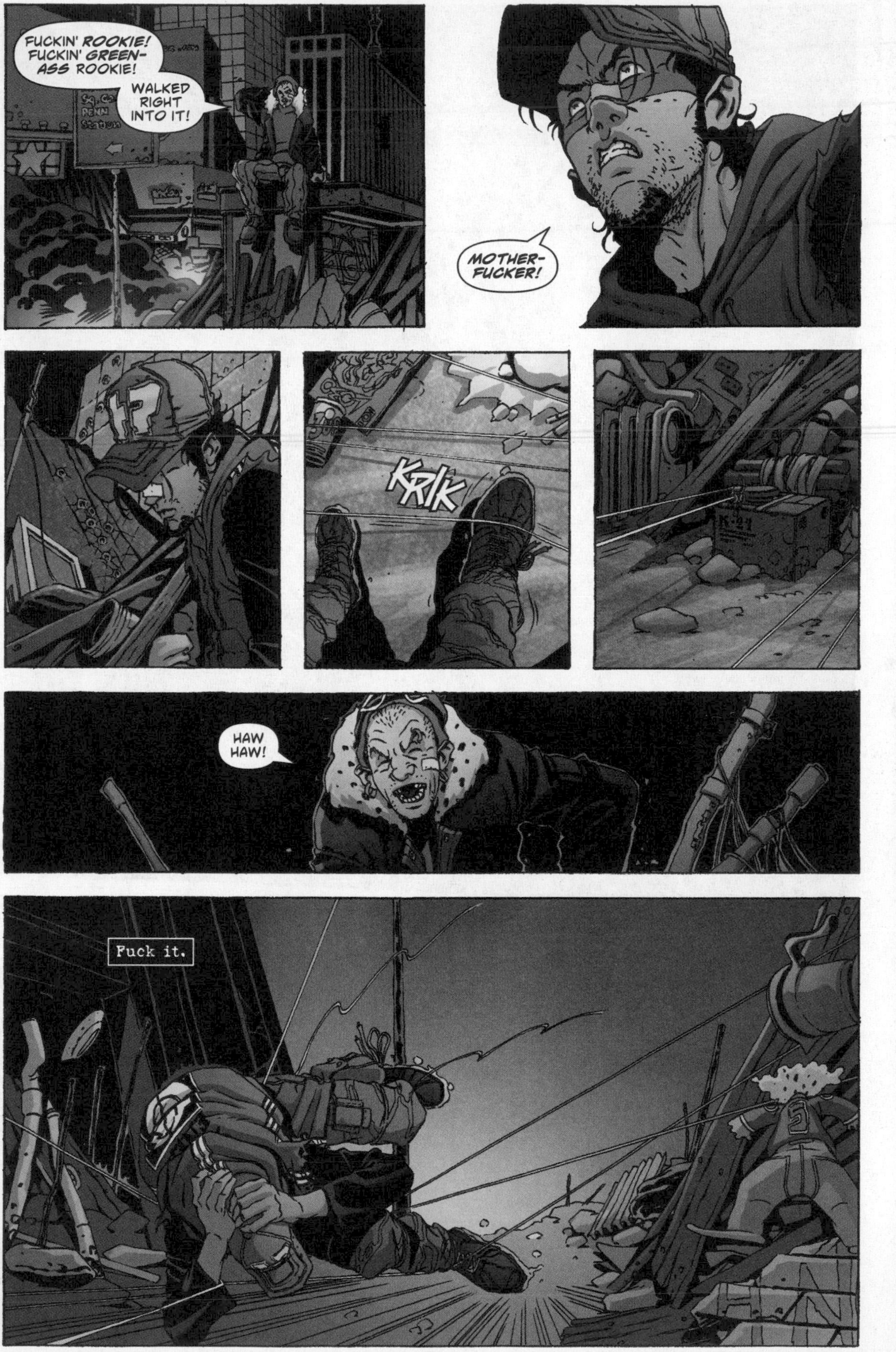
FUCKIN' *ROOKIE!* FUCKIN' *GREEN-ASS* ROOKIE!
WALKED RIGHT INTO IT!
MOTHER-FUCKER!
KRIK
HAW HAW!
Fuck it.

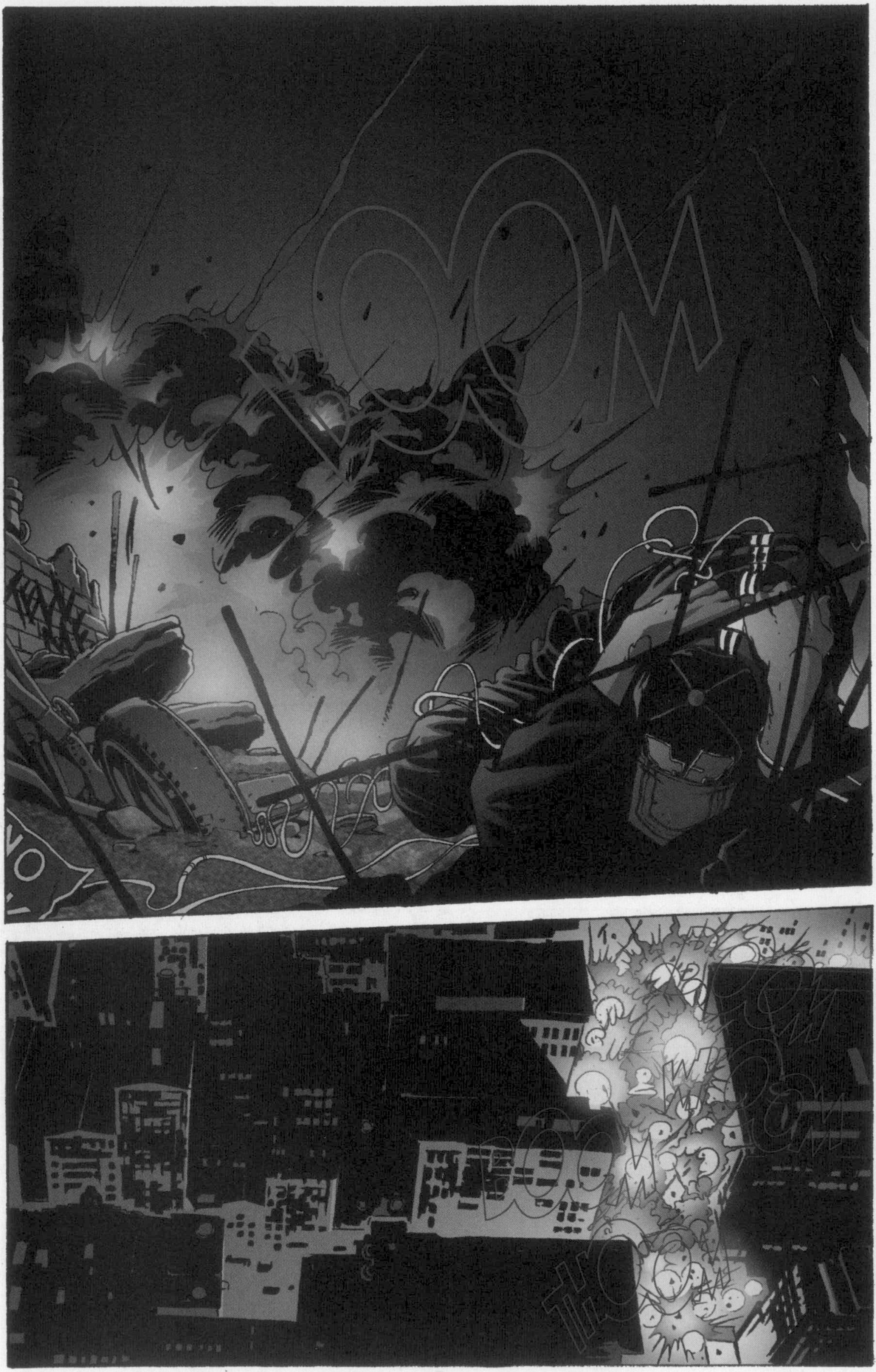
WOOOM
THOOM

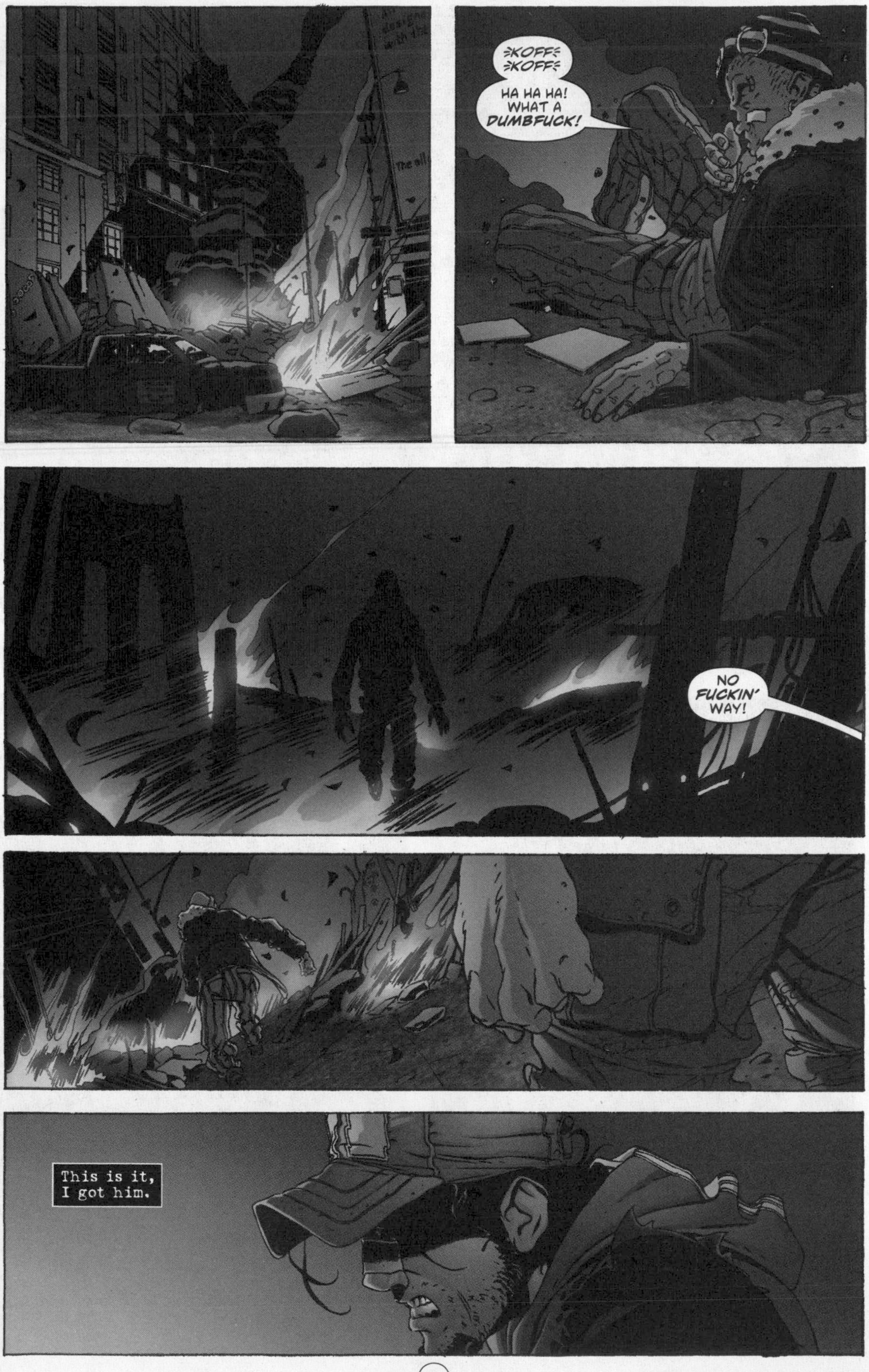
KOFF KOFF
HA HA HA! WHAT A DUMBFUCK!
NO FUCKIN' WAY!
This is it, I got him.

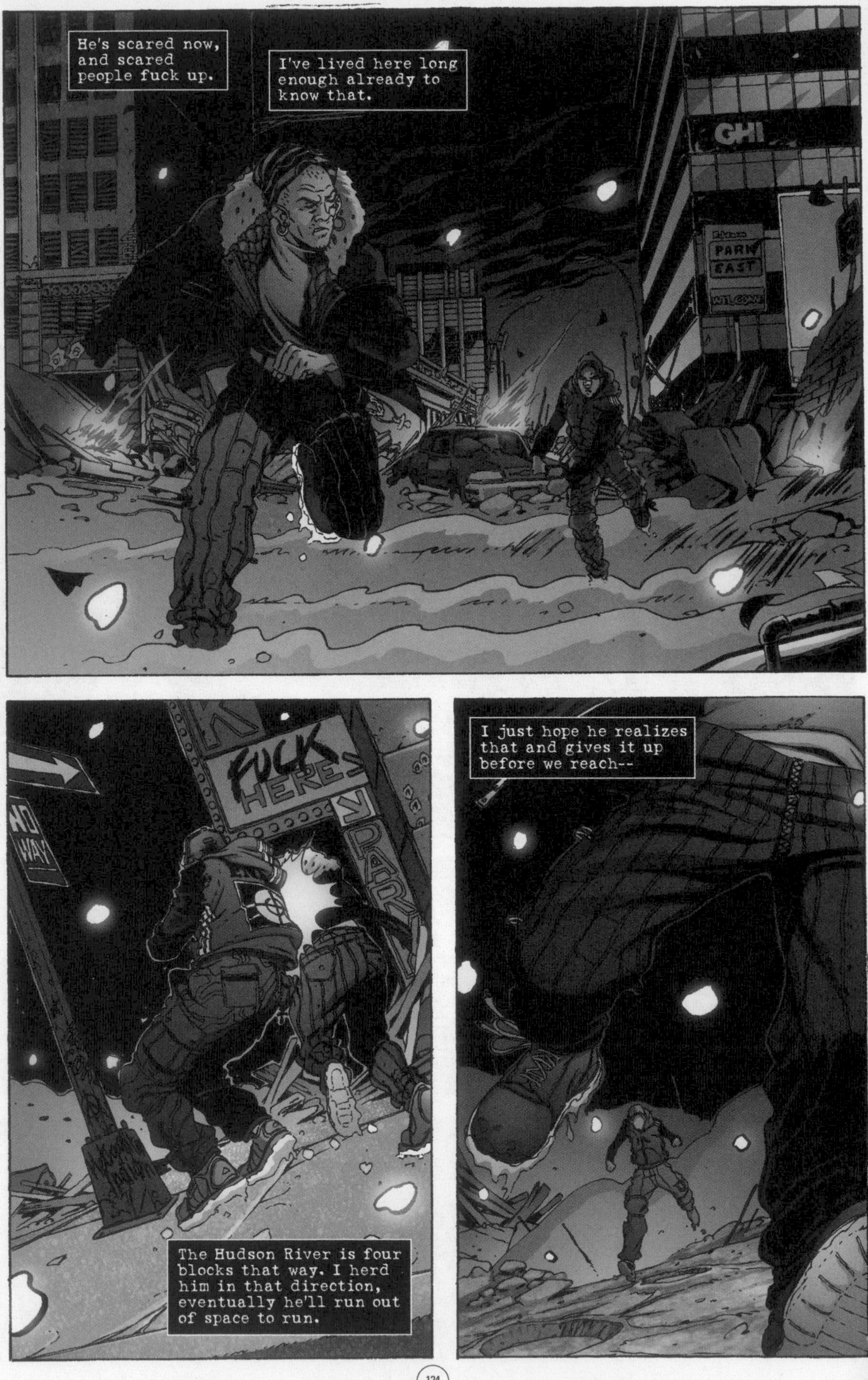
He's scared now, and scared people fuck up.
I've lived here long enough already to know that.
GHI
PARK EAST
FUCK
HERES
NO WAY
The Hudson River is four blocks that way. I herd him in that direction, eventually he'll run out of space to run.
I just hope he realizes that and gives it up before we reach--

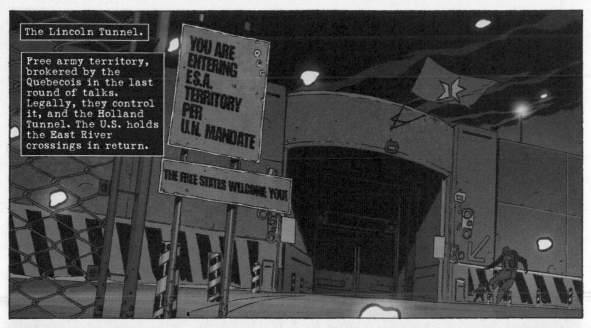

The Lincoln Tunnel.

Free army territory, brokered by the Quebecois in the last round of talks. Legally, they control it, and the Holland Tunnel. The U.S. holds the East River crossings in return.

YOU ARE ENTERING E.S.A. TERRITORY PER U.N. MANDATE

THE FREE STATES WELCOME YOUR

STAND STILL.

WHAT ARE YOU DOING HERE?

THIS GUY'S BEEN CHASING ME FOR BLOCKS, MAN. HE'S *CRAZY*, CHASING ME ALL OVER THE *FUCKIN'* CITY.

I DIDN'T DO SHIT BUT HE'S GOT IT IN FOR ME OR SOME-THING-- YOU GOTTA HELP ME, *PLEASE!*

PLEASE...

THAT TRUE? YOU CHASING THIS POOR KID, MR. ROTH?

...WHAT? HOW DO YOU KNOW--

WE GET LIBERTY NEWS OVER HERE, TOO, YOU KNOW. "NEWS FOR AMERICANS"? YOU'RE LOOKING AT THE TRUEST, MOST *BLUEST MOTHERFUCKING* AMERICANS YOU'LL EVER MEET.

TAKE OFF THE JACKET, KID. GIVE IT BACK.

I GOT FIVE MEN UP THERE WITH RIFLES AND ORDERS TO FIRE IF YOU DON'T.

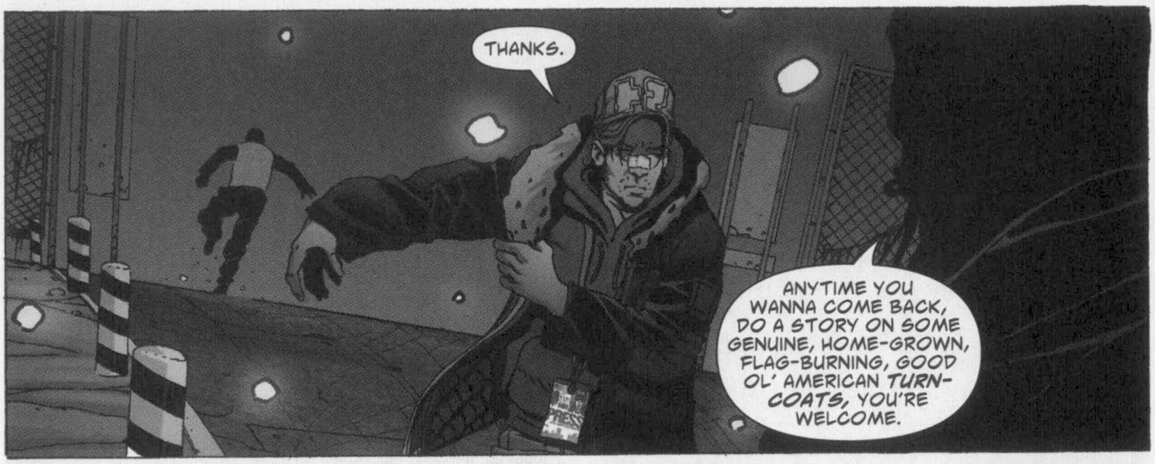
THANKS.
ANYTIME YOU WANNA COME BACK, DO A STORY ON SOME GENUINE, HOME-GROWN, FLAG-BURNING, GOOD OL' AMERICAN TURN-COATS, YOU'RE WELCOME.
PRESS

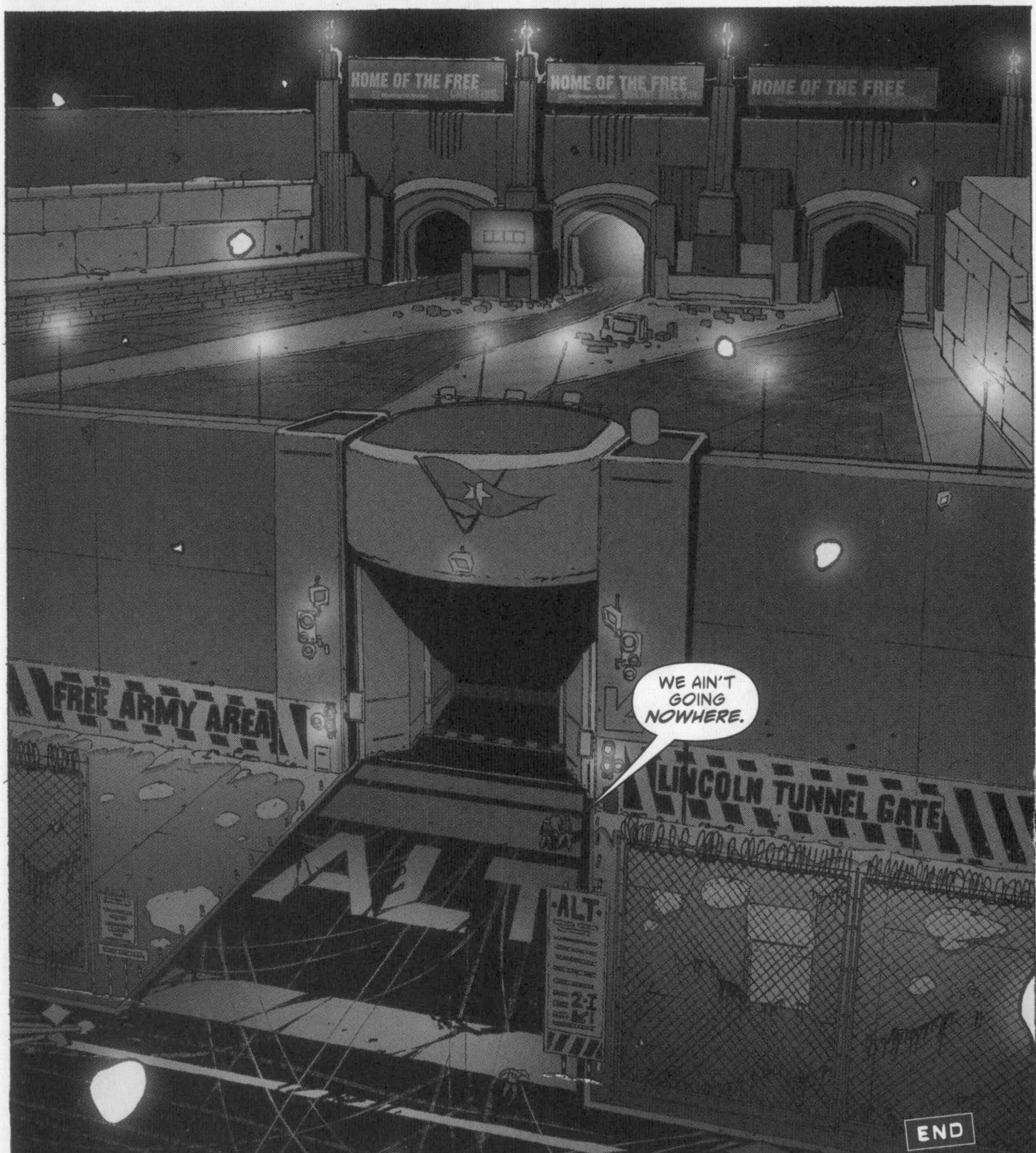
HOME OF THE FREE
HOME OF THE FREE
HOME OF THE FREE
FREE ARMY AREA
WE AIN'T GOING NOWHERE.
LINCOLN TUNNEL GATE
ALT
ALT
END